Tobias Deutsch

Human Bionically Inspired Autonomous Agents

Tobias Deutsch

Human Bionically Inspired Autonomous Agents

The Framework Implementation ARSi11 of the Psychoanalytical Entity Id Applied to Embodied Agents

Südwestdeutscher Verlag für Hochschulschriften

Impressum/Imprint (nur für Deutschland/only for Germany)
Bibliografische Information der Deutschen Nationalbibliothek: Die Deutsche Nationalbibliothek verzeichnet diese Publikation in der Deutschen Nationalbibliografie; detaillierte bibliografische Daten sind im Internet über http://dnb.d-nb.de abrufbar.
Alle in diesem Buch genannten Marken und Produktnamen unterliegen warenzeichen-, marken- oder patentrechtlichem Schutz bzw. sind Warenzeichen oder eingetragene Warenzeichen der jeweiligen Inhaber. Die Wiedergabe von Marken, Produktnamen, Gebrauchsnamen, Handelsnamen, Warenbezeichnungen u.s.w. in diesem Werk berechtigt auch ohne besondere Kennzeichnung nicht zu der Annahme, dass solche Namen im Sinne der Warenzeichen- und Markenschutzgesetzgebung als frei zu betrachten wären und daher von jedermann benutzt werden dürften.

Verlag: Südwestdeutscher Verlag für Hochschulschriften GmbH & Co. KG
Dudweiler Landstr. 99, 66123 Saarbrücken, Deutschland
Telefon +49 681 37 20 271-1, Telefax +49 681 37 20 271-0
Email: info@svh-verlag.de

Zugl.: Wien, TU, Diss. 2011

Herstellung in Deutschland:
Schaltungsdienst Lange o.H.G., Berlin
Books on Demand GmbH, Norderstedt
Reha GmbH, Saarbrücken
Amazon Distribution GmbH, Leipzig
ISBN: 978-3-8381-2709-5

Imprint (only for USA, GB)
Bibliographic information published by the Deutsche Nationalbibliothek: The Deutsche Nationalbibliothek lists this publication in the Deutsche Nationalbibliografie; detailed bibliographic data are available in the Internet at http://dnb.d-nb.de.
Any brand names and product names mentioned in this book are subject to trademark, brand or patent protection and are trademarks or registered trademarks of their respective holders. The use of brand names, product names, common names, trade names, product descriptions etc. even without a particular marking in this works is in no way to be construed to mean that such names may be regarded as unrestricted in respect of trademark and brand protection legislation and could thus be used by anyone.

Publisher: Südwestdeutscher Verlag für Hochschulschriften GmbH & Co. KG
Dudweiler Landstr. 99, 66123 Saarbrücken, Germany
Phone +49 681 37 20 271-1, Fax +49 681 37 20 271-0
Email: info@svh-verlag.de

Printed in the U.S.A.
Printed in the U.K. by (see last page)
ISBN: 978-3-8381-2709-5

Copyright © 2011 by the author and Südwestdeutscher Verlag für Hochschulschriften GmbH & Co. KG and licensors
All rights reserved. Saarbrücken 2011

Abbreviations

AGI	Artificial General Intelligence	*MOSES*	Meta-Optimizing Semantic Evolutionary Search
AGISim	Artificial General Intelligence Simulator	*OpenCog*	Open Cognition
AI	Artificial Intelligence	*PAD*	Pleasure, Arousal, and Dominance
A-Life	Artificial Life	*PAIAS*	PsychoAnalytically Inspired Automation System
ARS	Artificial Recognition System		
ARSi10	ARS implementation number 10	*PAM*	Perceptive Awareness Module
ARSi11	ARS implementation number 11	*PEAS*	Performance, Environment, Actuators, Sensors
BDI	Believe-Desire-Intention		
BFG	Bubble Family Game	*RePast*	Recursive Porous Agent Simulation Toolkit
CAAT	Cognitive Agent Architecture and Theory		
		PDL	Propositional Dynamic Logic
CogAff	Cognition and Affect	*PLN*	Probabilistic Logic Networks
DB	Database	*SDL*	Specification and Description Language
GOFAI	Good Old Fashioned Artificial Intelligence		
		SmaKi	Smart Kitchen
GUI	Graphical User Interface	*TCP/IP*	Transmission Control Protocol/Internet Protocol
GWT	Global Workspace Theory		
H-CogAff	Human-Cognition and Affect	*UML*	Unified Modeling Language
HMM	hidden Markov model	*VAB*	Virtual Animal Brain
HVAC	Heating, Ventilating, and Air Conditioning	*VRML*	Virtual Reality Markup Language
		WASABI	WASABI Affect Simulation for Agents with Believable Interactivity
ICT	Institute of Computer Technology		
LIDA	Learning Intelligent Distribution Agent		
		XML	Extensible Markup Language
MASON	Multi-Agent Simulator of Neighborhoods ... or Networks ... or something ...	*Zamin*	Zoological Agents for Modification and Improvement of Neocreatures

Table of Contents

1	**Introduction**			**1**
	1.1	Overview		1
	1.2	Methodology		2
		1.2.1	Lessons Learned from Artificial Intelligence	2
		1.2.2	Why Psychoanalysis?	4
		1.2.3	Objections to Psychoanalysis	5
		1.2.4	Modeling Process	7
	1.3	Context		8
	1.4	Problem Statement		10
		1.4.1	Motivation	10
		1.4.2	Research Considerations	11
	1.5	Approach		13
2	**State of the Art**			**15**
	2.1	Artificial General Intelligence Architectures		15
		2.1.1	Foundational Architecture Frameworks	16
		2.1.2	Project Architectures	19
		2.1.3	Evaluation and Comparison of Architectures	25
	2.2	Emotions, Drives, and Urges		28
		2.2.1	Theoretical Considerations	28
		2.2.2	Projects	30
	2.3	Embodiment		36
		2.3.1	Foundations	37
		2.3.2	Design Principles	39
		2.3.3	Virtual Embodiment	43
	2.4	Related Projects Basing on Psychoanalysis		44
	2.5	Artificial Life Simulation		52
		2.5.1	Simulation Platforms	52
		2.5.2	Related Projects	56
	2.6	Artificial Recognition System		62
		2.6.1	Project Origins	62
		2.6.2	The 1st ARS Model	64

| | | 2.6.3 | Bubble Family Game | 68 |

3 Model — 73
3.1 General Concept — 73
3.1.1 Psychoanalytical Theories Used — 73
3.1.2 Freud's 2nd Topographical Model — 77
3.1.3 Memory — 79
3.1.4 Embodiment in Psychoanalysis — 82
3.1.5 Four Model Design-Principles — 83
3.2 Beyond a Shallow Model — 84
3.3 Drives—the Connection to the Body — 87
3.3.1 Additional Drives — 87
3.3.2 Distribution of Drives — 89
3.3.3 Seeking System — 91
3.3.4 Primal Repression — 93
3.4 Final Functional Model — 94
3.4.1 Complete Model — 96
3.4.2 Innovations — 96
3.4.3 Function Modules — 97
3.4.4 Memory Access — 111
3.5 The Id and Parts of the Ego — 114

4 Platform, Framework, and Decision Unit Implementation — 119
4.1 Requirements Analysis — 119
4.2 Use-Cases — 122
4.3 Platform ARSIN World — 128
4.3.1 Concept — 128
4.3.2 Animals, Plants, and Energy Sources — 131
4.3.3 ARSIN Agent — 134
4.3.4 Inspectors — 138
4.4 Decision Unit Framework — 139
4.5 Psychoanalytically Inspired Decision Unit — 141

5 Results — 146
5.1 Environment Setup — 146
5.2 Use-Case 0 Revisited — 150
5.3 Step by Step — 152
5.3.1 Self-Preservation System — 152
5.3.2 Seeking System — 156
5.3.3 Libido Buffer — 158
5.4 Impact — 160
5.5 Minimal Model — 163
5.6 ARS Goes NAO — 164
5.7 Discussion — 165

6 Conclusion and Outlook 167
 6.1 Discussions 167
 6.2 Research Considerations Revisited 169
 6.3 Further Work 171
 6.4 Outlook 174

Bibliography 177

Internet References 193

A UML Notation 195
 A.1 Class Diagram 195
 A.2 Sequence Diagram 196
 A.3 Package Diagram 196

> A beginning is the time for taking the most
> delicate care that the balances are correct.
>
> Frank Herbert, Dune (1965)

> Science is what we understand well enough to
> explain to a computer. Art is everything else we
> do.
>
> Donald E. Knuth

1 Introduction

From the many approaches for building an intelligent decision unit for an autonomous software agent, using the human mind as archetype is the most promising one but the hardest to realize. Various sciences have gathered a vast amount of information on the human mind. An unmanageable flood of different theories, ideas, and approaches derived from psychology, neurology, and philosophy could be used as starting points. The problem is: They are piecemeal—no holistic model is provided (see Dietrich in [DFKU09, p. 100]). From all these sciences, only psychoanalysis offers a holistic model states Kandel in [Kan99, p. 505]. This thesis uses psychoanalysis as foundation to build some aspects of a decision unit for embodied autonomous agents.

1.1 Overview

The Artificial Recognition System (ARS) Project [1] at Institute of Computer Technology (ICT) [2] started to take shape about ten years ago with an article that discusses the opportunities and problems which arise when fieldbuses are used to control buildings with hundreds of thousands of nodes written by Dietrich [Die00]. The quintessence is the question how to deal with the immense flood of data produced by these nodes. The proposed answer is to use bionic[1] approaches.

The first project carried out at the ICT was the Smart Kitchen (SmaKi) [3], [Rus03, Fue03]. The kitchen was first controlled by the Perceptive Awareness Module (PAM) and later by pattern recognition modules. Although the system operated reasonably well, the interpretation of the data flood was unsatisfying (see Rösener [RHBP04, p. 350]).

To circumvent this shortcoming, a novel—more radical—approach was formulated by Brainin et al. in [BDK+04]: The creation of a system based on neurobiology, psychology, and psychoanalysis. With the pursuit of the idea of using psychoanalysis the project

---

[1] Bionic is defined in [DFZB09, p. 418] as "...translates biological principles into technical principles. The main idea is that evolution forced living organisms including fauna and flora to become highly optimized in order to survive. The principles and actual solutions those living organisms developed are transferred into technical systems."

gradually shifted its focus from the original task of building automation to the undertaking of formulating a decision unit for an automation system derived from psychoanalysis. In project ARS a decision unit is a special type of control architecture. This term represents the project's focus on human bionically inspired control architectures.

This thesis is part of the basic research project titled PsychoAnalytically Inspired Automation System (PAIAS) which is associated with ARS. The main purpose of PAIAS is to build a functional model[2] based on psychoanalysis using an interdisciplinary top-down modeling approach. Unlike the SmaKi, the target applications are autonomous agents populating an artificial simulated world. This intermediate step has been introduced to ease the implementation of the model. It is far easier to identify the drives and demands of animal-like creatures than to answer the question of what drives and what kind of body does a kitchen have.

To generate the functional model, a top-down modeling approach is followed. The psychoanalytical model of the human mind called second topographical model — Id, Ego, Superego — is used as topmost layer and starting point. From there, a finer grained, more detailed description of the system is generated with each layer added.

The focus of this work lies within the definition and description of the various modules of the Id. Especially, the generation of drives is of interest. Due to the fact that the Id needs a body, the design of the agent's body within the Artificial Life (A-Life) simulation is of great importance. Finally, the question of how such a system can be evaluated is handled by creating use-cases and test scenarios within the simulation.

A more detailed introduction into the ARS Project and the existing preliminary work is given in Section 2.6.

1.2 Methodology

If one follows a new approach, the reasons for this step have to be analyzed: First, the reasons why the old approach has been abandoned (Section 1.2.1); second, the reasons which lead to the new approach (Section 1.2.2). With the advent of a novel approach, objections to it arise. A list of common objections to psychoanalysis is discussed in the next Section 1.2.3. Interdisciplinarity is a big issue in project ARS. Thus, the methodological approach to the design process is sketched in the last part of this section.

1.2.1 Lessons Learned from Artificial Intelligence

One has to be careful, when using terms from human sciences. They tend to end as a label for something which has nothing to do with the original concept they described in the end.

---

[2] A functional model is a structured view on the functions of a system and how they are connected. The description is generated using four components: process, store, interfaces, and external entities. "Process" are the different functions within the system and they are connected by interfaces. An additional layer is the store — data is stored and retrieved from it. External entities are interacting with the system.

Introduction

Many Artificial Intelligence (AI) projects were and still are working on systems incorporating for example emotions and drives (cp. Sloman in [Slo04b, p. 128]). The definitions are taken from various fields like psychology, behaviorism, neurology, psychoanalysis, and folk psychology. Exemplary the projects from Velásquez [Vel97] and Breazeal [Bre02] are cited. Usually, the best fitting theories are taken; little or no attention is paid whether their underlying assumptions are consistent. After implementation, the system has some simple algorithms incorporated which are then labeled "love", "anger", etc. The control system uses them according to rules without knowing what they actually mean (cp. symbol grounding problem by Harnad [Har90]). Nevertheless, it is said that the system is able to feel the emotion "love".

The first failure in this approach is to misunderstand what terms and concepts provided by human sciences are. They are not the thing itself; they are just descriptions of something which has been observed. Hence, the term "love" already describes a model. Consequently, when using this term and implementing it, further abstractions have to be performed — for example, from the living human to psychoanalysis, from there to an object oriented analysis, further to an object oriented programming model, and finally, the implementation in some high level programming language (which is compiled in several steps to machine code). Hence, when labeling a certain behavior of an artificial system with the term "love" one should be aware that this label should in fact be named "observable behavior implemented after the model of the model of the ... of the model of love". The result is that AI projects tend to have a simplistic view on these concepts (see [Slo01a, p. 178]).

The second failure committed is, how these concepts are integrated into a control system. For example, if one takes the concept of memory from psychology and integrates it into a cognitive architecture based on Brooks' subsumption architecture (e.g. Ho et al. [HDN03]), several problems arise. The subsumption architecture was developed by Brooks [Bro86] to create autonomous robots operating on simple, reactive rules. Hence, its memory structures were omitted deliberatively. Thus, when introducing memory to this architecture, several questions have to be answered. For example, is the original design of the memory structure described with a certain type of architecture in mind (for example the human mind)? Is this architecture exchangeable with the subsumption architecture? Is the subsumption architecture designed to have a long-term memory and thus to store a model of the world?

The third failure made by researchers is to overlook or ignore the possibility of information overload in interdisciplinary projects (see [Wil96]). When operating outside their scientific community they are confronted with different knowledge bases, methods, and terminology [LBP06, p. 70]. Thus, when trying to incorporate theories from another profession, an expert from this profession has to be consulted. Interdisciplinary work cannot be done by reading books alone — it needs the personal cooperation of scientists of the fields of interest.

The fourth failure is, to mix systems which have an emotion and systems which show some behavior that is interpreted as an emotion by a human observer. Robots or software agents which show some emotional expression are sometimes labeled as having it (e.g. Breazeal in [Bre01, p. 584]). Creating agents having behavior showing emotions is an interesting and fascinating field of research with immediate applications in toy industry and in human-system-interface design.

The fifth failure is to state that a system feels something [Lor08, p. 4]. Such mental states are subjective experience [ST02, p. xiii]. I — the human observer — can only suggest that the person with whom I am talking with at the moment has a certain feeling, thinks about a special topic, etc. Thus, it is only possible to define that every mechanism identified to be necessary has been implemented (cp. [Fra03, p. 53]) and — up to some extent — one believes that the agent experiences a certain feeling.

Theories used in the described ARS model are primarily taken from psychoanalysis (and transformed into technically feasible terms in cooperation with psychoanalysts). Psychoanalysis' concern is on the psyche and not on the body itself. Nevertheless, it contains theories on the interaction between mind and body (cp. Section 3.1.4). Concepts for this part are taken carefully from embodied cognitive science (e.g. [CB97]). The goal of this work is to present a psychoanalytically inspired decision making architecture for a software agent. Thus, the focus is towards the mechanisms of emotions, drives, affects, etc. As long term goal, the system should be able to express its emotions and also to tell which emotions it currently feels[3]. Note that when writing in this work of an emotion of an artificial agent, it refers to whatever emerges from the mechanism mentioned before.

1.2.2 Why Psychoanalysis?

Taking a bionic approach to decision making raises the question which life-form from nature should be taken as archetype. Insects have interesting but limited capabilities. The mental capabilities of mammals — even the smallest one — are much more promising. For a start one would tend to take small, simple mammals like mice. Although a lot of research on the brain of mice has been done by behaviorists and neurologists, still little is known compared to the most complex mammalian mind known — the human mind.

If one takes the human mental apparatus as archetype for designing a decision unit, one cannot deny the complexity of the internal structures of this apparatus. Questions like "Why do I remember this and not that at the moment?", "Why do I have such an emotion?", "What is the structure of the mental apparatus?" immediately arise. Behaviorism can give no answers; psychology and neurology can only give limited answers.

Eric Kandel, 2000 Nobel laureate, stated that psychoanalysis is "[...] still the most coherent and intellectually satisfying view of the mind [4] (quoted in Solms and Turnbull [ST02, p. 304])." Psychoanalysis does not give us an absolutely complete and totally coherent view on the mind, but as stated in the quote above, more than any other science of the mind can give. Psychoanalysis as therapy is based upon a theoretical framework called metapsychology. Within this framework a functional model of the mental apparatus is described.

---
[3]Not to be confused with I — the designer — am attributing to the system that it feels something.
[4]Kandel continues his speech with a harsh critique where psychoanalysis fails.

Before continuing to answer the initial question "Why Psychoanalysis?", a short overview of the problems Good Old Fashioned Artificial Intelligence (GOFAI) is faced with is worth to be noted here. Push Singh published a widely recognized list of five points on his website [4]:

- First, AI is a widespread field of research without an umbrella unifying the various results.
- Next, simple explanations are searched for complex systems.
- The overall goal of AI — building a human like, flexible "intelligence" — is surrendered to highly specialized sub goals.
- Many researchers are dealing with building robots instead of creating software.
- Building systems which can deal with common sense knowledge is necessary; many researchers are trying to circumvent this fact.

Although the fourth point — robots instead of software — has to be relaxed due to the upcoming of embodied AI (e.g. Pfeifer and Scheier [PS99] and Pfeifer and Bongard [PB07]), the other four points are still valid today. Franklin [Fra97, pp. 516–517] states that using a holistic view on "intelligence" is necessary. Looking at isolated parts is not sufficient for building satisfying cognitive agents.

The authors of [DZ08] are taking critiques a step further — they are proposing a new — the 5th — generation of AI. In continuation to the first three points formulated by Singh, they demand that engineers have to build uniform, holistic models, preferable with a top-down modeling approach. As result the system architecture is not explained by the interaction of neurons. Further, an interdisciplinary approach — bringing together scientists from various fields — is an integral postulation for the 5th generation of AI.

Using psychoanalysis as an archetype will not solve all the problems of AI. But it offers answers to most of the questions which result from the above listed five points.

After arguing why psychoanalysis is the right choice for the task at hand, reasons why psychoanalysis has hardly been used before has to be discussed.

1.2.3 Objections to Psychoanalysis

There are lots of objections against psychoanalysis. In the following list, I shall address some central ones; all of which having been brought forward by other scientists during my work within an interdisciplinary project:

It is not a (natural) science. For example, Perner claims this in [Per97, p. 242]. While many psychoanalysts state that it is a science (e.g. Solms and Turnbull in [ST02, pp. 304–306], [DFZB09, pp. 17–21]), others are arguing that it is not (e.g. Colby and Stoller in [CS88, pp. 1–7]). Nevertheless, even the ones denying psychoanalysis the state of being a science say, that it can commit valuable theories and concepts to cognitive science [CS88, p. 153].

Psychoanalysis is based on subjective analysis. A point extensively discussed by Grünbaum in [Grü00, p. 288]. Objective sciences like neurology have no or at least very limited possibilities to measure internal mental states like feelings. Despite the lack of eligible measurements, feelings are real. At least their effect on the world is real. Feelings are producing e.g. certain facial expressions which have a real impact on other humans in our vicinity. Subjective analysis is the only possibility to describe mechanisms which are not observable by methods of objective sciences [ST02, pp. 296–297], [LBP06, p. 66].

Nothing in psychoanalysis has ever been objectively proven. Popper formulates this objection in [Pop63, p. 48]. The above two points are answering this objection: Psychoanalysis provides valuable insights which can only be gained by subjective analysis. And to disagree with the statement: The relative young field of neuropsychoanalysis aims directly at bringing results from an objective science (neurology) and results from a subjective science (psychoanalysis) together (e.g. [ST02, p. 300]).

There are several — partially mutual exclusive — models. Next to Freud's first and second topographical theories other important psychoanalytical theories are: Object-relation theory (Klein and Bion), psychodynamic (Jung), and structuralism (Lacan). Psychoanalysis is an ongoing and vivid science. Thus, existing models are modified, from time to time new theories appear, or old theories are merged into one. These changes are heavily discussed. Sometimes, this leads to (temporary) contradicting theories which are pursued. Below, the method with which the project ARS is approaching this issue is sketched.

Psychoanalysis is a lot about therapy. This statement can also be found for example at [5]. And so are almost all other sciences of the mind without an engineering background. Be it psychology, neurology, or linguistics — all of them deal a lot with real patients and how to cure them. What they have in common with psychoanalysis is that beyond therapy each of them is researching one or more models of the human mind or of parts of it.

A robot does not need sexuality. This is the line of argumentation Buller uses in [Bul05] to justify the usage of psychodynamics. Buller prefers psychodynamic to psychoanalysis among other things due to the non-existence of sexuality. It is not applicable to reduce the term sexual drive to reproduction needs or pleasure gain. Moreover, it refers to everything which enables development and life. The psychic energy produced by the sexual drives can also be transformed into creative activity. In later works, Freud uses the term Eros which represents the life instinct native in all humans. It is composed of sexual drives and self-preservation drives. Thus, a robot — if controlled by a psychoanalytically inspired decision unit — needs sexuality as its main motivational system.

The list given above is a short discussion of the topics at hand. Each point could be discussed in more depth easily and more points could be added too. Nevertheless, this discussion would exceed the limits and the scope of this thesis.

1.2.4 Modeling Process

In Section 1.2.1 it was stated that two failures committed by AI researchers are to mix incompatible theories and not to consult experts from the fields of interest. The ARS project in which this thesis is embedded in is taking these traps very serious. From the start the project followed and still follows a strict interdisciplinary approach. Psychoanalytic experts have been — and still are — integrated into the modeling and publishing process from the very beginning (e.g. Brainin et al. [BDK$^+$04]). In the first years, meetings every two month were held. Since October 2007 one to two psychoanalysts are part time employed by the project — thus, intensifying the interdisciplinary exchange. One has always to be aware of the fact that interdisciplinarity is a challenging task — not only the language but also the processes how to approach and to describe topics of interest can be different [LBP06, p. 70], [CS88, p. 7], [DFZB09, pp. 36–37].

The process of generating a technical model from psychoanalysis followed in project ARS is a four step repetitive algorithm with an additional initial step (see Figure 1.1):

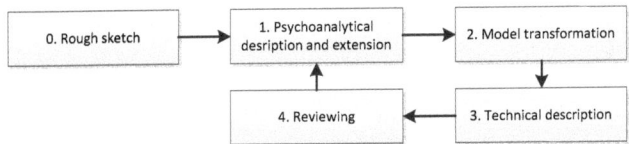

Figure 1.1: Modeling process

0. Psychoanalysts and engineers are describing in rough the control system.
1. Psychoanalysts are describing and extending the system in their own language.
2. Psychoanalysts together with engineers transform the psychoanalytical model into an intermediate one — tools like Unified Modeling Language (UML), Specification and Description Language (SDL), and feedback loops are used.
3. Engineers are describing all identified modules and interfaces in their own language.
4. Engineers together with psychoanalysts are reviewing the model for gaps and inconsistencies. (Continue with Step 1)

This approach is comparable to Cognitive Agent Architecture and Theory (CAAT) — a scientific loop proposed by Franklin in [Fra97, p. 507]. It consists of seven steps to create intelligent autonomous agents inspired by animals and humans. The main difference is the explicit distinction between an engineering step and an interdisciplinary cooperation partner — the psychoanalysts — step in the loop sketched in Figure 1.1.

The main method used for modeling in this project is top-down design. Thus, a look at the top-most level at the broadest possible view of the domain — the plain idea — is taken. In the next level, this idea is divided into several, more detailed parts. The total of these parts is equivalent to the idea plus a better description. This process is continued until the granularity of the description of the subparts is at the desired level. In the case of this project this would be a list of functions, their interfaces, and their interaction plus their exact description. The reason for preferring top-down to bottom-up is that designing a system with feelings starting from neurons is likely to fail (see Dietrich et al. [DLB+10, p. 723], [DBM+10, p. 80]).

Due to the fact that psychoanalytical theory covers infancy, childhood, adolescence, and adulthood the object of interest has been deliberately reduced: What is being described is a normal[5], fully developed adult of the age of 30 years. Thus, the body developments of the important first 20 years along with the mental development of these years are bypassed. Although these years are crucial for psychoanalysis, this design decision reduces the complexity of the task. Not all mental functions are present in infants. The development and integration of functions like Superego while growing up is skipped for the time being. In violation of the symbol grounding problem (cp. [Har90]) everything of these years has to be defined by the designer (e.g. body, rules, experiences). Please note, that the development is not totally abandoned in this approach. Psychoanalytic theories contain it implicitly. Concluding, the desired result of this research project is a technically feasible psychoanalytically inspired model and not the individual experience of an artificial agent.

As mentioned above, several psychoanalytical theories exist. Some of them are mutually exclusive. A uniform, generally accepted model is not available. This project focuses on the structural model as first described by Freud [Fre23]. As a result, only works not contradicting this model are used.

Off course, psychoanalytical theories — as detailed as they may be — can never describe every mental function in a resolution fine enough that every implementation oriented question can be answered sufficiently. Thus, whenever the division of a function into sub-functions has to stop at a premature time — no straight forward implementation of the function is possible — fitting algorithms and approaches from AI are used. One has to be careful not to perform a backward modeling to change the psychoanalytically inspired model to better fit the selected AI algorithm.

1.3 Context

The content of this thesis can roughly be fitted to the following two sciences: Cognitive science and a subset of AI called Artificial General Intelligence (AGI).

According to Gardner [Gar85, p. 37] (see Figure 1.2), cognitive science can be described as the collaboration of the following six sciences: Psychology, philosophy, AI, linguistics, anthropology, and neuroscience. Most of the pairings (e.g. AI and neurosciences) have strong interdisciplinary ties; whereas some pairings like AI and anthropology are only weakly tied. Project ARS focuses on the triangle psychology (of which psychoanalysis is a part of), neuroscience, and AI.

---

[5]Please note that this term is not used by psychoanalysis — they are using expressions like "non conspicuous".

Introduction

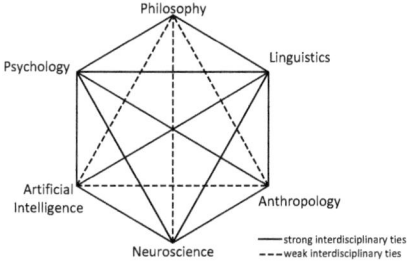

Figure 1.2: Gardner's hexagon [Gar85, p. 37]

The connection between psychoanalysis and neuroscience is represented by the usage of neuropsychoanalytical works like Solms and Turnbull [ST02]. This is a young scientific field founded by Solms [ST02] and Panksepp [Pan98]. The aim of it is to combine psychoanalysis with neuroscience. Thus, closing the gap that Freud opened deliberately over 100 years ago [Fre15b, pp. 174–175]. Freud — being a neurologist himself — discovered that using methods and measuring instruments available around 1900 will not be sufficient to explain the human mental apparatus. In order to be able to continue his work on the psyche, he decided to work with subjective observation of patients and with introspection for the time being. Today, neuropsychology aims at bringing scientific research results from the two very different approaches — neurology and psychoanalysis — into consistence.

Thus, the interdisciplinary work is between AI and neuropsychoanalysis. Currently, the focus is on transferring theories from neuropsychoanalysis to AI. In future, results of this engineering work should be offered to neuropsychoanalysis.

The engineering part of this project can be accounted to AGI. This is a subset of AI which aims at the general nature of human "intelligence" [WG06, p. 1]. This is in opposition to mainstream AI work — they usually aim at specialized "intelligence" in narrow defined domains. According to Franklin [Fra97, pp. 516–517], these specialized types of "intelligence" cannot converge to a unified, general one.

A precise definition for AGI does not exist. It refers to everything which supports the idea of creating human-level "intelligence". An AGI framework should at least include learning, memory, and a cognition cycle. While this fits for most AI frameworks too, not every AI framework is an AGI framework — narrow AI projects lack generality [WG06, p. 5]. Thus, the main difference between AGI and narrow AI projects are their goal and the scope of research. Three important points to identify an AGI project are:

1. A theory of "intelligence" as a whole has to exist.
2. An implementation of the theory has to exist or at least an implementation plan.
3. Some concrete results in form of publications or implementations have to exist.

Franklin lists in [Fra06, p. 37] additional features of AGI machines. Among them are *"[they] generalize their knowledge across different domains"* and *"[they] reflect on themselves."*

Further, he claims that to meet the requirements for learning, the framework should be embedded in agents. Autonomous agents are providing the necessary sensing and acting abilities [FG97, p. 27]: *"An autonomous agent is a system situated within and a part of an environment that senses that environment and acts on it, over time, in pursuit of its own agenda and so as to effect what it senses in the future."*

Which theories should be used and which techniques should be applied is of no concern to AGI [WG06, p. 2]. They can range from symbol manipulation systems to statistical approaches. This is reflected in the list of existing AGI projects given on [6]: SOAR, ACT-R, Novamente, NARS, PolyScheme, Joshua Blue, LIDA, OpenCog, and MindForth. All of these projects differ in methods and focus.

Comparing ARS with the (soft) requirements for AGI projects leads to the conclusion that it can be seen as a member of the above given list with some limitations/adjustments. Learning is postponed until a first full implementation of the model has been realized. Psychoanalysis does not provide a theory of "intelligence." It provides a general architecture of how the human mind works. This can be translated as being a theory of "intelligence." More than eighty articles and theses have been published until now. And an implementation is currently under development. The very open view on which theories and methods can be used for AGI systems is not shared. Dietrich et al. [DZ08] sketches the demand of a new approach to AI. It is argued that a top-down modeling process in combination with a functional model is the most promising approach to create systems with human-like "intelligence."

1.4 Problem Statement

In this section the implicitly sketched problem statement from above is made explicit. This is done in a two folded approach: The scientific motivation and the research considerations are developed. Although the research considerations are extracted from the motivation, they are also influencing the scientific motivation.

1.4.1 Motivation

Parallel to the advent of holistic approaches to bionically inspired control systems the decoupling of the decision system from the body was reverted. Early AI focused on data processing algorithms. Brooks [Bro92] and later Pfeifer and Scheier [PS97] are arguing that much processing time can be saved by utilizing pre- and post-processing capabilities of the body and its anatomy. For example, the position and the shaping of the ears help to focus on sound coming from usually important areas and filter non important frequencies. Both could be done by using algorithms running on the processor; this approach saves costly hardware resources. Another example is the use of elastic joints in robot legs providing adaption to uneven surfaces automatically.

This research direction is called embodiment. Its core idea can be summarized to two main components: How we think has been shaped by the body and the richness of the body, the control system, and the environment have to match. If an adult human loses one arm, the mind adapts to this situation (although never fully). This results in different thoughts and ideas and finally different actions than before. A typical example from AI (see [Pfe96, p. 9]) is that a two-wheeled robot with a simple gripper does not need a high resolution camera and huge processor capacities. The poor manipulation capabilities do not allow the robot to generate grounded symbols based on sensor-actuator coupling experiences.

An important feature — hinted by Chiel and Beer in [CB97, p. 554] — is usually not included in embodied systems: Rich internal systems. For example Pfeifer and Bongard discuss the interplay between the mind and the body in [PB07] by analyzing outer attributes like shape of the body and joints. Internal systems like the stomach and blood circulation are hardly mentioned at all. Nevertheless, real world bodies in nature include some kind of nervous system, some approach to digest nutrition, some internal sensor to monitor these processes, etc. These elements should not be ignored when looking at embodiment.

The influence of the body and its rich internal systems on decision making is an important part in psychoanalysis. The Id is responsible for collecting data from internal sources and preparation of this information to be included in the decision making process. The bodily demands are the driving force for activity.

The holistic model provided by psychoanalysis together with a rich body will produce systems that are able to maintain themselves — the body tells them what they need — while working on more complex tasks. The coordination between these two — partly contradicting — tasks emerges from affects generated by the Id. They are influencing decision making and memory retrieval. Further, currently non appropriate demands and perceptions can be blocked by the system. Part of the tasks of the Id is to "resurface" these blocked contents. Such, the demands can be satisfied at another time or by other means.

The motivation sketched above can be condensed to: The focus of this thesis is on the psychoanalytic instance Id and its interaction with the body.

1.4.2 Research Considerations

To guide the work on the above sketched topic, several considerations are formulated. They define basic assumptions and conditions. The first three statements are of more general nature. The next two aim at the core of this thesis. The last one deals with an implementation issue.

Statement 1.1. *The model of the human psyche as described by the theoretical framework of psychoanalysis — the metapsychology — can be transformed into a technically feasible model.*

The first condition — Statement 1.1 — is the basic assumption of the ARS project. It guides model development and leads to the description of the functional modules within the model, the interfaces between them, and the atomic data types of information passed through the connections.

Statement 1.2. *The technical model as described in Statement 1.1 can be implemented in a computer.*

Statement 1.2 is a consequence of Statement 1.1. It is important due to the fact that the theoretical work should be implemented in real world applications in the end. This implies that the implemented methods have to have similar functionality as described in the model. An empty shell with random results does not qualify for this task. Implementing a model helps to point out inconsistencies of the model. Thus, evaluation by building is an important method to evaluate the model. This leads to the next statement:

Statement 1.3. *A-Life simulations are best suited to perform evaluations of the implemented model based on Statement 1.1.*

Virtual creatures—autonomous agents equipped with a control system implemented according to Statement 1.2—populate a virtual world. They can interact with animate and inanimate objects as well as with other creatures. By defining use-cases which consist of a setup within this world and desired behaviors of the agents the validity of the model can be tested. This is not to be confused with designing the control system with behavioral patterns. These patterns are used solely to evaluate the model after it has been designed using neuropsychoanalytical theories.

Statement 1.4. *The Id implies a body and thereafter embodiment.*

According to psychoanalysis, the Id is developed first in a human being. It evolves from the body and represents bodily demands in the psyche. In the Ego, emotions and affects are the mechanisms through which the demands provided by the Id are perceived. Thus the body operates as motivational source. The autonomous agents from Statement 1.3 have to be extended to satisfy Statement 1.4. The psyche developed to keep the body alive in a hostile world. Thus, the body and the psyche are tightly interconnected. Hence, embodiment is introduced. Embodied autonomous agents have a (virtual) body with its own internal dynamics.

Statement 1.5. *The solution which satisfies Statement 1.4 satisfies Statement 1.1 too.*

Statements 1.2, 1.3, and 1.4 are focusing on the psychic entity Id. Other entities defined by Freud's 2nd topographical model like Ego and Superego can be modeled based on the same assumptions as well. The resulting overall model would suffice Statement 1.1.

Statement 1.6. *A subset of the implemented model (see Statement 1.2) exists which provides a simpler, but still operational system.*

The last statement — Statement 1.6 — deals with an implementation issue. The model consists of roughly 40 modules, 50 interfaces, 3 feed-back loops, a memory layer, etc. For some applications and during testing, not all of these are needed. A minimum set has to be identified which has to be present for all purposes. The performance of an agent with the full implementation compared to one equipped with the reduced one will show what functionality can be gained by the added complexity. Additionally, this set identifies the critical implementation path. Elements which are part of it have to be more robust than others. Even with a perfect implementation system locks due to the data feed into it cannot be excluded. Thus, when designing a technical system a core block and an extended block can be defined. In case of a lock in the extended block, the core block can continue to control the system while the extended block can be taken care of.

1.5 Approach

Based on the motivation, the research considerations and the sketched preliminary work given above, the task for this thesis can be condensed to:

> Extend and improve the existing psychoanalytically inspired decision making model with focus on the psychoanalytic instance Id. The developed model has to be evaluated using an A-Life simulation.

Although the main focus is on the Id, the whole second topographical model has to be looked at. Only the interplay of all three psychic instances — Id, Ego, and Superego — produces the desired AGI model. Thus, a holistic view during model development has to be kept. As a result all modules, their interfaces, and their interplay are dealt with. The modules related to Ego and Superego are sketched briefly. The same accounts for modules that realize body functions. Special care is given to all Id modules.

The implementation 'ARS implementation number 11 (ARSi11)/Deutsch'[6] is divided into three parts:

1. The A-Life simulation which operates as test-bed itself,
2. the virtual body of the artificial creature which hosts human bionically inspired decision system, and
3. the implementation of the decision system.

Although this work uses psychoanalysis as its foundation, psychoanalysis itself is out of scope of this thesis. The introduced concepts are examined only regarding their technical feasibility. The virtual body is designed to provide interesting internal dynamics. It is loosely inspired by nature and the human body. The creation of a more correct and

---

[6] ARSi11/Deutsch stands for ARS implementation number 11 done by Tobias Deutsch (=the author of this work). ARS implementation number 10 (ARSi10) has been done by Zeilinger in his PhD [Zei10].

Introduction

realistic body would be out of scope of this thesis, too. The introduced principles work similarly independent of the underlying organs.

The simulation is inspired by Todas' Fungus-Eater [Tod62]. He describes a reduced world with objects and other agents to interact with. To ensure that the designed world meets the research needs, a requirement analysis has to be done. With such an analysis, the simulation can provide all necessary needs to operate as test-bed for the use-cases. A use-case defines the conditions, start situation, desired outcome(s), and how to verify success for an experiment.

As the Id communicates bodily needs to the other psychic instances, a body is needed. The body is designed to operate within the artificial world. It provides actuators and sensors as well as internal systems (like a converter of external energy providing objects to internally usable energy). Similarly to using the human mind as archetype for the decision unit, the human body is — very loosely — used as archetype for the virtual body. It would be out of scope of this thesis to develop a body as rich and complex as the human one (or any living creature). A lot of simplifications, reductions, and 'shortcuts' are used. The human nervous system — which transports for example the information of pain from a body part to the brain — has to be reduced to a fast messenger system which transports binary information from source to target. Another example is vision: The field of view is fixed and object cannot be occluded. Further, information from visible objects are extracted directly from the coded objects and transformed on a symbolic level. Thus, low-level sensor data processing is bypassed. Nevertheless, the resulting body provides rich enough data sources for the Id.

The framework for the decision unit has two layers. The first one is a general purpose interface between the body and any type of decision unit. Thus, an arbitrary number of different decision units can be implemented and compared. The second layer to be described in this thesis contains the psychoanalytically inspired decision unit. It consists of a set of modules which are processed every simulation step in a fixed order. They send messages through interfaces between them and perform memory access via a memory layer.

The minimum set of these modules is determined by a developmental point of view. Other than the basic assumption in project ARS — the model is designed by using the psyche of a normal human adult of 30 years — the developmental process of the three instances is examined. The Id develops first, next is the Ego and finally the Superego is developed. The point in time when Statement 1.6 is satisfied is used as blueprint. Similarly to the final model, this minimal model is implemented too.

The above sketched test-bed is used to evaluate the introduced concepts. A use-case that focuses on the interplay between body and psyche is the general set-up. First, a step by step analysis of the implementation of the concepts is performed. Next, a broader perspective is taken and the impact of the novel concepts on the overall model is discussed. Additionally, the performance of the minimal model in contrast to the final model is shown. Finally, the first application of the model to a robot is shown and the gained insights discussed.

> AI can have two purposes. One is to use the power of computers to augment human thinking, just as we use motors to augment human or horse power. Robotics and expert systems are major branches of that. The other is to use a computer's artificial intelligence to understand how humans think. In a humanoid way. If you test your programs not merely by what they can accomplish, but how they accomplish it, then you're really doing cognitive science; you're using AI to understand the human mind.
>
> Herbert Simon: from Doug Stewart's Interview with Herbert Simon

2 State of the Art

Many projects using concepts from Artificial Intelligence (AI) and Artificial General Intelligence (AGI) exist. It is necessary to position this work in relation to them and to compare it with comparable fitting works. A third aspect in this positioning is the usage of psychoanalysis: How do other projects incorporate it? The focus of this thesis is on the interaction between the body and the control architecture. Thus, the fourth aspect is related to embodiment and bodily demands.

In Section 1.3, this work was assigned to the scientific research field AGI. This leads to the questions how cognitive architectures are defined and what projects exist in it? Also, the topic, how do other AGI projects evaluate their work? These three points are discussed in Section 2.1. Statement 1.4 defines that emotions, affects, and bodily demands are basic requirements. Not all projects dealing with this topic are related to AGI. Thus, this topic is dealt with in Section 2.2 by comparing how others have formalized and implemented them. A further conclusion from Statement 1.4 is that the whole system to be designed needs to be embodied (Section 2.3). The first three sections are independent of the leitmotif as stated in Statement 1.1—psychoanalysis. Not many projects exist that use psychoanalysis as their starting point/foundation. An overview of them is given in Section 2.4. As sketched in Section 1.5 and based on Statement 1.2 and Statement 1.3, an Artificial Life (A-Life) simulation is needed as test-bed for the modeled architecture. A short overview of agent based simulation platforms concludes the overview of work of others. The chapter is concluded with an overview about preliminary work already done in project Artificial Recognition System (ARS).

2.1 Artificial General Intelligence Architectures

AGI—introduced in Section 1.3—is a research area aiming at the development of systems capable of general "intelligence." A tool to achieve this goal is the usage of foundational architecture frameworks (Section 2.1.1). They describe necessary features and structures and can guide development. AGI architectures which have already been—partly—implemented are discussed in Section 2.1.2. A difficult task is the comparison of different projects. They differ in modeling approaches, application domains, and maturity. Also, the evaluation of a single architecture is a non-trivial task. Possible approaches to this problem are introduced in the last subsection.

2.1.1 Foundational Architecture Frameworks

The most important design choice is the overall architecture [Slo99, p. 35]. All further questions like memory usage have to be answered in context of this architecture. The archetype of the system described in this work is the human mind (see Section 1.3). This is necessary to design a system capable of human-like "intelligence" (cp. [Fra06, p. 37], [Bau06, p. 56], and [Slo99]). Despite the differences of AGI projects, most of them share a common foundational architecture as described in [Fra06]. It is a rough sketch of identified necessary elements and processes to accomplish the goal.

An architecture for human-like agents has to provide information on different levels of abstraction and their corresponding levels of implementation [Slo99, p. 36]. For example, a fully operational architecture may be composed of the following sub-architectures: An architecture for the underlying physical mechanisms, an architecture of a complex algorithm, and an architecture of concurrent software modules and how they are integrated. Next to the different levels of functionality, the architectures differ in terms of functionality. External and internal tasks — both necessary for the correct operation of the human-like agent — have to be modeled within these architectures.

[Slo00, p. 6] describes a three layered control architecture called Cognition and Affect (CogAff). Each layered is build atop the others. Figure 2.1(a) depicts the simplest architecture — the reactive subsystem. At this level, the system responses to all perceptions as soon as the triggering conditions are met. No inhibition, delay, or deliberation takes place. The cognitive cycle is immediate: Sensor data is perceived, processed, and immediately a corresponding action is performed on the environment.

Such a reactive system is fast, easy to implement, and reliable within the design space. The problem arises as soon as new situations arise. If a suitable reaction cannot be found using the pre-defined set of rules and triggers, the system may break down. Further, the combination of choices, rules, actions, and inputs is explosive in complexity. These problems are met with the introduction of an additional layer — the deliberative subsystem (Figure 2.1(b)). Next to some kind of planning mechanism, a memory, a motivational system, and an attention filter are added. Not every information perceived is now passed to the higher level mechanism; reducing the amount of data which has to be processed. The motivational system enables the agent to operate independently from external events. The available long-term memory relaxes the need to react to each event immediately.

Similarly to the reactive subsystem, the deliberative subsystem can fail. A meta-management layer (Figure 2.1(c)) can be added to evaluate the performance of the deliberative layer. The evaluation should be done relative to long term high level generic objectives. These could include rules like "do not try to solve a problem which has already turned out to be unsolvable." It has to be questioned if this meta-management layer does not introduce the "homunculus" problem: To operate as expected, the meta-management layer might

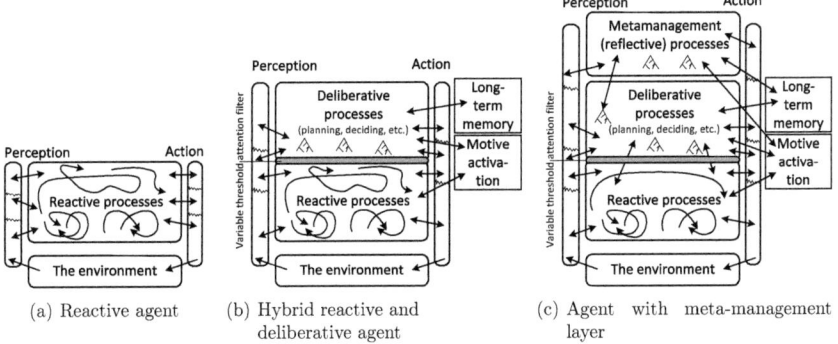

Figure 2.1: Three levels of control [Slo99, pp. 8–10]

need another meta-management layer which needs another meta-management layer which ... Thus, an infinite set of meta-management layers would then be necessary. Each additionally introduced layer can fail and another layer has to be added to control it. While the first two layers are necessary for human-like agents, the third one can be omitted if necessary [Slo99, p. 11]. Nevertheless, self-monitoring and self-assessing processes are important mechanisms which should be included. These processes have to be designed such that no additional layer which guarantees their correct functioning has to be added.

An important group of elements of CogAff are "alarms" [Slo01b, p. 42]. This kind of sub-system receives inputs from many parts of the rest of the system and is capable of triggering global re-organizations of activities. There can be several such sub-systems on one or more layers or across different layers.

Based on the foundational framework CogAff, an architecture called Human-Cognition and Affect (H-CogAff) has been designed [Slo04a, SCS05, SC05]. Extensions to the three-layer system are an alarm system in the reactive layer and a personal identity module. According to Sloman and Chrisley in [SC05, p. 19], no complete implementation of the H-CogAff-Architecture exists, yet. Nevertheless, partial implementations have been performed in the project group of Sloman.

The CogAff framework is useful for comparisons. Different architectures can be mapped to the three layers and the additional elements. It is less appropriate to be used as starting point for development of a control architecture [Lan10, p. 17]. The underlying mechanisms are described vaguely. Additionally, the interfaces between the modules are only sketched and the control flow is undefined.

According to [Fra06, p. 48], an agent has to perform cognitive cycles in an infinite loop. A cognitive cycle is the sequence of sensing, processing, and acting. Although CogAff provides a lot of information, this cycle is not described. A further missing part is the

State of the Art

definition of the interfaces between the various modules. Also, learning is not included. The foundational architecture described in [Fra06, p. 44] is more compact compared to CogAff. The layered approach and the alarms are not explicitly included. But the three missing — or at least not sufficiently explicit demanded — issues are included.

The demands for a foundational architecture described in [Fra06] are:

- The agent has to be situated in its environment. Thus, interaction between the agent and the environment has to be done via its sensors and actuators.
- The cognitive cycle has to run in an infinite loop.
- The agent has to decide what to do next.
- Incoming sensor data has to be processed to assign meaning to it.
- Reoccurring sequences of actions have to be grouped and stored in a memory.
- An associative long-term memory has to provide the system with information about past events.
- A mechanism responsible for focus of attention has to be present.
- The incoming data has to be filtered. This can happen at several modules like perception, attention, or action selection.
- Learning has to be an integral part of the architecture.

Figure 2.2 shows the foundational architecture which meets these requirements. The environment is sensed and evaluated in the Module **Perception**. The resulting **Percepts** are passed to the Module **Attention**. It is responsible for decision making using information recalled from **Episodic memory**. **Attention** module decides which data is passed to the **Procedural memory**. Using associations, fitting actions are retrieved from **Procedural memory**. They are passed to the last module — **Action selection**. It makes the final decision which action should be performed on the environment.

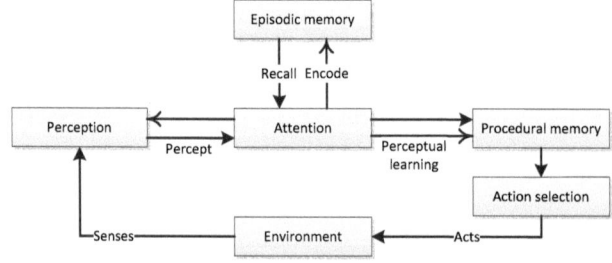

Figure 2.2: A foundational architecture for AGI [Fra06, p. 44]

Three types of learning are included in this architecture: Procedural, perceptual, and episodic. The current perception is encoded and stored to the episodic memory. New meanings like new object classes are extracted from the percept and passed back to module perception. In parallel, new sequences of actions can be passed to the procedural memory.

Although this foundational framework helps in clarifying design issues, its description contains a serious problem. A clear distinction between functions and data is missing. For example, attention is a function module, whereas episodic memory is a data module.

[Fra06, p. 47] performs a mapping of this architecture to CogAff. Reactive and deliberative layers as well as the long-term memory are present. The missing meta-management layer can be added if necessary. A realization of the architecture called Learning Intelligent Distribution Agent (LIDA) is discussed in the next section.

2.1.2 Project Architectures

Different AGI projects exist. For example, the website [6] lists SOAR, ACT-R, Novamente, NARS, PolyScheme, Joshua Blue, LIDA, OpenCog, and MindForth. The proceedings of the AGI Workshop 2006 [GW07] — which is the first publication of the AGI community — contains articles on the projects LIDA, Novamente, NARS, BICA-GMU, MOSES, and PLN. Out of this list, LIDA and Novamente are selected to be discussed in detail. The first one is selected due to its double role: part of the project defines a foundational architecture already discussed in the previous subsection, the other part of the project deals with a system designed and implemented for a specific task. BICA-GMU is comparable to LIDA [WG06, p. 11]. Novamente incorporates MOSES and PLN in its functional modules. Further, this project is the origin of OpenCog (Prime). Thus, both of them can be seen exemplarily for other AGI projects.

LIDA

Project LIDA [7] has two aims: A science aim and an engineering aim [FP06, p. 2]. The science aim is to better understand human cognition — more precise "a cognitive theory of everything [FP06, p. 4]." The engineering aim is to create and implement a fitting architecture. The science part is done by integrating various theories from neurology, psychology, and cognitive science. Used theories include situated cognition, perceptual symbol systems, working memory, memory by affordances, long-term working memory, the CogAff architecture, and transient episodic memory [FM04, BF09]. No superior scientific instance is providing a coherent model — its creation and evaluation is part of the work. This is in opposition to the approach of project ARS — the overall model is provided by psychoanalysis. The task of the interdisciplinary team is to point to inconsistencies and gaps.

The Global Workspace Theory (GWT) which has been integrated into LIDA [FRD+07] is a simple cognitive model making use of the interaction of dominant and non-dominant content. At a given point in time only one set of information can be dominant. Dominant content is distributed to other modules. Not dominant content can form coalitions to gain higher probability of being dominant. The functions necessary for a GWT implementation are: A coalition manager (contents can form new coalitions), a spotlight manager (selection of the dominant content), a broadcast manager (distribution of the dominant content), and attention codelets (recognition of novel or problematic situations). The broadcasted

State of the Art

dominant contents are guided and constrained by contexts which cannot become dominant like perceptual contexts, goal contexts, and conceptual contexts [Fra03, p. 48], [BF07, p. 959]. In this way the relevance problem encountered in AI can be solved [FRD+07, p. 4].

Cognition is modeled with a cycle (described below). Such a cognitive cycle is a sequential processing of the cognitive modules starting from perception and resulting in an action. A single run is responsible for data processing and simple but fast reactive acting. Cognitive processes of higher order like reasoning or imagination are multi-cyclic. Thus, they need several cycles to finish their calculations.

In Figure 2.3 the cognitive cycle of LIDA is shown. A single run consists of the following nine steps ([RBDF06, pp. 245–246], [FRD+07, p. 6], [BF07, p. 959–960]):

1. External and internal stimuli are processed by the sensory memory module. Through association meaning is attached. The result is a percept codelet.
2. In the module perceptual associative memory, the current percept and still existing percepts from previous rounds are combined to higher-level percepts.
3. In the workspace, perceptions, associations retrieved from episodic memory, and declarative memory information are put together to cues which are stored in long term memory.
4. These contents form coalitions which compete for dominance. This is guided by attention codelets provided by the module attention codelets.
5. Based on GWT, the dominance broadcast takes place in module global workspace.
6. The dominant content evokes fitting responses from procedural memory in the procedural memory module.
7. Additional content which is not dominant is used to bind resources in the action selection module.
8. Finally, an action which is to be performed in this cognitive cycle is selected by the action selection module.
9. LIDA performs the action on the internal or external environment.

Content not processed in action selection can be used in the next cognitive cycle. They are transferred from action selection to perceptual awareness memory via the re-afference connection. A reactive connection between sensors and actuators is realized with the dorsal stream connection (Interface Encode). In this way immediate reactive action can be taken.

Four types of learning are present in this model [RBDF06, pp. 247–250]: Perceptual learning, episodic learning, procedural learning, and attentional learning. Supported by dominant content, new information is added to these memories. Entries of transient episodic memory can be added to declarative memory by consolidation.

An interesting aspect of LIDA is that information is represented by codelets. A codelet is an active, special purpose process [FP06, pp. 1–2]. It is implemented with only a few lines of code. Thus, they carry information and can perform actions.

State of the Art

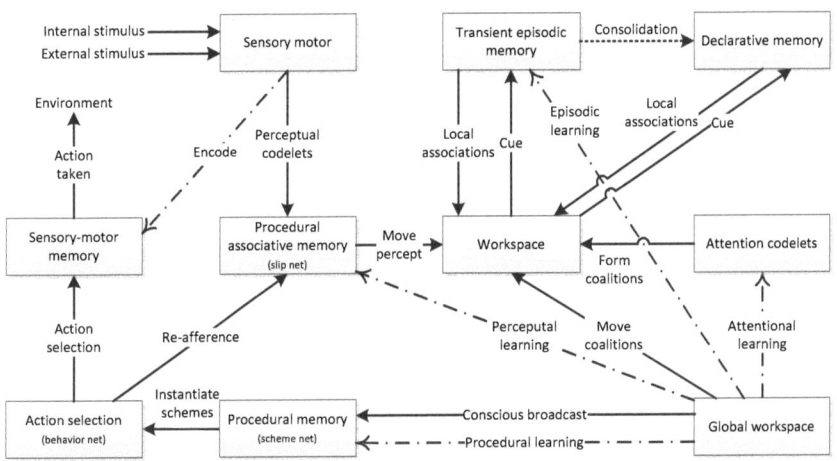

Figure 2.3: The LIDA cognitive cycle [BF09, p. 26]

The application LIDA is designed for job distribution in the US-Navy [Fra06, p. 46]. More than 200000 employees need job reassignments regularly. This is usually done by human job brokers. The employee writes an e-mail to his/her broker with information like employee-number, preferred next job, and preferred next location in natural language without any special formalism. The broker looks into the job record and the list of open assignments. Based on this information two to three new job assignment suggestions are sent to the employee. Finally, the employee selects the preferred job. The implemented LIDA based job distribution agent performs comparable to its human counterparts.

LIDA is a solid model for a control architecture based primarily on neurology and psychology. Its focus on GWT is manifested by two central modules in the model: Workspace and global workspace. Both have six interfaces while all other modules have between two to four interfaces. Further, the Module global workspace is responsible for the important tasks learning, focus of attention, and coalition building. A more detailed model would bypass this accumulation of tasks and lead to a better understanding how these tasks should be accomplished. Next, a clear distinction between functions and data is — deliberately — avoided. The codelets are both: Functions and data. While this concept seems to be influenced by the human brain, a description of how they operate and what benefits they provide is missing.

OpenCog Prime / Novamente

Another project with a long development history is Open Cognition (OpenCog) Prime/Novamente[1] [8]. It originates in a theory called PsyNet [Goe06, p. 452]. The basic assumption

---
[1]The names OpenCog Prime and Novamente are exchangeable. Novamente is older and originates in a closed source project started by Novamente LLC. OpenCog Prime is an open source implementation of

21

State of the Art

is that the mind is made of patterns [GP07, p. 80]. These patterns are represented by Atoms interconnected with Hebbian Links. MindAgents operate on these Atoms. This basic structure is used for all modules of the architecture; only differing in knowledge stored in the Atoms and the set of MindAgents used. According to [GP07, p. 64], Novamente is up to 2/3 build upon narrow AI; extended by new, self-developed concepts with AGI in mind.

OpenCog Prime is implemented using the OpenCog Framework [HG08]. This framework provides a collection of libraries for AGI applications. Additionally, a collection of cognitive algorithms is provided. The framework is designed to interact with the Artificial General Intelligence Simulator (AGISim).

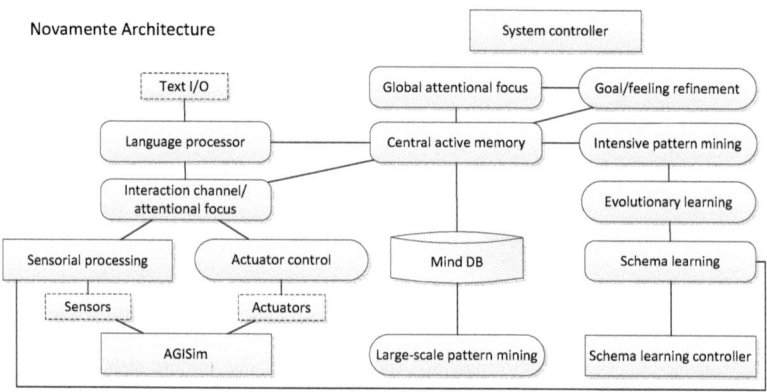

Figure 2.4: High-level cognitive architecture for OpenCog Prime [Goe07, p. 227]

DB ... Database

The Novamente Architecture depicted in Figure 2.4 describes a high level structure [Goe07, p. 227]. Interfaces to the simulation environment AGISim — sensors and actuators — and to external human operators or knowledge base — Text I/O — exist. The Language Processor contains language related Atoms only and is used to process information provided by Text I/O interface. Sensorial Processing is responsible for sensations, patterns, perceptual schemata, and attention allocation. The latter is also performed by Actuator Control along with action schemata control. These three modules are connected to Interaction Channel Attentional Focus. This is an active memory containing high-importance Atoms related to the three interaction modules. The Central Active Memory is responsible for goals, feelings, cognitive schemata, declarative knowledge, inference, and attention allocation. It is also the only interface to the Mind Database (DB). This database stores the Atoms and decides if they are kept in volatile memory or stored to disk. Large-Scale Pattern Mining performs greedy data mining on the stored Atoms. The module Global Attentional Focus serves as the active memory which contains only high-importance Atoms. Using data from

---

the Novamente architecture. The differences between them — except for some low level implementation details — are ignorable [Goe09, p. 1].

this module and the Central Active Memory module, Goal/Feelings Refinement performs inferences on it. Intensive Pattern Mining uses information provided by the Central Active Memory for two tasks: Evolution (generation of new knowledge) and inference (generation of new relations between existing knowledge). Next, specialized hardware is used to accelerate genetic algorithms used for evolutionary learning. This module uses data directly fetched from Sensorial Processing too. Schema Learning operates similarly to Intensive Pattern Mining, but with focus on schemata. Once new or adapted schemata are generated, they can be used as replacement for existing schemata. This exchange is performed by Schema Learning Controller. The System Controller is related to each module and is responsible for resource allocation.

According to [GP08, p. 2] this architecture can be roughly compared with the above discussed LIDA. The interesting part of Novamente is that each module consists of the same structure called Novamente cognitive unit. Figure 2.5(b) shows the structure of it. It consists of an arbitrary number of Novamente units which are interconnected. Further, all atoms stored in the local databases of these units may be interconnected within this cognitive unit. A Novamente unit (Figure 2.5(a)) — or Novamente Machine — consists of a database called atom space and several mind agents. A scheduler is responsible for the execution of the agents. Each agent performs different tasks on the atoms stored in the atom space.

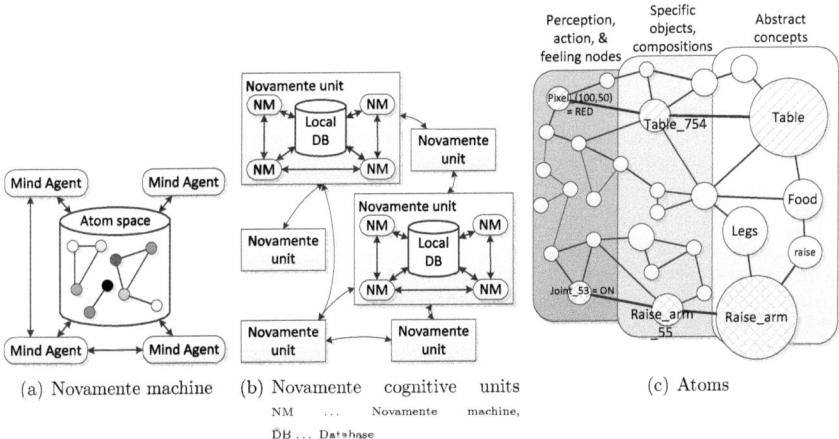

(a) Novamente machine (b) Novamente cognitive units (c) Atoms

NM ... Novamente machine,
DB ... Database

Figure 2.5: Sub elements of the Novamente cognitive architecture [Goc07, pp. 224–228]

Atoms are connected junks of information which are organized in different levels of complexity (see Figure 2.5(c)). The perceived information of the color of a certain pixel (pixel at (100,50) is red) is connected to a specific object (table_754) which is connected with an abstract concept of a table. The net generated by this connected atoms is the content of the Atom Space.

MindAgents serve different purposes [Goe07, p. 227], [GP07, p. 95]. They can work as "system maintenance" agents. For example, one agent is responsible for caching Atoms to the disk. The others operate as "cognitive"' agents. The agent Concept Formation creates new ConceptNodes (Atoms which represents concepts).

Although the ultimate goal is to create a fully operational AGI system, the current implementations focus on two issues: ´Collaborative learning [GP08, GP09] and to follow roughly Piaget's child development steps [GHB+06], [Goe07, p. 218], [GB07]. A third — more practical — application is within bioinformatics — a system to analyze genes [LGP04, p. 60].

Collaborative learning aims at speeding up learning a system to interact with its users. This is done by usage of a shared knowledge base. Each agent has its own personality and memory of events (which is not the knowledge base). According to the personality, information from the shared knowledge base is used sooner or never used at all. The application described in [GP09] uses a subset of the above described architecture called Virtual Animal Brain (VAB) implemented into dogs. Humans can interact with the dogs in the virtual reality environment Second Life. After one user has successfully taught his dog how to sit after several tries, this knowledge is transferred to the common knowledge base. If another user tries to teach her dog something using similar gestures or commands like the first one, her dog may retrieve the fitting information from the shared pool and starts to sit after much less tries than the first dog. Due to parallelizing and diversification the system can learn much faster and more stable than in a sequential approach. VAB is an intermediate step to natural language learning.

The second focus of current implementation efforts is on Piaget's child development stages. The basic steps defined by Piaget according to [GHB+06, p. 28] are: Infantile (imitation, repetition, association), pre-operational (abstract mental representations), concrete (abstract logical thought in context of the physical world), and formal (abstract deductive thought). Based on these four steps, a novel set more fitting to non-human cognitive structures was defined [GHB+06, p. 28]: Infantile (simplistic hard-wired inference control schemata), concrete (inference control schemata that adapt behavior), formal (carry out arbitrarily complex inferences), and reflexive (self-modification of internal structures).

In a simulation environment called AGISim ([GHB+06], [Goe07, pp. 238–240], [HGS+07]), a human controlled "adult" humanoid robot teaches a computer controlled "child" humanoid robot. Current focus is on the "A-not-B-error" as defined by Piaget. An object is first hidden in place A and sometimes hidden in place B. Depending on the developmental stage the "child" robot can correctly identify where the object has been hidden. Thus, the computer controlled robot is in its pre-operational stage.

The currently implemented architecture is shown in Figure 2.6. It resembles an intermediate step towards a completely functional and robust "artificial baby" [Goe07, p. 240].

The base of this system is the implemented Novamente core system consisting of AtomTables, MindAgents, Scheduler, etc. A perception module which performs stochastic conjunctive pattern mining to extract reappearing patterns in data streams provided by

State of the Art

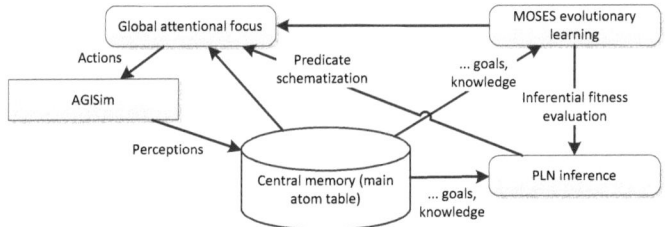

Figure 2.6: Current implementation of the architecture [Goe07, p. 230]

AGISim ... Artificial General Intelligence Simulator; MOSES ... Meta-optimizing semantic evolutionary search; PLN ... Probabilistic Logic Networks

AGISim. One of the previously learned actions is executed by the Schema Execution module. Learning is implemented in two modules: Meta-Optimizing Semantic Evolutionary Search (MOSES) and Probabilistic Logic Networks (PLN). MOSES — a supervised learning algorithm — supports learning by imitating the human controlled virtual robot. PLN is used to reason about abstract knowledge. The connection between the Novamente core and the AGISim environment is implemented using a proxy. A natural language processing front end is provided to bypass learning and to edit the knowledge directly — at the cost of losing the groundedness of the stored information.

The project follows the path sketched by the developmental stages. Once one stage has been mastered, the next — more complicated stage — is approached. According to [9] the long term goal is to create an AGI system with intellectual capabilities comparable to a scientist and beyond.

Other than project LIDA, OpenCog is not developed for a single purpose and is not being used in a production system currently. This is reflected by the many different models created by this project. Each uses a different subset of the developed concepts and focuses on a special topic. A clear road map or methodology how to proceed is missing. The used concepts are not discussed regarding their compatibility. Nevertheless, some concepts like the developed atom space are worth mentioning. The atom space is a three layered information representation module comparable to the symbolization layers of project ARS discussed in Section 2.6.1. Other concepts like the Novamente machine or hardware accelerated genetic algorithms are not grounded cognitive science. MOSES and PLN are statistic and probability based algorithms and are thereafter to be accounted to AI instead of AGI. The model depicted in Figure 2.6 shows the central role these two concepts have. To conclude, OpenCog has some interesting concepts but in general its focus is on building clever gadgets instead of developing a control architecture based on the human mind.

2.1.3 Evaluation and Comparison of Architectures

Development of an AGI system leads to the problem of evaluating it. AGI systems differ in which knowledge is used as foundation, the development approach, the target application, development progress, etc. Further, development of such a system may take several years (see [WG06, p. 3]). Thus, questions like is architecture A preferable to architecture B in general and for given problem C in particular are hard to answer. Although all AGI systems aim at general "intelligence," their current progress and focus on a special application — like LIDA and OpenCog Prime in the previous section — make comparisons difficult.

The imitation game [Tur50, p. 433] — better known as Turing test — could be used to compare two architectures which are at a comparable level of implementation. Human users rate if the communication partner at the other side the wall is a human or a computer. The architecture that gains the best ratings is better than the other one in the domain the Turing test has defined.

Critique on the Turing test is that every form of human communication which cannot be expressed by written words is excluded [GL09, pp. 368–369]. Even more serious, emotions are excluded as not being relevant for "intelligence." AGI systems incorporating them will be rated lower due to this system immanent design decision. The design niche for architectures which can be tested by the Turing test is very small [Slo99, p. 41]. Thus, most AGI architectures might not be applicable for such a test.

Another approach is to perform a comparison by answering questions regarding design decisions. This is especially appropriate if the overall architecture is available but the implementations are either not at comparable levels or a common test domain cannot be found. For example, one system focuses on natural language processing and the other on threat assessment in large buildings — the intersection between these two implementations might not be sufficient for a test setup like defined by the Turing test. Further, the resulting behavior is not the only criterion for comparison. In [Slo99, p. 36] a list of internal processes which are of interest is given. For example, the adaptivity of the system depends on the ability to adapt its strategies. For this, internal monitoring, evaluation of its decisions, and analysis of the system performance are needed.

In [Slo00, p. 4] a model to classify models of minds called CogAff-Grid is introduced. The architecture discussed in the previous Section 2.1.2 is strongly related to it. It defines three layers — reactive mechanisms, deliberative reasoning, and meta-management — and perception and action on each layer. Architectures from cognitive sciences, AI, and AGI can be mapped into this grid.

This kind of mapping is performed in [SC05, p. 159]. Figure 2.7(a) shows the application of a typical subsumption architecture as described by Brooks in [Bro86] to the grid. Subsumption architectures are solely reactive driven — thus, perception, central processing, and action are performed in the lowest layer only. Another example is depicted in Figure 2.7(a) — the so called "Omega architecture." Architectures fitting to this category are not using the possibilities provided by higher level perception and action modules. Every input is passed through the lowest level of perception, walks the central processing levels up and down, and finally produces an output at the lowest level for actions. The shape of such a system is comparable to the Greek letter Ω.

Although this method is suitable to group architecture according to similarity of the data flow pattern in the CogAff-Grid, it does not provide any method to discuss architectures belonging to the same group.

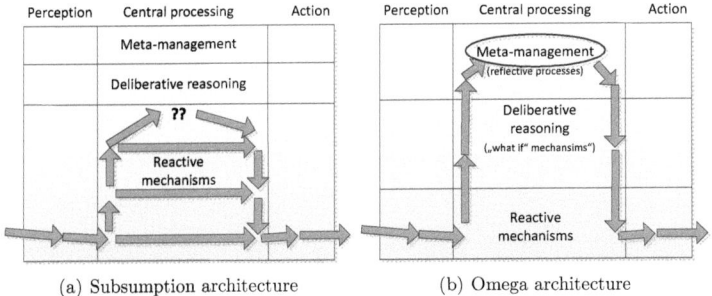

Figure 2.7: CogAff-grid [SC05, p. 159]

In [FGSW06], Franklin et al. compare four contemporary AGI designs — including the two above described (LIDA and OpenCog Prime) — with the help of 15 questions. The questions asked in this comparative treatment range from the type of target environment to is the system able to show creativity. A similar approach is performed by Coward and Sun in [CS04]. Two cognitive architectures — CLARION and RA — are compared by description of the systems and presentation of the answers to some questions in a structured approach. As far as possible, the description of both architectures follows the same structure. The same accounts for the question and answer session. The downside of these two approaches is that the evaluation and comparison is not done by using measurable variables but by interpretation of the given answers.

Another structured comparison between agent based systems can be done using the Performance, Environment, Actuators, Sensors (PEAS) framework described by Russell and Norvig in [RN03, pp. 38–44]. The task environment a system is designed for is described by the four components: Performance measure, environment, actuators, and sensors. This description framework is designed to compare tasks. Thereafter it is only limited applicable to comparison of two control architectures. In fact, for the same task environment different control architectures can be used.

A different approach is described by Hanks et al. in [HPC93]: Performance of controlled experiments in testbeds. A testbed can be a simulated environment for agents providing all resources needed for a given task (for example [HGS+07]). The different architectures have to perform the same task in this simulator. The performance is first measured automatically by some implemented goal function which rates the success of the agent. Afterwards, a human interpretation of the different performances of the agents has to be undertaken. Although this leads to the same problem as with the comparative treatments described above, the interpretation is guided by the actual performance. Another advantage is that such a testbed can support development. The richness of the environment and the difficulty of the task can be increased as the project continues.

Results gained from testbeds and Turing tests are valid for a small, restricted application. Extrapolation to more general insights has to be supplemented with convincing arguments

[HPC93, p. 26].

None of the listed approaches is sufficient for an exhaustive comparison and evaluation for an AGI architecture. Each method covers only a small part of the whole. A combination is necessary [BF07, p. 955]. For example, a testbed to demonstrate various features to perform as predicted in combination with thorough discussion of the developed model is necessary. Theoretical design issues together with practical proofs lead to possible new insights.

2.2 Emotions, Drives, and Urges

This section analyzes how other projects design the technical implementation of whichever emotion theory they use. It does not try to compare different emotional theories. This has to be done by psychologists, psychoanalysists, philosophers, and neurologists elsewhere.

2.2.1 Theoretical Considerations

Emotions are — in a very general point of view — some kind of internal state of the agent used in deliberation. They can be emergent (e.g. [Pfe94, p. 46]) or explicitly designed (e.g. [Pic99, 188–189]). Drives are some kind of mechanism which communicate some kind of bodily needs or urges to deliberation (e.g. [VM97], [Bre02, p. 45]). Emotions and drives are used as motivational system. The theories used for emotions and drives in the various projects origin in many different sciences — for example Buller [Bul02, p. 17] bases on psychoanalysis, Velasquez [VM97] uses several fields (neuropsychology, neurobiology, psychology, ...). Thus, when talking about topics like emotions, drives, urges the terms are highly overloaded. Sloman [Slo04b, p. 129] suggests to group all these terms under the umbrella of the term 'affect'. This does not solve the problem — 'affect' is used in different definitions in [Can97, p. 153] and [Pal08, p. 65]. Sticking to a consistent holistic background — as suggested in Section 1.2.4 — for a project is the only solution. Nevertheless, when approaching the engineering step — transformation of the theories from human sciences to computer programs — looking at other projects can give valuable insights.

Pfeifer [Pfe94, p. 55] gives an interesting argument against using emotion theories in control system. He argues that emotions theories are highly contradictory and no that unitary model satisfying all sciences exists. Starting from Toda's Fungus-Eater Experiment [Tod62], the argument Pfeifer develops is that what it is we are interested in are the mechanisms behind the emotions. In his view, emotions are emergent phenomena and can be excluded from system design. In contrast, emotions are intrinsic to theories from human sciences like neurology, psychology, and psychoanalysis. Thus, when using a bionic approach emotions and drives cannot be omitted. Using the same arguments but in a reverse order Picard [Pic99, p. 68] argues that if a system is built with all mechanisms necessary for emotions, then it has emotions. Further, Aubé [Aub98] develops from the same starting point — Toda's Fungus Eater — the conclusion that emotions are necessary and should be included in design process.

According to [Pic99, pp. 47–84], four different types of computers in respect of affects can be identified:

1. Computers that recognize emotions
2. Computers that express emotions
3. Computers that have emotions
4. Computers that have emotional "intelligence"

The first two do not need an architecture build on emotional theories. They can utilize behavioral and statistical approaches. This is different for the other two. Systems that have emotions need to build on some theoretical foundation. Computers that have emotional "intelligence" are extending computers that have emotions such that they are able to deliberately influence their current emotional state by setting actions which influence this state.

Computers that have emotions are defined to consist of five components [Pic99, pp. 60–75]. They need to have emergent emotions. Thus, the resulting observable emotions must not be implemented in a behavioral approach. Two different types of emotions have to be present: Fast primary emotions and cognitively generated emotions—a differentiation taken from [Dam94, pp. 131–139]. Further, the system has to be able to have emotional experiences. This includes being aware of its own emotional state derived from observation after past actions taken and physiological hints like heartbeat. Further, implicit situation assessment is needed—the knowledge that something is good or bad without knowing why. Concluding, if the system designed in this thesis is to be assigned to the third type of affective computers it needs to incorporate the above mentioned five points.

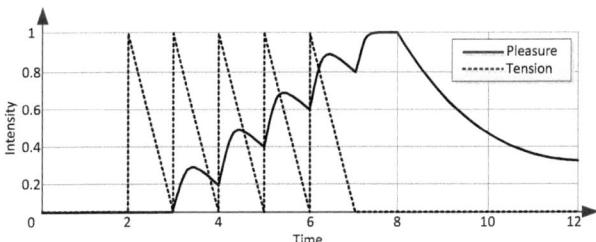

Figure 2.8: Accumulation of pleasure via repetitive discharging of a tension [Bul09, p. 325]

A typical approach to representing emotions and moods is the curve depicted in Figure 2.8. A tension is applied to the system which is released immediately. The reduction of tension is experienced as pleasure. While tension is reduced almost immediately after the source of the tension disappears, pleasure has much slower response decay. Thus, when tension is applied and released in high frequency, pleasure is accumulated to a maximum value. The reason for the delay between the reduction of unpleasure and rise of pleasure until unpleasure being reduced to zero is to simplify the example. It is to mention that

State of the Art

the tension shown in this figure can hardly be mapped to any bodily tension source. The repeated jump discontinuity raising the tension from 0 to 1 in zero time seems to be an oversimplification of the observed processes. Thus, the practical relevance of this model has to be questioned.

Picard [Pic99, pp. 144–160] is using a bell metaphor for this approach. Nine properties for a signal representing an emotion are given: Response decay, repeated strikes, temperament and personality influences, nonlinearity, time-invariance, activation, saturation, cognitive and physical feedback, and background mood. To model this signal a *sigmodial nonlinearity* is suggested (Equation 2.1):

$$y = \frac{g}{1 + e^{(x-x_0)/s}} + y_0 \qquad (2.1)$$

The current value of the signal y is calculated by the gain g of the curve, the steepness s of the slope, and the input x. Thus, the signal quickly responses to impulses and converges towards g from x and decays slowly to 0 afterwards. The formula takes as input only four of the nine listed parameters. The other five influence the input parameters or describe the general behavior of the system.

The problem with this approach to modeling an emotion signal is that it is a behavioristic approach. The desired behavior of the signal is defined with the nine components and does not emerge from a functional description. Interestingly, this approach even contradicts with statements from the same author in the same book. As written above, Picard [Pic99, pp. 60–75] demands that emotions are emerging from the system underneath.

Drives are usually modeled to show the deviation of the desired value (e.g. [VM97]). A typical equation is $d_{i,t} = |v_{i,actual} - v_{i,target}|$. The drive tension d for drive i at time t is defined by the absolute value of the difference from the target value of the corresponding bodily system v to the actual value.

2.2.2 Projects

Many different possibilities to formalize emotions and drives exist. Among them are projects which have a logical perspective [Lor08], using state charts [Pic95, p. 7], using equations [VM97], or are using categorizations [Tur09, p. 287]. In the following, three prototypical projects are introduced.

Hidden Markov Model

A possible approach to model an emotional system is to use a hidden Markov model (HMM) ([Pic95, p. 7], [Pic99, 188–189]). Figure 2.9 shows a HMM with three states, each representing a distinct emotion. Each state — Joy, Distress, and Interest — has transition probabilities to the other two. For example, $Pr(I|J)$ defines the probability that the state changes from Joy to Interest. Further, each state has a measurable form $(O(V|?))$.

STATE OF THE ART

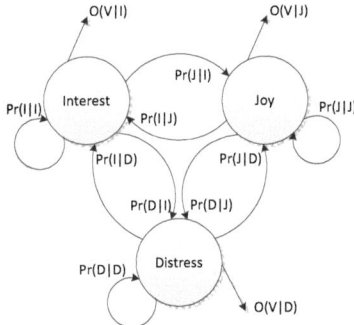

Figure 2.9: Emotional states modeled with HMM [Pic95, p. 7]

This approach creates a one-dimensional, discrete emotion space — only one emotion can be active at a given state. Human psyche is not a state machine changing from one well defined state to another. Thus, even if the HMM is extended to allow blends of emotions, using a HMM is an oversimplification of the used emotional theories.

Cathexis

In [VM97, VFK98], Velasquez sketches a computational model of emotions called Cathexis. It reacts to external and internal stimuli and produces corresponding actions. This is done by the interaction of three systems — emotion generation system, behavior system, and drive system. The system is inspired by a wide range of scientific fields [Vel98b, pp. 70–71], [VM97]: neuropsychology, neurobiology, psychology, AI, and ethology. The aim of Cathexis is to develop a model where old and new theories of emotions and "intelligence" can be tested. Other than the HMM from above, Cathexis is a two dimensional model with several primary emotions on one axis and their intensity on the other.

Figure 2.10(a) depicts the overall architecture. There are two interfaces with the world: External stimuli (input) and actions (output). External stimuli are processed by the three systems emotion generation system, behavior system, and drive system. All three systems are interconnected and influence each other. Only the behavior system can send commands to the motor system which finally manipulates the world through actions.

All systems are built by a set of specializations of the basic computational system [Vel98a, p. 2]. The basic system as described by Formula 2.2 consists of a set of k inputs which are connected to releasers (R) and their weights (W):

$$A_i = f\left(\sum_k (R_{i,k} \cdot W_{i,k})\right) \qquad (2.2)$$

31

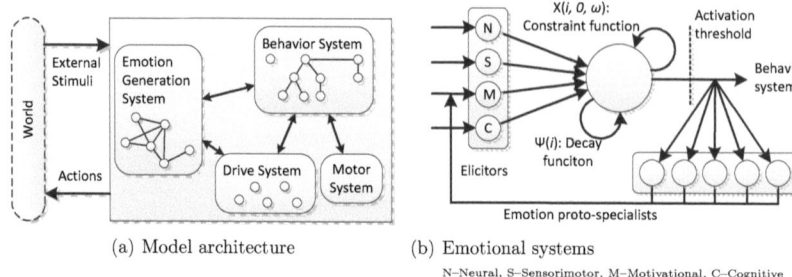

Figure 2.10: Cathexis — a computational framework for emotion-based control [Vel98b, pp. 71–72]

Thus, the system A_i is described by the weighted sum of all inputs applied to a limiting function f. For example, the drive $i = 1$ is triggered by two sources in the body. Source $k = 1$ is twice more important than source $k = 2$; the first source sends the value 0.5 to its releaser and the second one sends 0.2 to its releaser. The function f guarantees that the resulting value is within the range $[0, 1]$. This leads to $f(R_{11} \cdot W_{11} + R_{21} \cdot W_{21}) = f(0.5 \cdot 2 + 0.2) = f(1.2) = 1$. Thus, the value of system A_1 has reached its maximum of 1. The given formula is identical to the ones used for artificial neural networks.

Drives represent urges that arise from internal stimuli — the control systems. For example, the hunger drive represents the amount of food needed. The result of Formula 2.3 is compared to a desired value. The difference sets the drive intensity. No saturation or limitation of the result is needed, thus function f from Formula 2.2 can be omitted. The drive D_i at time t is determined by the weighted sum of the control systems.

$$D_{i,t} = \sum_{k} (C_{i,t,k} \cdot W_{i,t,k}) \tag{2.3}$$

A more complex system is the emotion generation system. It consists of a distributed network of self-motivated subsystems. Each represents a basic emotion like anger, fear, or surprise. Each node can have several input channels. They can be split into the following four categories [Vel97, p. 11]:

Neural: Internal information sources like neurotransmitters, brain temperature, or hormones.
Sensorimotor: Feedback from muscles, facial expression, body posture, and other sensorimotor processes.
Motivational: Influence from other emotions or drives.
Cognitive: All information and processes in the cognitive system which activate emotions (e.g. appraisal of events, beliefs, and desires).

The inputs belonging to the first three categories are natural releasers; if part of the fourth category the input is a learned releaser.

Figure 2.10(b) shows a typical emotional system node. On the left hand side are the four inputs which are influencing the current value (large circle in the middle). Further, a decay function (*psi*) and saturation function (*chi*) are applied to it. The decay function reduces the intensity of the emotional system with each time step. Thus, if no releaser is activated, the value converges to zero. *chi* assures that the intensity cannot go above a threshold value ω. Results from other emotional systems can influence the intensity (inhibitory or exhibitory). The sketched behavior is formalized in Formula 2.4:

$$I_{e,t} = \chi \left(\psi(I_{e,t-1}) + \sum_k L_{e,k} + \sum_l (G_{e,l} \cdot I_{t,l}) - \sum_m (H_{e,m} \cdot I_{t,m}) \right) \quad (2.4)$$

The intensity value of the Emotion I_e at time t is determined by the decayed value of the last step $\psi(I_{e,t-1})$ plus input releasers which are not emotions ($\sum L_e$). Exhibitory weighted emotion intensities are added to the value (G) while weighted inhibitory emotion intensities are subtracted (H). I is the weight of the incoming emotion intensities. Finally, the saturation threshold is guaranteed by function χ.

The basic emotional systems are coexisting and are updated in parallel. Mixed emotions like grief are emerging from the interaction of the basic systems.

Emotional systems have a high decay rate. Thus, they influence the behavior system for a short time only. To enable longer lasting influence moods are introduced. They are similar to emotions but have a much lower decay rate. Moods have much less influence compared to emotions but over a longer time. They can bias the behavior system towards a certain direction.

The temperament of an agent equipped with Cathexis can be configured using various parameters. This is done mainly by changing the thresholds, decay rates, and saturation values. For example, by reducing the activation threshold and the decay rate for the emotion fear a much easier frightened agent is created.

The behavior system operates similar to the emotional systems. Releasers receiving input from different sources — external perception, drives, emotions, and moods — are combined with input from other nodes. They can inhibit or exhibit the behavior. For example, 'wag the tail' is likely to inhibit 'run'. On the other hand, 'play with human' is likely to exhibit the more basic behavior 'search human'.

$$B_{j,t} = \sum_n (R_{j,n} \cdot W_{j,n}) + \sum_l (G_{j,j} \cdot B_{t,l}) - \sum_m (H_{j,m} \cdot B_{t,m}) \quad (2.5)$$

Equation 2.5 describes the behavior system. The likelihood of behavior B_j at time t is defined by the weighted releasers R plus the exhibitory inputs G minus inhibitory influences H. B and W are the weights.

More than one behavior can be active at any given time. The motor system tries to execute all behaviors above a threshold. If two mutually exclusive commands are equally important, the system will produce no action at this time step.

The clear and precise formalization using equations is a good approach in an interdisciplinary project. The concepts of one discipline are translated into the language of the other one. Also, the concept of using a basic computational system (Equation 2.2) as foundation for all other systems is interesting. Nevertheless, it is questionable whether drives, emotions, and behaviors truly share a common basic algorithm.

It is not clear which emotion theory is used or how the whole system is rendered from the various sciences listed. Especially the technical realization is unjustified. This is confirmed in [Vel97, p. 12]. Here the mechanism for the moods is motivated by "*[...] common observation that moods seem to lower the threshold [...].*" Thus, the implementation is done by making a common mistake done in AI — well defined concepts are flawed by the integration of folk psychology (see also Section 1.2.1).

Further, the model is build following a behavioral approach. Not the functions from which an emotional system emerges are identified; the desired behavior is formulated and then implemented. It is questionable how such a behavioral approach can result in a system which satisfies the above listed goal: Test old and new theories about emotions.

WASABI

WASABI Affect Simulation for Agents with Believable Interactivity (WASABI) is an affect simulation architecture developed by Backer-Asano and Wachsmuth [BKW07, BAW09, BA08]. Its core is the three dimensional emotional space Pleasure, Arousal, and Dominance (PAD) (see Figure 2.11(b)). The three axes are pleasure, arousal, and dominance [BKPLW08, p. 42]. Pleasure — or valence — represents the valence of the overall emotional state. The activeness is put to the arousal axis. The terms pleasure and valence as well as activeness and arousal are used as synonyms in this project. Dominance depicts how much control over the situational context exists.

Within PAD-space, two different types of emotions are located — primary emotions and secondary emotions. They are built according to Damasio's differentiation of emotions (see [Dam94, pp. 131–139]).

In WASABI, primary emotions are inborn affective states. Each one is defined by one or several points in the emotional space. For example, the primary emotion Happy is defined by the four points $(80, 80, \pm 100)^2$ and $(50, 0, \pm 100)$. Hence, the first point defining happiness in PAD is to be found at pleasure=80, arousal=80, and dominance=100. Interestingly, the primary emotion Angry is located at the same point. The current primary emotional state is determined by calculating the distance of the current emotional state in PAD-space to all points of the primary emotions. Nine primary emotions exist in WASABI: Angry, Annoyed, Bored, Concentrated, Depressed, Fearful, Happy, Sad, and Surprised.

---

[2] The three axes have a value range of -100 to 100

STATE OF THE ART

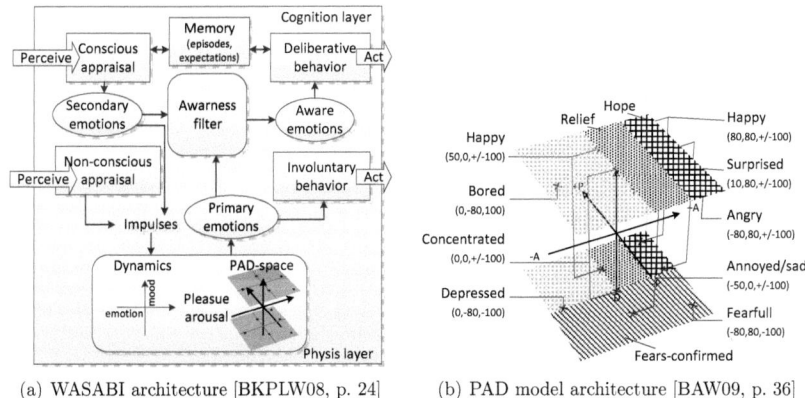

(a) WASABI architecture [BKPLW08, p. 24]   (b) PAD model architecture [BAW09, p. 36]

Figure 2.11: WASABI — an affect simulation architecture

Secondary emotions are represented by three dimensional areas in PAD-space. Similarly to primary emotions, a secondary emotion can be defined by several, non-overlapping areas. Each area has an intensity value attached. Currently, three secondary emotions exist in WASABI: Hope, Fears-confirmed, and Relief.

Emotions — primary and secondary — can directly influence deliberation. If they pass the awareness filter (see Figure 2.11(a)) they become aware emotions and as such can be processed and stored to memory. Independent of their awareness level, emotions are influencing the agent constantly. Primary emotions are hard-wired with involuntary behavior; secondary emotions are influencing the mood/emotion dynamics.

An interesting aspect of WASABI is the mood/emotion interaction. A mood is a long lasting emotional background state [BA08, p. 88]. Other than emotions, moods are more diffuse and cannot be distinguished. The two dimensional dynamics component has valence of emotions on one axis and valence of moods on the other one. The valence for each axis is determined by non-conscious perception appraisal and secondary emotions. The value of each axis tends to return to zero. This motion is independent from the other axis. According to [BKW04, pp. 156-158] the dynamics of moods/emotions are modeled after a two spring system with different spring constants for each axis. It is possible to add a third axis — boredom. If the mood/emotion value stays within a small area around the origin, the agent is bored. With time, the boredom representing value decreases towards -1. If -1 is reached, the agent has reached its maximum possible boredom. As soon as the mood/emotion value leaves this area, boredom is reset to 0.

$$K(x_t, y_t, z_t, t) = (p(x_t, y_t), a(x_t, z_t), d(t)) \quad (2.6)$$
$$p(x_t, y_t) = 1/2 \cdot (x_t + y_t) \quad (2.7)$$
$$a(x_t, z_t) = |x_t| + z_t \quad (2.8)$$

The mapping of the current emotional state to PAD-space at time t is done with Function K as defined in Formula 2.6 [BKW04, p. 159]. x_t, y_t, and z_t on the right side of the formula are coordinates of the three dimensional mood/emotion dynamics diagram (mood valence, emotion valence, and boredom); x_t, y_t, and z_t on the left side are responding to the three coordinates of PAD-space pleasure, arousal, and dominance. Pleasure — defined as the overall valence of the system — is the average of the two values in mood/emotion space (see Equation 2.7). Equation 2.8 defines arousal as the deviation of the emotional state from zero and the degree of boredom. Thus, if the agent is in a high emotional state but highly bored, arousal stays low. Finally, dominance ($d(t)$) is determined by a heuristic [BA08, p. 92].

The result of the above sketched emotional architecture is a system which incorporates primary and secondary emotions as well as moods. All components have influence on deliberative and involuntary behavior. The cycle (impulses affect the mood/emotion system which is the base for calculating the current position in PAD-space which again results in primary and secondary emotions which are partly used to produce actions but also are part of the impulses) is modeled in an interesting approach. Only a single system exists which defines the current emotional state — the moods/emotions dynamics. Other than for example Cathexis described above, WASABI has not a distinct value for each emotion, but a categorization component — the PAD-space. Distinct emotion valences are calculated with a distance metric.

What is missing in this architecture is the integration of bodily needs/drives. Although they can be integrated using the "non-conscious perception" input, a more explicit integration would be favorable. The main weakness of this approach is to be found in dominance function $d(t)$. Strong cognitive abilities are required to determine whether a current situation can be controlled or not. This problem is bypassed using a heuristic function which is hand-crafted for a special application. Thus, the used implementation approach is interesting but lacks clarity on how a general solution can be achieved.

Summary

In general, all three discussed architectures are modeled following a behavioral approach. The desired signal response is defined first, the mechanism to achieve it later. Sigmoidal signals are a good example for this. Cathexis uses a simple version of sigmoids whereas WASABI implements a two-step approach with a two-dimensional sigmoid signal in the first step which is translated into PAD-space in the second step. The problem is that the emotions/drives valences are decaying each time step without any cause. It would be preferable if — similar to the initial rise which is triggered by an event — the reduction is caused by an event, too. This concept of a functional approach could be used.

2.3 Embodiment

One of the primary tasks of the psychoanalytic entity Id is the mental representation of bodily needs. Even more important, according to Freud in [Fre23], the Ego requires a body too: "The Ego is first and foremost a bodily Ego; it is not merely a surface entity, but is itself the projection of a surface [Fre23, p. 25]."

Thus, when designing a control system inspired by the second topographical model, the corresponding body has to be considered as well. In AI and cognitive science, researchers are faced with similar topics: Is a body necessary? How should the body be designed? What are the implications of a certain body? The following three subsections are elaborating these questions and put them into context of ARS.

2.3.1 Foundations

The motivation, why to look into embodiment when trying to model a cognitive system is best given by the quote from Pfeifer and Scheier [PS99, p. 649]: *"Intelligence cannot merely exist in the form of an abstract algorithm but requires a physical instantiation, a body."* Further, Ziemke states in [Zie01, p. 76] that off-line cognition — the "thinking" process is decoupled from the environment — is body based. Thus, abstract concepts are metaphors grounded on bodily experience (an extension to the symbol grounding problem [Har90]).

Although it seems to be obvious what embodiment means — especially in the case of physical agents — the exact definition of embodiment and its implications are not. One of the first attempts to define embodiment has been undertaken by Quick and Dautenhahn [QD99, p. 3]. The basic idea is that the body is a coupling device between a system (e.g. brain, control unit, piece of software) and an environment (e.g. the real world). The degree of embodiment is given by the amount of perturbatory channels existing. Thus, the number of sensors reading information from the environment and the number of actuators manipulating the environment give information on how well the system is embodied within the environment.

According to Riegler in [Rie02, p. 341], the definition provided by Quick and Dautenhahn in [QD99] is not sufficient, a stronger definition for embodiment is needed. The system has to be sensitive to the structural coupling. Otherwise, for example a fly walking on a Rembrandt painting would fit to the definition of embodiment — the fly would be embodied within the painting.

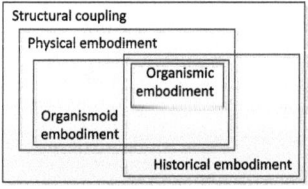

Figure 2.12: Notions of embodiment and their interrelations. [Zie01, p. 81]

Ziemke defines five notions of bodies required for embodied cognition [Zie01, pp. 77–81]. The broadest notion — structural coupling — includes the definition discussed above. The body and the environment have some structural connections. If as a result of agent-environment interaction the agent has gained competence within the environment, the requirements for the notion historical embodiment are met. While structural coupling and historical embodiment make no restrictions regarding physical or non-physical bodies, the notion of physical embodiment excludes everything which is non-physical including software agents. Organismoid embodiment refers to organisms like body forms. It includes every living organism as well as e.g. dog shaped robots. Thus, such bodies share some body characteristics with bodies of natural organisms. The strongest notion of embodiment provided by Ziemke is organismic embodiment. Only autopoietic[3], living systems fall into this category. Man-made machines are allopoietic[4] and heteronomous[5]. Figure 2.12 depicts the interrelations of the five notions. While structural coupling contains all other notions, organismic embodiment presupposes them. Historical and physical embodiment can coexist.

The agents who are developed in this work would qualify as organismoidial embodied if the physicality can be relaxed. They 'live' in a simulated world which provides some simplified physical constraints. In Section 2.3.3, the issue how much physicality is needed is discussed.

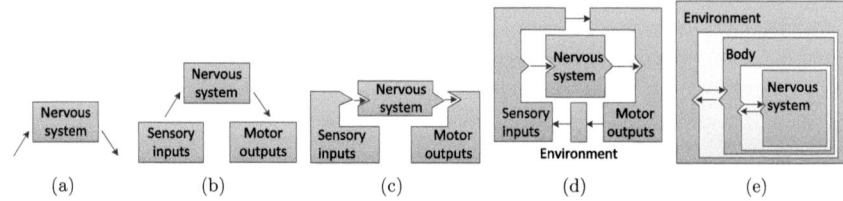

Figure 2.13: Interactions between nervous system, body, and environment [CB97, p. 554]

Another useful categorization is done by Chiel and Beer in [CB97]. Like Russell and Norvig [RN03, pp. 32–54] did for the definition what an intelligent agent is, the authors develop more and more complex views on the interaction between the nervous system, the body, and the environment (Figures 2.13(a) to 2.13(e)). The simplest view is shown in Figure 2.13(a). The behavior of the system can be explained solely by the nervous system alone. In Figure 2.13(b) no concepts for body and world exist; input and output is added into the explanation of the behavior. Still, input, system, and output are independent modules. This changes in Figure 2.13(c) — a co-evolution between sensors, system, and actuators is assumed. Thus, more detailed sensors go along with better processing power and more possibilities in acting on the world. In the next stage — Figure 2.13(d) — sensors can

---

[3]Autopoiesis — Greek for auto (self)-creation — describes a self-construction and self-maintaining system.

[4]Allopoiesis — Greek for other-creation — refers to a system which produces something different than itself.

[5]This is a critic on the usage of the term autonomous for artificial agents by Ziemke. Heteronomous here means, that the rules these agents have are man made rules. Even with self-organizing, learning, adaptive machines this problem is valid — although no explicit rule may be present, the mechanisms which enables the agent to create its own rules is man made.

directly influence actuators and a feedback from the actuators to the sensors through the environment is present. Finally, the most complex view is depicted in Figure 2.13(e). The nervous system is embedded within a body which is embedded in the environment. Between each layer bi-directional communication exists. All three entities are rich, complicated, highly structured dynamic systems, which are coupled with one another, and adaptive behavior emerges from the interactions of all three systems.

Taking the psychoanalytically described human mind, as archetype for building the model can be considered as building a rich, complicated, highly structured dynamic system. Thus, applying category (e), the body and the world have to be of fitting complexity. This view is also affirmed by Pfeifer and Bongard in [PB07, pp. 161–164]: *"[...] one of the aspects of the principle of ecological balance is that the complexity levels of sensory, motor, and neural systems should match."*

"Intelligence requires a body" is the simplest meaning of embodiment. Sensory-motor coordination is an example for a more sophisticated point of view provided by Pfeifer et al. [PIG06, pp. 15–16]. Behavior in natural agents can be modeled as sensory-motor coordination. The same accounts for adaptive artificial agents. Next to the simple control concepts needed for good designed sensory-motor systems, the information structure induced in the various sensory channels is important. Thus, perception and learning profit from the sensory-motor coordinated interaction with the environment an agent performs. This is called "information theoretic implications of embodiment." Sensory-motor coordination is useful especially in the case of learning. Pfeifer and Scheier [PS97] show how this principle can be used for robot learning.

2.3.2 Design Principles

Embodiment is used to emphasize and study the agent's interaction with the world. The objects of study are complete agents. This kind of agents have to fulfill the following four demands: 1. they have to be independent of external control (autonomous), 2. they have to exist as a physical entity in the real world (embodied), 3. all information about the environment has to be gained from its own perspective through its own sensory system (situated), and 4. they have to have the ability to maintain all their necessary resources by themselves (self-sufficient). In this way they can truly operate independently in a real world setup.

In [PB07, pp. 95–96] a list of five essential properties is given which can be derived from the four demands for cognitive agents:

They are subject to the laws of physics: Each real world agent (artificial or biological) is subject to the laws of physics. When it moves it has to overcome friction, gravitation, etc.

They generate sensory stimulation: Every action produces new stimuli. Moving changes our perspective to the world. Each body part we move produces some kind of sensor sensation (e.g. we feel the muscles move).

State of the Art

They affect the environment: This is not only done by deliberate actions like moving an object. Moreover, every movement of the agent affects the environment. For example, the wheels leave rubber markings on the floor; the heat of the motors affects the environment temperature.

They are complex dynamic systems: And thus *"[they] tend to settle into attractor states."* Each dynamical system has a tendency to settle into attractor states. For example, horses have different types of movement: Walk, trot, canter, and gallop.

They perform morphological computation: Some calculations are outsourced to the body. For example, the shape and position of the ears work as filters; the human knee adapts to the ground each time the foot hits it.

To guide the design of embodied agents, Pfeifer has proposed the design principles for autonomous agents [Pfe96, pp. 5–11]. Based on four different viewpoints on agent design — functional, learning and development, evolutionary, and societies of agents — listed in [Pfe96, p. 5], Pfeifer and Bongard [PB07, pp. 357–358] set up four categories of design principles: Agent design principle, design principles of development, design principles of evolution, design principles for collective systems.

Currently, the focus of project ARS is on fully developed agents which are provided with a large amount of predefined knowledge. Learning, growth, and evolution will be skipped for the time being. The fourth category — collective systems — consisting of the design principles level of abstraction, design emergence, from agent to group, homogeneity-heterogeneity are only of partial interest in this thesis. The last point is corresponding with the configurability of the agent like shape, abilities, and psychic parameters. The other three are out of scope for this thesis. Roesener et al. discusses in [RDL+09] the points emergence and agent to group from a psychoanalytical point of view. The only remaining category is agent design. The eight design principles (see [Pfe96, pp. 5–11], [PS99, pp. 299–326], [PB07, pp. 89–140]) of this category are:

1. Principle "Meta principle": The basic problem of embodied design is: The desired ecological niche and the desired behavior of the robot are known. How has the agent to be designed to meet these specifications? How should the agent be constructed?

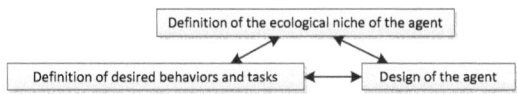

Figure 2.14: Meta principles and their influences

These questions can be reformulated to any given tuple of the three tasks depicted in Figure 2.14 to ask what the third component should look like. The usual view point in cognitive science is to define the ecological niche and the tasks first. The behavior of an agent is bound to a certain ecological niche. Thus, it cannot be described independently. This is reflected by the term "task environment" which combines the behavior and the ecological niche.

2. Principle "The complete agent principle": Intelligent agents have to be complete. Thus, they are autonomous, self-sufficient, embodied, and situated.

3. Principle "The principle of parallel, loosely coupled processes": Intelligence emerges from agent-environment-interactions. These are based on parallel, loosely coupled, asynchronous processes which are themselves coupled to the sensory-motor-mechanisms of the agent.

4. Principle "The principle of sensory-motor coordination": The true shift from classical AI to new AI is the introduction of sensory-motor coordination — the shift from pure symbol manipulation to a sensory-motoric interpretation of the behavior. Perception of objects cannot be decoupled from sensory-motor coordination if it is necessary to manipulate the object (e.g. What is on the rear side of a cube?).

5. Principle "The principle of cheap design": Good design has to be cheap. Cheap has not to be taken literally. The meaning of cheap in this context is: Take advantage of physics in the system-environment-interaction. Take advantage of the specialties of the given niche. Deploy efficient design wherever possible.

6. Principle "The redundancy principle": Redundancy is not reduced to adding a second sensor of the same type, more important, a certain type of diversification is meant by it. For example, the collision of a robot should not only be perceived by an acceleration sensor, but additionally by a bump sensor and a proximity sensor.

7. Principle "The principle of ecological balance": The design of the sensors should never be done without considerations regarding the motoric system and the physical environment of the agent. It makes no sense to install a vision sensor which is able to detect grasshoppers in grass, if the environment is an office building. The same accounts for the actuators.

8. Principle "The value principle": An autonomous agent has to have mechanisms for unsupervised, continuous learning and must incorporate a value system. Both — learning and value system — have to be self-organized and the agent has to have the possibility to decide whether a certain action was good or bad (in context of the situation and the desired outcome).

Figure 2.15 depicts how the design principles are related. Regular lines are showing strong correlations (e.g. parallel processing and cheap design) whereas dashed lines are marking contradictions (redundancy vs. cheap design). What can be seen is that sensory-motor-coordination is the most important principle not only due to the reasons explained above, but also due to its strong interconnection with other principles.

State of the Art

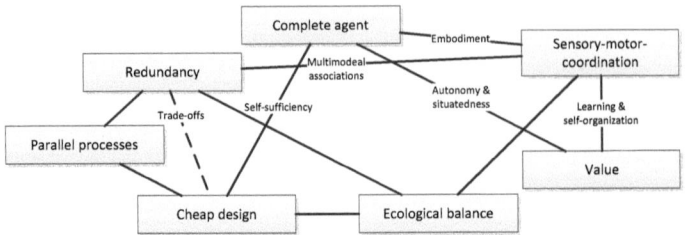

Figure 2.15: Relations between the design principles [PS99, p. 318]

Another set of design principles is provided by Franklin in [Fra97, pp. 508–510]. Its focus is on:

1. Drives — A build-in motivational system is necessary to drive the agent.
2. Attention — A complex environment perceived through several sensors might overload the agents' decision unit. Some mechanism to direct the focus is needed.
3. Internal Model — Frequent sampling of the environment should be used whenever possible. If not, build an internal model of the world.
4. Coordination — In multi-agent environments, coordination among the agents is necessary. This is not necessarily done via high cost communication.
5. Knowledge — Knowledge should be put into the lower levels of the agent, if possible. For example, the information about how to access the motor control interface is stored in the topmost level. The only function which accesses this information is located at the lowest level. This distribution concept would only overload the communication channels between the levels. To store the information where it is needed is a more promising approach.
6. Curiosity — To support unsupervised learning, curiosity has to be present. This results in a more or less random behavior during learning phases.
7. Routines — Frequently used action sequences should be transformed into routines. This reduces the processor load.

The principles given by Franklin in [Fra97, pp. 508–510] are dealing with every aspect of the agent including the decision making. The set defined by Pfeifer in [Pfe96, p. 5] focuses on the design of the body and what parts of decision making can be outsourced to it. The following principles are — at least partly — similar: The first principle in [Fra97, p. 508] — Drives — is equivalent to the value principle. Attention is a subset of the sensory-motor coordination. Internal model is related to the principle of cheap design. It takes advantage of system-environment interactions whenever possible. Coordination refers to the principle from agent to group mentioned above. It is important in collective systems. Curiosity is loosely related to the value principle. Some emotional theories are defining a basic emotional system called seeking (e.g. [Pan98, p. 50]). Routines can be matched to cheap design up to some extent. The main controller is used more efficiently by moving action sequences to another subsystem.

2.3.3 Virtual Embodiment

Derived from the first essential property for embodied, cognitive agents listed above — "They are subject to laws of physics" — a problem regarding virtual embodiment in simulated worlds arises: If 'embodiment' can only be used for agents in the real world, can the design principles be applied to a virtual world? Brooks states that *"[...] to build a system that is intelligent it is necessary to have its representations grounded in the physical world [Bro90, p. 5]."* This implies that only physical bodies can provide sufficient embodiment — a software body cannot provide an interface to the physical world. If it would, then these interfaces would have to be physical and part of the body and thereafter, the body would be physical.

Pfeifer and Bongard [PB07, pp. 90–92] give six real world challenges which are important reasons why a virtual world is not the real world:

- Data acquisition/processing takes time in the real world.
- The real world is not a completely accessible environment.
- Data collected from the real world is always noisy and error prone.
- Everything in the world is continuous. Clear, discrete states do not exist.
- The real world forces the agent to perform several actions in parallel.
- The real world has its own dynamic; forcing the agent to constantly act.

Concluding, Pfeifer and Bongard [PB07, pp. 90–92] state that *"[...] the real world is a highly complex dynamical system, making it intrinsically unpredictable because of its nonlinear nature and its sensitivity to initial conditions"* and *"[...] the real world is challenging and 'messy'."*

Further, simulations are providing numerous possibilities to bypass real world problems. Design decisions for real world robots differ from simulated ones [PB07, pp. 221–222]. While the real world robot has to deal with partially covered objects, this problem can be bypassed in a simulation if this problem is not a central research question. Another example is the passing of one object from one robot to another. In the real world, the robots have to do the right things at the same time. A virtual world has only discrete time steps — no matter how fine the granularity is, the simulated robots have a higher chance to act simultaneously.

A more relaxed view on physical embodiment is formulated by Kushmerick in [Kus97]. He provides a framework where the physical attributes of a body are examined from a computational point of view. If all required physical body functions needed for embodiment can be described in computational terms, a software body is sufficient. The framework consists of two sets of simplifications: Type I, algorithms which can be more efficiently implemented in a body should not be implemented in the decision unit, and Type II, having a body can affect which problem needs to be solved in the first place. Several — more specific — subtypes of Type II are defined. For example, Type II-b "exploiting task invariants to simplify reasoning" thus, rely on the world continuity and structure. A small deviation of the path or a wrong turn might result in another solution. Returning to the starting point is rarely necessary. The author claims, that application of these definitions to Brooks' claims about embodiment show that all physical requirements can be replaced by computational ones.

This view is supported by Franklin in [Fra97, p. 517]. The embodied design paradigm is concluded with the definition that they can be applied to physically embodied agents, software agents in real computational environments, and to A-Life agents in A-Life simulations.

Chrisley [Chr03, p. 139] claims that for intelligent systems a body is not necessary. Moreover, all physical AI systems like robots are embodied per se. Embodiment is nothing novel to AI, the important contribution when talking about embodied AI is the introduction of the explicit concept embodiment. This provides clarification and a formal background.

Although the claim from Chrisley [Chr03] that a body is not necessary cannot hold (cp. Section 2.3.1), his conclusion — embodiment provides a formal background — is valid. A virtual embodiment can be created using the design principles given in Section 2.3.2. But the designer has to be aware which simplifications are done deliberately and which are existing systematically. Further, a system created in a virtual world cannot be directly copied into the real world. Concluding, existing research projects similar to project ARS are using virtual embodiment to implement and test their theories. For example, Goertzel and Pennachin [GP09] create a virtual dog in a social simulation tool called multivers. The virtual body which is designed for this thesis is introduced in Section 4.3. The reasons why embodiment is important for a psychoanalytically inspired control architecture are discussed in Section 3.1.4.

2.4 Related Projects Basing on Psychoanalysis

The interdisciplinary approach — psychoanalysts and engineers working together for a long period — along with development of a reference implementation makes it — next to many other properties — unique. Up to my knowledge, no research project comparable to ARS exists. Nevertheless, related projects which are using psychoanalysis up to some extent have influenced the work and are a valuable source of information.

Although, no community among researchers using concepts from psychoanalysis for projects in cognitive science or AI exists, various projects with different research objectives can be found. Applying a rough categorization, they can be divided into three groups:

Theoretical issues: Important issues and questions regarding psychoanalysis and cognitive science or AI are raised. But no architecture has yet been developed or implemented.
Existing model in context with psychoanalysis: A cognitive architecture has been developed using some theories (except psychoanalysis). The result is critically analyzed in respect of psychoanalytical theories.

Psychoanalysis as foundation: The project uses psychoanalytical theories as starting point from which the architecture is built.

Projects which can be assigned to the first group — "theoretical issues" — are [CS88], [Tur89], [RR96], and [LBP06]. They have in common that one or more psychoanalysts — and in case of [LBP06] a psychoanalysts and an engineer — elaborate on how can psychoanalysis be used in context of AI.

The first work — written by Colby and Stoller — has been published in 1988 [CS88]. The main focus of the work is on the usage of psychoanalysis in cognitive science. Both authors are psychoanalysists who are seeing psychoanalysis not as a science; whereas cognitive science is one [CS88, pp. 1–7]. Nevertheless, they conclude that psychoanalysis is still able to contribute to a science of the mind by incorporating its theories into cognitive science. Moreover, if cognitive science does not include concepts like fantasies and feelings of real people, it will never be a true science of the mind [CS88, p. 153]. The most important psychoanalytical ideas which should be used are unconscious processes and defensive strategies.

Despite their long list of criticism about psychoanalysis, Colby and Stoller give a list of sixteen points where psychoanalysis is good at in their opinion [CS88, pp. 35–37]. The most important points are *"1. Never before has there been such an opportunity for collecting naturalistic information on subjective experience."*, *"3. No other field has tried to take every detail [...] and fit each to the others."*, *"10. No other field has explored the intricate connections–conflicts and mediations–between biologic drives and external forces [...] and how these struggles become internalized and fixed as permanent character structure [...]"*, *"15. Even those put off by psychoanalysis grant that it has provoked many long-lasting excitements in the world of ideas."*

Farrell (1981, p.25) as cited in [CS88, p. 38] defines the following four attributes for psychoanalysis:

1. *"Psychic Determinism. No item in mental life and in conduct and behavior is 'accidental'; it is the outcome of antecedent conditions."*
2. *"Much mental activity and behavior is purposive and goal oriented in character."*
3. *"Much of mental activity and behavior, and its determinants, is unconscious in character."*
4. *"The early experience of the individual, as a child, is very potent and tends to be pre-potent over later experience."*

All four points are crucial for the task of transforming psychoanalysis into an implementable cognitive science model. Especially the first point — psychic determinism — is the key for implementing such a system. Most other mind sciences are describing mental activities with stochastic functions.

The authors are describing an analogy between the poorly understood human mental systems and — the far better understood — computer systems [CS88, pp. 15–17]. The mental apparatus is described as a three layer system with the following layers: Neural, symboling capacities, and semantic. The corresponding computer layers are: Hardware, instruction set, and programs. The assumption leading to this analogy is that the human mental system is to be seen as a symbol processing architecture. While the defined layers for the mental apparatus could be argued, the mapping to the computer layers is wrong. Neither is the instruction set equal to symboling capacities nor are programs semantic information in the sense as semantic is seen within the mental apparatus.

To conclude, the authors of [CS88] have put their main effort to extract general points where psychoanalysis is well or not so well suited for cognitive science projects.

Turkle suggest that AI and psychoanalysis can form a new alliance in her article [Tur89]. Both of them are having at least one thing in common: Self-reflection and thus subjectivity. Freud developed his theories using self-observation and introspection. According to Turkle, many AI developers stated that in the end they thought about how they solve a certain problem and use this approach as reference. Thus, facing a similar problem — which mechanisms may solve a given problem/behavior — both are using the same principle: Answering "How do I solve it?" This leads to another similarity: Both are dealing with inner states. This would be of no interest in behaviorism. In [Bau06], an AI researcher elaborates on how he creates a problem solver for a game called Sokoban. This is done primarily with introspection — answers to questions like "How would I [the researcher] solve the current sub-problem?" are analyzed and added to the overall model. It has to be criticized that engineers perform the task of introspection. This should be done by people educated for this task — for example psychoanalysts.

According to Turkle, two approaches in AI are interesting: Emergent AI like connectionism and information processing like agent/object oriented programming. Especially the later one is of importance — Freud used information like terms in his description of the reflex arc in [Fre95]. Analogue to Minsky's Society of Minds, she elaborates on societies of inner agents (or microminds)[6]. Her further analysis of Minsky's work yields the fact that he is using vast array of agents: Censor agents, recognition agents, anger agents, etc. Thus, Minsky recognizes Freud as a colleague in "society" modeling. Freud too wrote about censor agents. These censors are according to Minsky an essential part for modeling human thought and for building intelligent machines.

Further, she notices that Newell stated that censors in large and complex information-processing system are necessary, but can be replaced by clear unambiguous rules stated in advance. If looking at society theory driven systems, contradiction and conflict is intrinsic to them — without a censor, no "intelligence" can emerge.

As an example, of how AI can help psychoanalysis, she depicts how recursions could be applied to Kleinian theories. Further she hints, what kind of programs AI researchers could develop to support Kleinian psychoanalysts. From an engineering point of view, these examples are not directly portable.

---

[6]In pure Freudian psychoanalysis, only one such agent is known — the Superego. Other branches of psychoanalysis, like the one founded by Melanie Klein, are suggesting more inner agents.

Turkle concludes her proposal with a summary of the similarities of AI and psychoanalysis. They are to be found in theoretical issues: "*[...] the challenge to the idea of the autonomous, intentional actor, the need for self-reference in theory building, and the need for objects such as censors to deal with internal conflict [Tur89, p. 261].*"

Next in line of the works looking at psychoanalysis and AI from a theoretical point of view is from Rodado and Rendon [RR96]. They are focusing — similarly to Turkle — on the early works from Freud, "Studies on Hysteria (1893)" and "Project for a Scientific Psychology (1895)." Originating in neurology, the described model is very similar to connectionism, which is already used in biological psychiatry today.

Both books are tempting for engineers — in the first one Freud still uses formulas and has not abandoned the attempt to describe complex mental functions in neurology terms yet. The other book — being published several decades after he stopped working on it — can be viewed in the same manner. Many theories of these early books were changed or abandoned in his later work. Thereafter, although the language and the methodology of these two books seem to be a good starting point, one has to be cautious to the fact that many theories are outdated and far from being complete. Very soon, one wants to add other, newer theories that complete the model, but faces the incompatibility with Freud's later work. The ARS project research team went through this process and finally abandoned most of these early books.

Other than these two books, Rodado and Rendon are focusing on parallel distributed processing as the tool to use. In their point of view, this tool is an artificial system composed of large numbers of simple computing units — very similar to neural networks. The four main characteristics of such a system are: Parallel scheduling of concurrent processing mechanisms, local concurrent interactions result in emergent behaviors, no central control mechanism is necessary, and focus is on learning instead of pre-programming. Their argument is "*[...] the spontaneity, unpredictability, and above all self-organizing properties of these nonlinear dynamical systems are well suited for explaining the notoriously similar characteristics of humans [RR96, p. 397].*" Although, this is true in principle, it does not explain how to create a system complex enough to show such behaviors and still operates stable enough.

One of the few examples of true interdisciplinary work between psychoanalysts and engineers has been done by Leuzinger-Bohleber and Pfeifer [LBP06]. Leuzinger-Bohleber — a psychoanalyst — gained experience on interdisciplinary research in a project together with neurologists. The challenges met can be generalized to any interdisciplinary work. Although both fields may seem to use the same terminology, often they were referring to different concepts. Further, divergent scientific traditions and philosophies make cooperation hard. Thus, it is important to stay open minded and a lot of effort is necessary to keep the group together to reach the long term goal of new scientific insights for both groups.

The authors claim to have published many articles which try to apply concepts from embodied cognitive science to central issues of modern psychoanalysis. The difference between embodied cognitive science and cognitive science is that the first one tries to identify mechanisms underlying intelligent behavior too. New insights have to be searched through "understanding by building." Thus, the theories have to be applied to e.g. a robot.

Although Leuzinger-Bohleber and Pfeifer are writing that cognitive science is "understanding by building" it seems that most — if not all — of their work regarding psychoanalysis and cognitive science is theoretical. Nevertheless, spin-offs like their contributions to embedded cognitive science have undergone this "understanding by building" process.

The only member of the second group defined at the beginning of this section is the work by Minsky. He has developed a multi-layer model of human "intelligence" based on the interactions of simple, mindless agents which form a society. Hence his model has the name "Society of Mind" [Min88]. Starting from there, he investigated how his theories fit to psychoanalysis (see [Min05, p. 4], [Min06, pp. 86–88]). One of his major motivations was to figure out "which actions not to take." Most works in cognitive science and AI focus on which action is the optimal one. Soon the number of possible branches of the decision tree exceeds the available resources. Early termination of one branch might result in the loss of an optimal solution. Thereafter, deciding which branches to expand and which to terminate is a nontrivial decision problem — which would need another decision tree. According to Minsky, this issue is rarely discussed in psychology. Freud's writings are one of the few sources available.

Analogue to Minsky's Society of Mind, the human mind can be described as an organization of multi-level processes. Values, Censors, and Ideals together with instinctive behavioral systems are used as inputs for processes like self-conscious emotions, self-reflective thinking, reflective thinking, deliberative thinking, learned reactions, and instinctive reactions. Using this approach, the machine could reflect what it was recently thinking about. According to Minsky, this system is consistent with early theories of Freud, especially with his second topographical model. The vague transformation provided in [Min05, p. 4] is a system with three modules "Values, Censors, Ideals, and Taboos", "Commonsense Thinking and Reasoning", and "Innate and Acquired Urges and Drives". They are equivalent to Superego, Ego, and Id.

In [Min06, p. 86–88], Minsky describes what he calls "the Freudian Sandwich" — the application of his models and concepts to psychoanalytical theories. Freud's theories are describing a system where ideas have to overcome certain barriers to come into effect. Thus, the system not only describes how thinking about a certain topic/idea works, moreover, it shows how non-fitting ideas are handicapped from being processed. According to Minsky, all ideas which have overcome the barriers are labeled to be conscious. The two main categories of ideas which are not able to become conscious are: repudiated ideas and repressed ideas. Ideas which are known to be blocked are repudiated. Thus, one can still remember rejecting it, but the idea itself is rendered powerless — meaning it has no further influence. Ideas rejected at an earlier stage are repressed. Here, neither the idea itself nor the fact of rejecting is known. However, the idea is still active and tries to "disguise" itself. Thus, it still can become conscious, although not in its original shape.

Inside Freud's three-part model (Superego, Ego, and Id), many resources are working in parallel. Conflicting goals/purposes is an innate property of this system. According to

Minsky [Min06, p. 88], "[...] the human mind is like a battleground in which resources are working at once — but don't always share the same purposes. Instead, there often are serious conflicts between our animal instincts and our acquired ideals." Thus, a constant struggle to produce acceptable compromises is going on. Functions which are working to the above described principles — repression and repudiation — are helping in this process. If they are successful, no censors or critics are aroused. In Freudian terminology this is called sublimation; in cognitive sciences this is sometimes called 'rationalizing'.

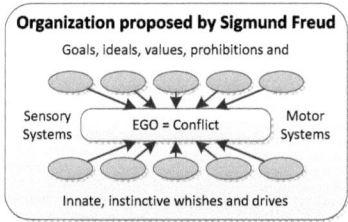

Figure 2.16: Minsky's Freudian sandwich [Min06, p. 88]

Figure 2.16 is a rough sketch how the organization of the mind can be described in agent terminology. Sensor inputs (left side) are processed together with goals, ideals, etc. (Superego; top) and instinctive wishes, drives etc. (Id; bottom) in the Ego module. There the conflicts between Superego and Id are mediated. Finally, the motor system processes the commands produced by the Ego.

Minsky states that few modern cognitive psychologists are appreciating psychoanalytical concepts and architectures. Nevertheless, Freud was one of the first to figure out that the everyday problems are too complex to be described on a centralized process. Thereafter, the human mind is a product of different activities including conflicts and inconsistencies. It is important to mention that these interpretations of psychoanalysis are more fitting to the object theory developed by Klein than to the work of Freud.

The last group — psychoanalysis as foundation — uses psychoanalysis as a starting point. Thus, psychoanalytical theories are selected, analyzed, transformed, and finally implemented into a technical gadget.

The architecture Volitron developed by Buller is the most important member of this group discussed here. It is based on theories from Freud, Piaget, and Minsky. Starting from psychoanalysis, Buller inserts fitting concepts whenever necessary. For example, the nature of psychic forces is not defined. A concept called "memes" is used [BJLS05, p. 198]. To be more precise, Buller uses psychodynamics, not psychoanalysis, as foundation. The first one is a subset of the latter. In [Bul05, p. 70] the listed four principles of psychoanalysis are:

- Fundamental role of unconscious processes
- Existence of conflicting mental forces and defense mechanisms
- Existence of the Oedipus complex

- Key role of sexual drive and aggressive drive

In psychodynamics, the last two assumptions are not considered. A further difference is that psychoanalysis is a theory and a therapy while psychodynamics is only a theory. The key concepts of psychodynamics are tensions and defense mechanisms. A rise of a tension is felt as unpleasure and the lowering as pleasure. This results to the following contradiction: according to Bullers interpretation of psychoanalytical theory, his model does not use sexual and aggressive drives — instead of drives, tensions are used. The term tension as used by Buller is similar to the term drive. The sexual drive — or libido — and the aggressive drive — or death drive — are inert to all drives according to meta-psychology. Thus, the fourth point is present in his model.

Psychodynamic is described in a narrative way. It has to be converted into more technical terms. An example taken from [Bul09, p. 323] is the conversion of the term "pleasure." The definition given by psychodynamics is: *"Pleasure is a measurable quantity that reinforces certain reactions and behaviors of a creature and constitutes an attractive purpose of actions the creature may plan and undertake."* Buller then defines the formula which describes the definition as: $p' = \lambda(-q') - p/T$. Where p is the pleasure volume (or intensity), q is the causing tension, λ a function which returns 0 iff its argument is below a threshold, and T is a time constant. The resulting behavior is equivalent to the first law of psychodynamics as defined in [Bul09, p. 323]: *"Pleasure volume rapidly rises when a related tension plummets, whereas it slowly decays when the tension either rises, remains constant, or diminishes with a relatively low speed."* The other three laws are produced similarly.

In [Bul05, pp. 72–73], Buller gives an enumeration of ten assumptions which an agent has to fulfill to be called a psychodynamic agent. The most important aspects can be summarized to: An agent is operating only for its own pleasure, with pleasure produced by discharge of a tension. Within the body and the brain several tension accumulating devices are present — the higher a tension gets, the more unpleasant the agent feels. If more than one tension becomes high, they fight to suppress the others. Thus, the winner gets discharged first. Through interaction with its caregiver and other agents, an agent learns when an action is positively judged by others and thereafter feels pleasure in such a case.

Although Volitron has never been implement in full-scale, parts of it have been implemented and tested successfully. What is missing is a critical examination of used psychoanalytical concepts and their transformation by an interdisciplinary team. Nevertheless, the work of Buller is one of the few which use a predefined methodology for the transfer of the narrative description of psychological phenomena into technically feasible terms.

Another interesting project is "Modeling Human Mind" by Nitta et al. [NTMI99]. The authors divide human psychic abilities into intellectual (like learning, judging, and estimating) and non-intellectual (like emotion and unconsciousness) activities. While much effort has been put into the research of the first set, the second set has been widely ignored. Starting from this assumption, a "personality model" based on psychoanalysis is developed. According to Nitta et al. in [NTMI99, p. 342], a crucial part of the human personality is defined by the defense mechanisms. They formulate defense mechanisms using inductive probability.

The used psychoanalytical terms are: Ego, Superego, Id, defense mechanisms, conflict, anxiety, repressions, and (psychic) energy. The used narrative definitions are shallow and imprecise. An example given: *"Id is associated with the drives of* want to do something, *and Superego is associated with the drives of* must do something." [NTMI99, p. 1]. While the definition for Id is acceptable, the definition for Superego faces a serious problem. "Drive" is the concept of connecting psychic contents with bodily needs. The Superego consists of something comparable to rules, commandments, and ideals [DFZB09, pp. 69–70]. Thus, the term drive cannot be used in the context of Superego. Similar problems are to be found with any definition given. Further, not much more information on the nature of e.g. Id are given. Especially in the case of defense mechanisms — which are the most important terms according to the authors — a more thorough discussion of the underlying psychoanalytical theories is necessary.

The framework developed by the authors operates according to this basic flow of operations: $Trigger \rightarrow Conflict \rightarrow Anxiety \leftrightarrow Defense$. External world events trigger Ego events — the so called anticipated events e, which are a subset of all possible events and thus a realization of focus of attention. The above mentioned drives from Superego and Id are personality dependent events (s and u). The occurrence of s and u events influence the conditional probability which generate Ego events a from e.

Conflict for any Ego event a is defined by $0 \leq P(a \cap \bar{a}) \leq 1/4$. If this equation system is not true — hence, the probability is above $1/4$ — a conflict for the event a occurs. If the sum of all conflicts is above a certain threshold α, the next stage in the model is activated (anxiety). Depending on another threshold β — which defines the mental strength to deal with conflicts — the defense mechanism might be necessary to deal with the situation. The only defense mechanism implemented in this work is repression. A more desirable, fictionally anticipated event is generated, the probabilities of all other such events lowered and the process is restarted.

After each cycle, α and β are raised in case of no repressions performed and lowered if the defense mechanisms were necessary.

The result of this model is a system which is able to fade out too many undesirable events. Next to the above already mentioned critique on the shallow usage of psychoanalytical terms, the system uses only a very minor subset of psychoanalysis. For example, only one out of twelve defense mechanisms is used (cp. Schuster and Springer-Kremser [SSK97, pp. 51–62]).

The last project to mention in this section is "A Design of the Mental Model of a Cognitive Robot" by Park et al. [PKP07]. The authors defined a mind sketch model of consciousness and unconsciousness based on Freud's mind model. This is combined with the emotion theories from Ortony and Turner [OT90]. Further concepts used are: Neural networks, fuzzy petry nets, AI, and kohonen networks. No argument is given how the used theory model fits into Freud's mind model. The same applies for all concepts. The authors — similar to [NTMI99] — are more interested in building a system that solves a certain problem than in analyzing the used concepts.

To summarize this survey: It can be clearly seen that in the last two or three decades the idea of combining psychoanalysis with computer science has been formulated and pursued by scientists from both sides. Unfortunately no scientific community dedicated to this idea has been formed yet. Instead, all approaches are isolated, short-term ventures of very small groups or individuals. Up to my knowledge, ARS is the first project on which an interdisciplinary team has been working for several years. Thus, most of the work this thesis can build upon has been produced by its very own project.

2.5 Artificial Life Simulation

The psychoanalytically inspired decision unit is to be tested in an A-Life simulation. The term A-Life was coined by Chris Langton: *"[...] the study of man-made systems that exhibit behaviors characteristic of natural living systems [Lan89, p. 1]."* To build an A-Life simulator, a suitable simulation platform has to be chosen (Section 2.5.1). Next, an overview of simulators suitable for the task at hand is given in Section 2.5.2.

2.5.1 Simulation Platforms

Simulation platforms provide a framework for agent based simulations. They usually provide schedulers, agent communication, visualization tools, and different types of maps. A-Life simulations like the Bubble Family Game (BFG) (see Section 2.6.3) can be developed more efficiently using such a framework.

The basic requirements which have to be met for this project are: A standard programming language like Java or C++, suitable for simulations with hundreds of agents, support of complex decision units within each agent, viability for social system simulations, a suitable 2D visualization, and a good inspector support to display internal states of the agents.

The compared simulation platforms are: AnyLogic, Swarm, Recursive Porous Agent Simulation Toolkit (RePast), and Multi-Agent Simulator of Neighborhoods ... or Networks ... or something ... (MASON). The first one is added due to project development reasons — the previous version of the A-Life simulator BFG was implemented in AnyLogic. The other three are included due to the fact that they are the common intersection between articles comparing agent based simulation platforms ([RLJ06], [Ber08], and [Poz06]).

All three comparisons are reviewing NetLogo next to Swarm, RePast, and MASON too. Although this is a good and powerful tool, it has been removed from the list of possible candidates. Its origins lie within education and are thereafter not suitable for complex simulations [RLJ06, p. 916]. Berryman [Ber08] additionally adds battlefield-specific platforms like BactoWars or EINSTein which do not fit into the niche of this project (socially interacting agents). Breve — a popular 3D simulator — focuses on topics like evolution of pedal motion using genetic algorithms. According to Pozdnyakov [Poz06, p. 4], it is not suitable for social simulations.

AnyLogic [10] is a multi-purpose simulation kit developed by XJtek. It is completely written in Java and embedded into a customized eclipse development environment. For A-Life simulations, five of the numerous abilities are of great interest: Discrete, event-based processing, agent based simulation, easily generated 2D graphic output, and good support for drawing charts. Further, AnyLogic provides many tools for rapid prototype development.

The development environment allows two approaches for implementing a model: First, drag and drop with no or very limited need for programming. Elements which can be used for this are state charts, timers, triggers, differential equation solvers, and others. Second, program everything in Java using the base AnyLogic simulation class as parent class. A mixture of both approaches is possible, too.

Although its suitability for agent based modeling in principle, AnyLogic is not the tool to use in larger — regarding complexity and/or number of agents — projects. Our experience gained from developing the BFG [DZL07, DZLZ08] showed several problems. The most severe ones are: The framework is overloaded and thus slow, debugging abilities of the development platform Eclipse are deliberately reduced, state chart definitions cannot be split over several files and nested state chart definitions is not possible which make development of complex systems difficult.

Swarm [11] is a simulation toolkit for the simulation of complex adaptive systems. The basic entity is the so called Swarm. A Swarm consists of a set of agents and a schedule of actions. A Swarm can consist of a set of Swarms. Thus, hierarchical systems are easy to design. Further, Swarm provides components for building models and to perform experiments on these models. This includes analyzing, displaying, and controlling the experiments. Experiments can be run with a Graphical User Interface (GUI) or in batch mode. Swarm makes no assumptions on the model being implemented. Thus, it is a multi-purpose simulation toolkit.

In Swarm, agents are designed as objects. Each agent can be "probed". Thus, all important aspects of the computation are observable. The core libraries of Swarm ensure that any object can be probed easily. Atop of the probes graphical tools for object inspection can be used while the system is running. Measurements can be performed using observer agents. *"The core of a Swarm simulation is the modeled world itself [MBLA96, p. 6],"* thus, the environment itself is Swarm containing the agents or Swarms which reside within the world.

Swarm provides three types of libraries: First, there are simulation libraries — swarmobject, activity, and simtools — which are "the center of the Swarm modeling paradigm." Swarmobject provides memory management, support for probes, and other tools. Activity is responsible for scheduling of actions. Simtools provides support for execution, display, and data analysis of the simulation. Second, the software support libraries provide container classes, infrastructure for the Swarm object model, random number generators, and basic support for a GUI. The third type consists of model-specific libraries that provide support for a very specific and limited domain. Examples are space (different environments), ga (genetic algorithms), and neuro (neural networks).

Swarm — being the father of the simulation frameworks [RLJ06, p. 620] — offers as its main advantage a small and well modeled framework. The main disadvantage is the usage of the Objective C programming language. It is lesser known than C or Java and uses some — for not experienced Objective C programmers — hard to understand concepts.

RePast   [12] — Recursive Porous Agent Simulation Toolkit — was originally concepted to be a Java implementation of Swarm. According to Railsback et al. [RLJ06, p. 611], during design phase the authors of RePast decided to use only a subset of Swarm and to add new capabilities. Some of these enhancements are start and reset the model from a GUI, a multi-run manager feature for series of experiments, and a totally new scheduling concept.

RePast is now in its fourth generation (RePast Symphony), extending the original framework by a comprehensive GUI [TNH+06, p. 85]. It supports 2D and 3D visualization, point-and-click model configuration and operation, access to enterprise data source, and easy integration of external data sources.

Similar to AnyLogic, the modeler can get support from the framework during design phase. In a four step process, the model grows from model pieces written in Java, to a complex, interconnected simulation model. Such, an experienced modeler can offload most of the repetitive tasks to RePast.

In comparison to the other three frameworks, it is the most complete one. The main disadvantages of it reside in questionable design decisions like scheduling is not sufficiently configurable or incompatible collection classes [RLJ06, p. 621].

MASON   [13] — Multi-Agent Simulator Of Neighborhoods... or Networks... or something... — is a new framework. It has been designed from scratch based on analysis of existing frameworks like TeamBots, Swarm, Ascape, RePast, StarLogo, NetLogo [LBP+03, pp. 1–2], [LCRPS04, p. 1].

MASON is a discrete-event, single core simulator and visualization toolkit developed entirely in Java. It is designed to be flexible enough to support a wide range of applications but has a special emphasis on swarm simulations. Thus, it is designed to support up to millions of agents. To accomplish this goal, emphasis has been put on slim design with no support for domain-specific features like physics models, robot sensors, graphs, and charts. Further, it is not intended to be used by inexperienced users.

Figure 2.17 shows the basic concept of the MASON framework. The main two blocks are the simulation model itself and the visualization. Utilities like graphs or other statistical analysis are deliberately excluded from the framework. The simulation module is responsible for four important parts: The event scheduler, the space, agents, and objects. Agents and objects are located in the space. Different types of fields — like 2D planar, 2D toroidal, directed networks — can be used. The scheduler takes care of which agent should be called in the current time step. Visualization is separated from the simulation. The module has its own representations — 2D and 3D portrayals — for each object or agent to be displayed. Due to performance reason, it is important that the simulation model can be run without

State of the Art

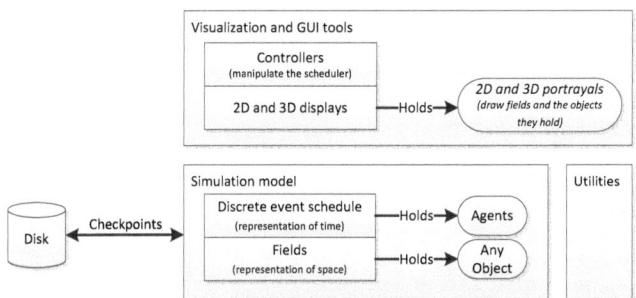

Figure 2.17: Basic concept of MASON [LCRPS04, p. 2]

any visualization. In MASON this is accomplished by designing the visualization/GUI module as wrapper for the simulation core.

An important feature of MASON is the possibility to checkpoint the current simulation run to the disk and recover it. Recovering can be done on any other machine which is capable of running MASON. Further, it can be decided whether to use visualization or not upon recovery. To the same disk, different model runs can be checkpointed. The user is free to choose to which system the run should be recovered.

Main advantages of MASON are its slim core, its expandability, and the execution speed. Disadvantages are the need for experienced programmers, the lack of development tools, and the restriction to a single core.

Comparison From the four analyzed frameworks the first two do not meet the requirements and can be eliminated from the list. AnyLogic is not suitable for development of large projects. Swarm fails to use a standard language like Java or C++. Although MASON deliberately fails to meet the last requirement — inclusion of chart drawing support — this shortcoming can be easily eliminated by usage of Java libraries like JGraph. Thus, MASON and RePast fulfill all requirements.

The two comparisons performed by Railsback et al. [RLJ06] and by Berryman [Ber08] are formulating a small simulation to be implemented in each tested framework each. The first one implements a so called "ridiculously simplified model" in 16 steps and compares the performance and the easiness of the implementation for each step with each framework. The second one implements a simple battle simulation with spatial distribution of the agents. The results are comparable: MASON and RePast are the winners under certain circumstances like availability of experienced programmers and the need for computation intensive simulations.

Based on the experiences gained with AnyLogic — a closed simulation environment provides too many restrictions for complex scenarios — together with the fact that RePast performed slightly slower than MASON in the comparisons and the design flaws of RePast mentioned above, MASON is chosen to be the foundation of the A-Life simulator described in Chapter 4.

2.5.2 Related Projects

The previously developed simulator BFG (see [DZL07, DZLZ08]) has proven to be a valid testbed and verification tool for the psychoanalytically inspired decision unit. The key points of it are: A continuous 2D world, several types of agents, many action possibilities, complex sensors, different objects of interest like statues, different types of energy sources, and several implementations of simple decision units. A detailed description of it is given in Section 2.6.3.

Although many A-Life simulations for different research projects exist, only few review articles comparing them exist. Other than with simulation frameworks (see previous section) each project is developing its own, very specialized A-Life. Zadeh et al. [ZLL04] gives an overview on A-Life simulations which can be used for agent based simulations. The starting point of this survey is: "How a general purpose artificial environment should be designed to be suitable for cognitive studies?" They analyze the simulators of nine projects — ranging from fish flocking behaviors to verification of some isolated psychological theories — regarding their practicability. The below described simulation called Zoological Agents for Modification and Improvement of Neocreatures (Zamin) has been adapted by the authors to meet the found requirements.

Simulations like Conway's Game of Life [Gar70] or Schelling's urban migration model [Sch71] do not provide sufficient interaction possibilities with the environment. Although the results show a complex behavior, the sensors and actuators are reduced to cell based functionality (e.g. is neighbor cell occupied, migrate to neighbor cell). On the opposite end of simulation complexity range game adaptions as for example described in (e.g. [BL06, pp. 190–192]). Commercially successful game engines like Unreal Tournament — which are made open source by the developers after some time — can be modified to fit the project's requirements. The problem lies within the very nature of the original games the engines were written for: They best fit for hide-and-seek scenarios. Other setups — like social interactions — are more difficult to realize.

The following three A-Life simulations have been selected due to the fact that they meet many of the above mentioned key points or they have other interesting features. The Fungus-Eater originate in a thought experiment where robots are put onto a remote planet to collect ore. Zamin provides complex mechanisms together with a simple, discrete cell environment. The third project provides many objects of interest for the agents. These objects may change their function during season changes (summer and winter).

Fungus-Eater

The Fungus-Eater [Tod82, pp. 89–99] is a model of a robot — not a real robot though. It is a thought experiment. The "intelligence" of this robot is far inferior compared to human intellect. If at all, it can be compared with the abilities of a rat.

The background story of this thought experiment is: On a remote planet named Taros, large quantities of uranium ore in form of small pebbles have been discovered. The planet itself is not very interesting and very remote. Next to the uranium ore, stone pebbles and fungi are the only objects found on the totally flat surface. Fitting autonomous robots have been designed to collect the ore. They are equipped with a biochemical reactor to transform the fungi into energy. Thus, they are given the name Fungus-Eater. Their task is to collect the ore and return it to the base station. Whenever necessary, fungus has to be eaten.

Toda created this thought experiment in 1962 [Tod62]. Robots able to perform these simple tasks were not available, then. The focus of his interest was how people are behaving in such restricted conditions. Nevertheless, the sketched robots and their expected behavior are well suitable for A-Life simulations and real world robots. The basic setup contains only one robot. Later, additional robots and robot predators are introduced to enable social interactions.

The differentiation of the objects of interest into two groups — uranium ore and fungus — is interesting. The first group is the one with the highest priority. It is the Fungus-Eater's main purpose to collect ore. The latter one is only important as means to fulfill the prime objective. Each action, especially traveling on the ground, costs energy. This applies even to sensing and thinking. Eaten fungus is stored in the stomach and converted into energy on demand. Without eating fungus, no ore can be collected. Thus, it can be said that the Fungus-Eater is survival driven although survival is no inherent value of it.

As mentioned above, everything costs energy. Thereafter, searching for an optimal solution could turn out to be more expensive than performing an inferior but faster found solution. A compromise between precision and time has to be found.

Although finding ore is the prime objective, locating or knowing the location of the next fungus is of greater importance. Otherwise, the robot will not be able to meet its tasks on long hand terms. This has immediate influence on the sensors of the robot. First, the fungus-detection device range should usually exceed the one of the ore-detection device. Second, the sensitivity/range of a sensor does not have to be fixed — it should be adaptable. A larger range consumes more energy.

Like on any other planet, Taros is exposed to a day/night shift. The vision sensor, which is working perfectly well during day, needs support by a spotlight during night. Again, there is a trade-off between collecting ore and increased energy consumption during night.

Thus, the Fungus-Eater is always in constant struggle between its two utility functions: Collecting ore and having enough energy reserves to get to the next fungus.

Wehrle [Weh94] is one of the first who has implemented the Fungus-Eater experiment. The Autonomous Agent Modeling Environment has been used for this purpose. It provides regions, manipulable objects with arbitrary properties, attractors, agents with different dynamic morphologies, different types of generic sensors, actuators and attractors, communication protocols, and building blocks for autonomous control architectures.

According to Wehrle, Toda's definition of microcosm/micro worlds is closely tied to the concept of autonomous agents.

Next to the above described abilities of a single agent, a kind of flocking behavior of several agents is introduced: They keep distance to avoid conflicts and they keep in loose touch to help each other in this potentially hostile environment. The observed behavior is that the robots flock in groups of two to five members. They are circling around fungi until the fungi reserve of one or more has been filled. Then each robot searches either new areas or areas known to have uranium ore.

The Fungus-Eater implemented by Wehrle are equipped with six sensors of which three are long range sensors (ore detector, fungus detector, and Fungus-Eater detector) and three short distance sensors (collision detector, fungus detector, and ore detector). Three effectors are available: Collect ore, locomotion, and consume fungus. Each Fungus-Eater selects one of four possible behaviors: Approach ore, approach fungus, distance regulation, and explorative behavior. The consume fungus and the collect ore effector are directly connected to their correspondent short distance sensor.

This work has been of great influence on project ARS in early stages (e.g. [Roe07, 102-103], [DZL07, p. 996]) and still is a valuable source of information, ideas, and concepts. Toda has created a detailed thought experiment with a setup that enables to test not only basic functionalities like collecting and navigation. In the next two chapters of his book [Tod82, 100–153] he extends the experiment to complex social settings. Also the description of the sensors and actuators are a valuable source.

Nevertheless, the Fungus-Eater experiment is just a thought experiment and as such a good source of ideas. It can only be used as a starting point. The implementation described above realizes just a fraction of what Toda has described. Further, the described possibilities for social interaction are limited. For the task at hand this is a crucial element.

Zamin

Target of project *Zoological Agents for Modification and Improvement of Neocreatures* (Zamin) is the development of a cognitive A-Life platform which is fast and realistic [HS02, p. 1009]. Fast in the sense that results are calculated within reasonable time and realistic in the sense that observed emergence of behaviors in real organisms can be traced in this system.

Zamin [ZSH04, p. 1674] is a simple toroidal world divided into cells. Figure 2.18 shows a typical Zamin environment. Agents called Ayros and Sentinels roam between trees. Each agent has an energy level. Eating a plant increases, being attacked by another agent decreases the level. Ayros are the agents of interest. They are plant eaters and hunted by Sentinels. Their properties are passed from one generation to the next by using genomes. The actions an Ayros can take are: Stepping ahead, turning left or right, sexual or asexual reproduction, attacking other creatures, resting, and eating — either plants or the flesh of dead creatures. Each step at maximum one action can be executed. Ayros having a

STATE OF THE ART

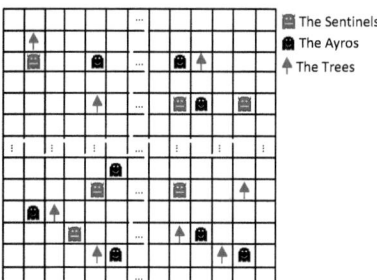

Figure 2.18: Zamin world [HS03, p. 602]

complex decision unit and can evolve over generations. Sentinels are hard coded — their only purpose is to produce threats to the Ayros.

The properties of an Ayros are: Energy, last consumed energy, and age. All three can be sensed by an internal sensor. Agents have to have a minimum level of energy to stay alive and to be able to act. Vision is the only external sensor. The type and some properties of the closest object within the field of view are returned. In case of a plant, the properties include distance, relative angle and the energy level of the plant. For other Agents, like Ayros or Sentinels, additional properties like carnivorousness, age, and tiredness are returned.

To support unsupervised learning, Ayros have a built-in pleasure system. Pleasure levels are defined using mappings from sensory input S to pleasure P — (S,P) tuples. Pleasure can be within a range of +1 (max. pleasure) to -1 (max. pain). The rules for this mapping can be defined — e.g. direct proportional mappings or fuzzy rules. The pleasure rules can change using evolution.

Communication can happen in direct information transfer from one Ayro agent to the next. As reward, energy is transferred back from the receiver to the information provider. The receiver can use the experience on performed experiments directly. Another form of communication is the broadcast of a message consisting of a sequence of characters [HSZ+04, p. 161].

This A-Life simulator has a closed material and energy system. Thus, once created, no energy or material is added. Simple organisms can absorb materials directly; agents must eat simple organisms or animals. Agents release energy and/or waist as result of their activity. How energy which is converted into movement or heat is brought back into the closed energy cycle is not explained in the available publications.

The project Zamin has several interesting aspects: The closed material and energy system, the complex reproduction system, and an agent type specialized to put stress on the agent of interest. The rather limited total number of possible actions together with the very simple sensors is to be questioned in context with ARS. The aimed complex decision unit is over-sized for the provided body complexity (see Section 2.3).

59

Complex Dynamic Virtual Environment by Ho and Dautenhahn

The reason to build this world was to analyze various topics connected with autonomous autobiographic agents. In [HDN03, p. 183], Ho et al. are focusing on control architectures with characteristic memory functions trace-back and locality. In [HDNB04, p. 362], they investigate multiple autonomous autobiographic agents which share their world knowledge. Finally, in [HDN05, p. 574] they compare purely reactive agents with agents incorporating short term memory and/or long term memory. Autobiographic agents have some kind of episodic memory which enables them to recall experienced events.

The environment is created to compare agents with different control architectures. Focus is on one hand that the agents have to maintain their homeostasis (glucose, moisture, energy, body temperature) and on the other hand that they have to search their environment for possibilities to maintain their homeostasis.

In general, the world is a bounded surface with different areas, different types of food, and two seasons (summer and winter). Each season results in a different world temperature, different types of food available, and different accessibilities of structures. Additionally to this complex world, two algebraic non-trivial characteristics have been modeled: Non-commutativity and irreversibility. Non-commutativity describes that the result of a set of actions depends on their order. Irreversibility refers to some events which cannot be 'undone'. Hence, reestablishing a previous state in the world by performing the same set of actions in reverse order is not possible.

A special object in this world is the stone. It can be found and picked up in the desert. It can only be used to crush a cactus. It is the only tool in the world.

The four food types are: Mushrooms, apple trees, cacti, and water. A mushroom provides a lot of glucose in both seasons. Apple trees provide a lot of glucose and moisture, but only in summer. A cactus provides little glucose and moisture in both seasons. Thus, cacti are the only source for moisture during winter. If not consumed in the sequence: Pickup stone, crush cactus, and eat cactus, the penalty is an energy loss instead of glucose and moisture gain (the needles injured the agent). Water provides moisture but only in summer. Sources for water are river, lake, and the waterfall.

Figure 2.19(a) is a screen shot of the simulated world. It shows the different areas existing in the environment and their spatial distribution. The area types are: Oasis, desert, mountain, river, lake, waterfall, and cave. An oasis is a warm and flat area with apple trees in summer. The desert is a hot and flat area with cacti all year long. Mountains are warm and steep with mushrooms at the peaks. The river is a cool area. In summer agents can swim in all directions in the river except upstream. In winter, the river is frozen. All frozen areas can be passed in any direction by foot. The lake and the waterfall are cool areas and, similar to the river, they freeze in winter. The waterfall connects the river with the lake. As soon as the agent enters the waterfall from the river, the downstream current picks up the agent. Finally, the agent falls into the lake. Neither in winter nor in summer can this movement be made undone. Hence, it is not possible to get from the lake back to the river using the waterfall; another route has to be chosen — irreversibility of event

STATE OF THE ART

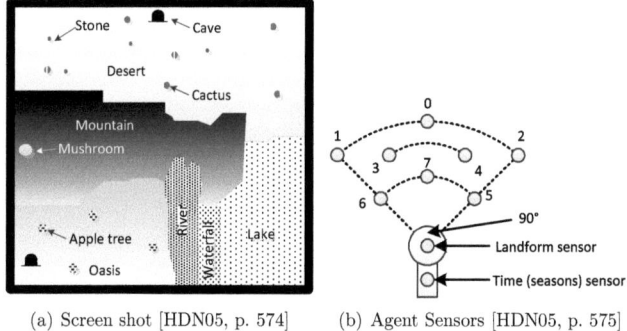

(a) Screen shot [HDN05, p. 574]   (b) Agent Sensors [HDN05, p. 575]

Figure 2.19: Complex dynamic virtual environment

sequences. The last area type is the cave which provides a normal temperature all year long. It is the only place where the agent can rest — energy can be regained in caves only.

The agents roaming in this world have a finite lifespan (zero energy equals death). Their basic behavior is to wander around the world. Their possibilities to interact with the world are: Moving (back and forth, rotate left and right; land and water movement is equal), eating (food and water), looking (for objects and landforms), picking up (stone), and crush (cactus). The agent's body is highly abstracted. It consists of a head and a tail.

The body has a homeostasis built of four parameters: Glucose, moisture, energy, and body temperature. Glucose is the agents "stomach". Apples, mushrooms, and cacti are refilling it. Each simulation step, the glucose is reduced by a fixed value. The agents "water reservoir" is represented by its moisture level. Apples, cacti and unfrozen water are refilling it. Each simulation step, the moisture is reduced by a fixed value. Energy is the agent's "battery". It can be refilled by staying in a cave. Each simulation step, the energy is reduced by a fixed value. If a cactus is touched without being crushed by a stone first, energy drops too. The agent has an ideal range of body temperature. Each landform has its own world temperature influenced by the current season. If the landform is hotter than the agent, the body temperature gets higher; if cooler it gets lower. Thus, if the agent is hot, it has to move to a cooler place and vice versa.

Figure 2.19(b) is depicting the available external sensors of the agents roaming in this world. The 90° arc contains nine object and landform sensors. Thus, the agent gets a list of nine tuples containing the detected landform and, if present, the detected object. Further, the agent has a sensor to detect, whether it is summer or winter. The internal values (glucose, moisture, energy, and body temperature) are available in absolute numeric values.

The implementation details are: The world is defined using Virtual Reality Markup Language (VRML), the programming language is JavaScript. The agents are programmed using principles of the agent programming language Propositional Dynamic Logic (PDL).

STATE OF THE ART

This A-Life simulator is the most fitting one found. It allows complex action sequences using tools, provides different energy sources which are not always accessible, etc. The main arguments against it are its usage of JavaScript as programming language and the sources are not available. JavaScript's missing type declarations and low performance render it unfit for larger projects.

2.6 Artificial Recognition System

The motivation of project ARS [1] is to build automation systems which are able to deal with complex situations. For example, in building automation hundreds of thousands of computer nodes equipped with sensors and actuators will be used to control a large office building soon [DS00, p. 348]. Applying classical AI approaches to the resulting immense amount of data may lead to systems which are unable to extract important features [PP05, p. 56]. Nature has developed various approaches to deal with the data flood every creature equipped with sensors has to cope with. One of them is the human psyche. ARS uses the human mind as archetype for the control structure of such building automation systems. The theoretical functional model provided by psychoanalysis — the meta-psychology — describes the human psyche most complete compared to other sciences of the mind [Kan99, p. 505]. Complete in terms of from sensing to acting and that no black-boxes like in behaviorism are present. Not every subsystem is explained and there exists no uncontradicted unified functional model.

First, a brief overview on the projects history is given (Section 2.6.1). Next, the predecessor stages of the current model are described to give a better understanding on various design decisions (Section 2.6.2). Concluding, the first two A-life simulations called *Bubble Family Game* (BFG) version 1 and 2 are discussed in the last Section 2.6.3. They were in use from 2005 to 2008.

2.6.1 Project Origins

Project ARS started more than ten years ago with the invited talk by Dietrich [Die00]. The first step was to equip a kitchen with sensors and actuators using a field bus system ([Rus03] and [Fue03]).

Figure 2.20 shows parts of the sensors the kitchen is equipped with and the visualization of the perception system. The large black rectangles are pressure sensors. The position information is merged with movement sensors, distance sensors, door sensors, and machine activity sensors to a representation of persons in the kitchen. The representations include not only their current estimated position, but also their activity history and the believe of the system what the person will do next.

Part of the representation is the perception the system generates using its sensors. The basic scheme is depicted in Figure 2.21(a). On the left, raw sensor data is collected and merged to a symbol. Next, this symbol is matched against a set of templates. Finally,

STATE OF THE ART

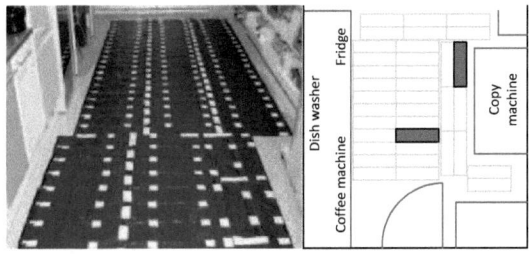

Figure 2.20: *Smart Kitchen* (SmaKi) [DLP+06, p. 117]

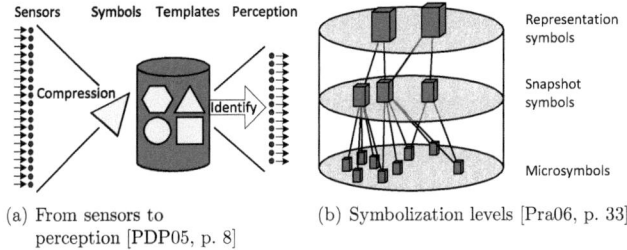

(a) From sensors to perception [PDP05, p. 8]

(b) Symbolization levels [Pra06, p. 33]

Figure 2.21: Symbolization

for further data processing the most likely templates for the given symbols along with the likelihood are the result of the perception.

The above described approach does not consider time. This can be overcome by introduction of different layers of symbols [PDHP07, p. 27]. Each layer takes as input symbols from the layer one level beneath. Figure 2.21(b) shows a three layer system. The lowest one contains micro symbols. Each micro symbol is more or less equivalent to a sensor. They are timeless — they only represent the current sensor values (e.g. kitchen door is open). The next layer — snapshot symbols — is more complex. The symbols of this layer incorporate information from various micro symbols (and even other snapshot symbols). They are designed to represent short scenarios which usually last for a few minutes. For example, a person enters the kitchen, fetches a coffee with milk, and leaves. Representation symbols — the topmost level — are long lasting symbols. Using snapshot symbols, they collect a rich history of e.g. a person's working day at office.

Another approach for scenario detection is presented by Bruckner in [Bru07]. Hidden Markov models are used to represent different possible (long term) scenarios. During learning phase, states like sensor X is active between 6:00 and 6:30 and paths connecting such states during a whole day are generated. These paths are condensed to a minimum set which still can describe all different activities which may occur. For example, an office is busy between 8:00 and 17.00 at a normal wookday, and deserted all day long on Sundays. These two scenarios can be detected by two different sensor activity paths.

STATE OF THE ART

Within ARS, a second approach to the above described multi-level-sensor-fusion system — from sensor values to representation symbols — has been elaborated. Velik describes in [VLBD08] a sensor fusion approach based on the work of the neuropsychologist Luria — a three layered perception model. The three main differences to the other approach are: The introduction of the novel concept of neuro-symbolic networks, the introduction of different modalities, and the feedback between layers. A neuro-symbol incorporates characteristics from a neuron and a symbol.

Using these mechanisms, a safety and security aware environment can be generated. A typical example is the "child in danger" scenario. The task of the automation system operating the kitchen is to perceive the situation correctly. Is the stove operating and hot? Is there a child present? Are adults taking care of this situation already? If the system detects that in fact a child is alone in the kitchen and it can hurt itself seriously at the hot plate it will generate an alarm. Eventually — if no operator reacts — it will put the system into a safe state. In this example, turning off the hot plate would be a possibility. Security can be generated by attaching a persistent representation symbol to every person entering the office building. If an unusual or novel pattern is detected within this symbol, a human operator can be informed to assess the situation.

One problem arose during development of the Smart Kitchen (SmaKi) — the immense flood of data to be interpreted. Early in this project (see [BDK+04, p. 1219], [RHBP04, p. 349], and [DKM+04, p. 93]), the need for alternative approaches for data processing and data fusion has been recognized. This lead to the novel approach — using psychoanalytical theories for AI — of project ARS. Pratl and Palensky give a first sketch of this bionic approach in [PP05] and [PPDB05]. The next section will give a detailed introduction into the first psychoanalytically inspired decision making model developed by project ARS.

2.6.2 The 1st ARS Model

The decision making model developed by project ARS is based on psychoanalysis. To ensure that psychoanalytically terms are well understood and used correctly, an interdisciplinary approach has been chosen: Engineers work together with psychoanalysts.

Figure 2.22(a) shows the basic data and control flow of the model. The `perception` collects data from the world. After converting it to perceived images, the `pre-decision` performs basic evaluation on them. They invoke certain drives and emotions. If a drive or an emotion is too strong, an immediate reactive action has to be performed (the dashed arrow from `pre-decision` to `action`). Parallel, the emotionally evaluated perceived images are transferred to `decision`. First, the images are connected to scenarios, which allow deliberation on time dependent, chained observations. Next, based upon these scenarios and the emotional state the system is in, decisions are made. Another important task is to inhibit reactive actions if necessary. Finally, `action` executes action commands received by `decision` or `pre-decision`, resulting in an altered world.

Perception is not passed directly to decision making. It first runs through an emotional filter and through the focus of attention filter. In Figure 2.22(b) the basic scheme of this

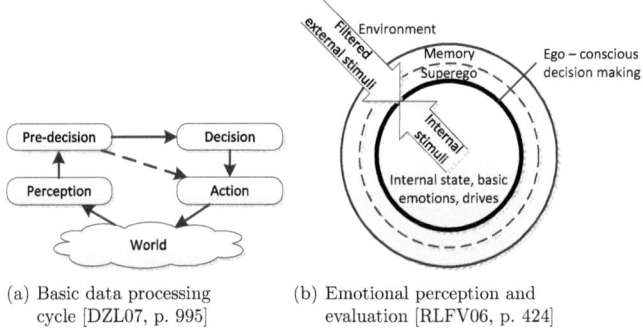

(a) Basic data processing cycle [DZL07, p. 995]

(b) Emotional perception and evaluation [RLFV06, p. 424]

Figure 2.22: Basic concepts

emotional perception and evaluation is sketched. Internal stimuli — basic emotions, drives, and internal states like fatigue — are passed unfiltered to the Ego — the place where decision making happens. External information is first transformed into symbols using memory. As explained in the previous section, received sensor data is compressed into symbols which are matched against already known templates. This results in the fact, that one can only recognize what one already knows (in case of a system that is not able to learn). If it is able to learn, only small innovations can be made in each learning step. The focus of attention can boost the weight of templates (this function is not depicted in Figure 2.22(b)); the system is expecting to see or is searching for. The Superego filters the perceived images according to social commandments. Finally, the decision making — in this case the Ego — uses the incoming, filtered stream from outside and the unfiltered internal stream as base for its decisions.

Within this model, the four basic emotional systems defined by Panksepp [Pan98, p. 52] are used. They are: Seeking system, rage system, fear system, and panic system. Each system is hardwired; appearing in all mammals soon after birth. The seeking system is — at least at a low level — always active and pushes the agent to show at least a searching behavior. The rage system causes aggressive behavior. The fear system enables the mammal to avoid threatening situations. The last one — the panic system — is responsible for feelings of loss and sorrow.

Complex emotions — all emotions that are not available in mammals soon after birth — are influenced by basic emotions and basic bodily states. Complex emotions typically identified in humans would be hope, joy, disappointment, gratitude, reproach, pride, shame, etc. They are generated and processed in the higher cognitive functions.

The work of Burgstaller et al. [BLPV07, Bur07] describes how this emotional system can be implemented. It is an integral part of the first ARS model described in this section.

The symbolization as depicted in Figure 2.23 is designed analogous to the approach depicted in Figure 2.21(a). Sensor values are condensed to symbols (or micro-symbol in the notion used in the previous section). The set of currently perceived symbols is matched against all predefined/previously stored template images. Such an image is defined by which symbols have to be available (mandatory and optional) together with a probability gain by each symbol detected (the sum is limited by 1). The set of perceived images is this list of template images together with the probability value for each image.

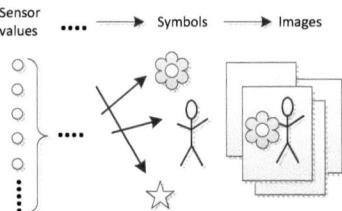

Figure 2.23: From sensor values to images [PPC09, p. 204]

Based upon the data processing cycle described above (Figure 2.22(a)), a more detailed cycling has been developed (see Figure 2.24(a)) [PPC09, pp. 197–216]. The agent's body is the interface between world, internal states, and decision making. The decision making unit has four major blocks: Pre-decision (basic-emotions and drives), decision (deliberative reasoning), sensors (internal and external), and actuators (internal and external). Pre-decision as well as decision have inner cycles which means that the results of the last calculation step are influencing the outcome of the current step. Pre-decision is influencing the decision by the current emotional state and the decision can perform a back-pressure to the pre-decision unit with the result of the complex emotions. Both influences are primarily performed by re-evaluation of active images. Sensors are producing perceived images which are passed to the pre-decision as the current perception. Pre-decision and decision can apply filters to this process. Actuators are getting commands from both control units. The body executes them and thereafter changes the state of the world.

Figure 2.24(b) is the final view. Everything is put together what is necessary for a psychoanalytically inspired decision making unit. Environment, internal state, sensors, and actuators are matching the above described elements (environment equals world and internal state is a subset of the body).

The perception interface module converts the sensor data into perceived images which are stored in the image memory. Sequences of perceived images are resulting in perceived episodes (the algorithm to produce them is similar to the one for the template images as described above). The entries of the semantic memory are predefined.

In the pre-decision currently perceived images are emotionally evaluated. The current basic emotional system is dependent on the different drives (which map bodily needs), the complex emotions, the previous value of the basic emotions, and the images perceived. Basic emotions together with drives can evoke reactive actions. In psychoanalytical terms, the pre-decision is the technical realization of a model of the Id. Thus, it produces demands.

State of the Art

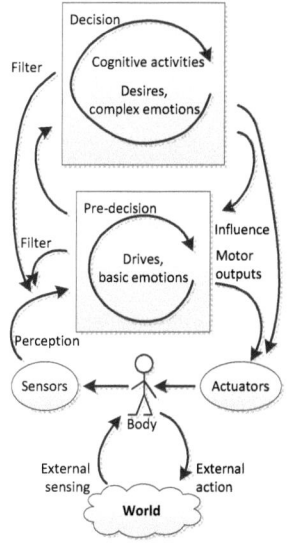
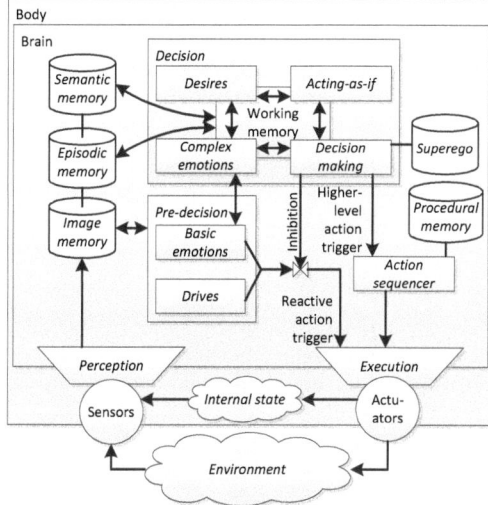

(a) Cycles and feedback mechanism of the old ARS model [PPC09, pp. p. 200]

(b) Old ARS model [PPC09, pp. p. 202]

Figure 2.24: Two views on the old ARS model

The decision module is more complex than the pre-decision module. Next to the perceived images, also the currently active basic emotions, drives, perceived episodes, and access to the semantic memory are used. The working memory connects the four modules desires, acting-as-if, complex emotions, and decision making. Complex emotions — also called social emotions — include other agents in the world and are based upon basic emotions. Desires are something the agent wants to be fulfilled due to an active complex emotion. A desire contains next to what is being desired one or more plans how it is possible to get it [LBP+07, p. 308]. Acting-as-if evaluates all active plans and tests the plausibility for success. Decision making has to mediate by the demands generated by the pre-decision and the commandments of the Superego. A further task of the decision making is to deliberately inhibit reactive action commands coming from the pre-decision. The totality of the four modules can be seen as the Ego.

The Superego is a storage of rules. It contains commandments and ideals. They are requested by decision making.

The output of decision making is high level action triggers. The action sequencer uses the procedural memory — which stores sequences of simple actions as routines — to select which action has to be performed according to the currently active action trigger.

The execution module translates the actions provided by the pre-decision and the action sequencer into motor commands. Further it has to decide what to do in the case that the two incoming signals contain mutually exclusive actions like lift leg versus lower leg. Finally, the action module executes the incoming commands and influences the environment and the internal state.

Although the above described model was produced using an interdisciplinary approach, it still has problems regarding terminology and incompatibilities of used concepts [DFZB09, 53–54]. Thus, based on the lessons learned, a new model has been developed which is described in Chapter 3.

2.6.3 Bubble Family Game

The Bubble Family Game (BFG) has been designed as testbed for the above described psychoanalytically inspired model. The idea has been to generate an artificial world in which artificial creatures roam. The minimum requirements for such a world are that there should be different kinds of agents (artificial creatures), different types of food, points of interest, and different landscapes. These four points are sufficient to provide social interaction, danger, joy, a world to be explored, objects which can be used for map generation, surfaces which makes it harder—if not impossible—to reach a destination crossing them.

The first version of this simulator—BFG 1.0 described in [DLP+06]—was implemented using a Java based simulation framework called AnyLogic. It contained a subset of the previously listed requirements: Two groups of similar agents (which are called Bubbles) are either searching and consuming food or are fighting against each other. It helped to test and develop early versions of the drive model and image perception. The most important limitations were the a priori division of the agents into two groups, the monolithic character of the software itself (distribution to several processors was not possible), and the interface between body and mind was not precise enough.

Based on the lessons learned from the first version, the 2nd BFG (see [Roe07, 102–123], [DZL07], and [DZLZ08]) simulator was developed. The world was designed to be more complex, allowing more different kinds of interactions. The simulator core—which includes the game logic and the pseudo physics engine—was detached from the software parts responsible for all agents.

Figure 2.25(a) shows a screen shot of a typical situation within the A-Life simulator. The screen is divided into two parts: On the left hand side is the simulated world, on the right hand side are game controls and inspectors which display internal states of the selected agent.

Using Transmission Control Protocol/Internet Protocol (TCP/IP) connections, different types of visualizations can be connected. Each one is placed in its own container. The container provides the connection socket. Next to the 2D visualization depicted in Figure 2.25(a), two other user interfaces were implemented: A 3D view on the environment (Figure 2.25(c)) and a 3D view on the internal states of a Cognitive Agent (Figure 2.25(b)). Next to displaying the world and/or selected values, all three user interfaces are providing basic interaction with the simulated world (e.g. drag and drop of objects).

STATE OF THE ART

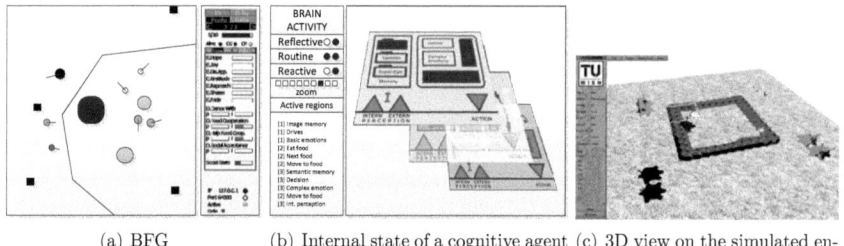

(a) BFG (b) Internal state of a cognitive agent (c) 3D view on the simulated environment

Figure 2.25: BFG 2.0 GUI [DZLZ08, pp. 1087–1089]

Within the world, several different types of agents are shown: Simple and complex Bubbles, small and large energy sources, surfaces, and obstacles. The Bubbles are agents equipped with more or less sophisticated decision units. The body shape is a circle with a line pointing towards the direction the agent is looking at. The size of the circle is directly proportional to the weight of the agent. The different colors are representing the different groups — or families — each Bubble is belonging to. The black squares are small energy sources. Each Bubble can consume energy from them by standing atop of them and performing the action eat. Large energy sources — the white square with a black border — can only be consumed in teamwork. Two or more agents have to perform the action eat simultaneously. The small gray squares are obstacles. Depending on the type assigned to them, they can represent points of interest, stones, landmarks, etc. Finally, the polygon represents a surface. Each surface represents a different landscape — for example grassland or desert. For some landscapes agents need to have special abilities to move through them.

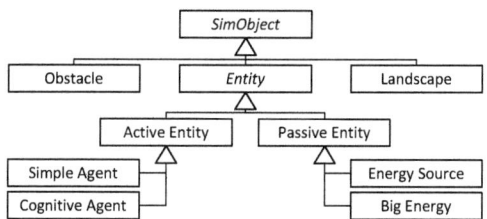

Figure 2.26: Bubble Family Game entity class tree [DZLZ08, p. 1088]

All agents are specializations of class `Active Object` (see Figure 2.26). As such they are provided with processes which update their internal state and have sensors and actuators to interact with the environment. A feedback on the success of an action is given in the next step. Common properties for all agents are energy level, active sensors, active actuators, and a flag if the agent is alive.

Each agent type has its own set of algorithms. Their purposes range from refilling the amount of food an energy source stores to complex, pro-active decision making. Objects

State of the Art

of the first type are grouped to be descendants of `Passive Entity`. This class provides an abstract function which is called each turn. Embodied autonomous agents are descendants of `Active Entity`. This class provides action patterns like move to visible object X and an interface called `Cerebellum`. Decision units for these agents use this interface to access sensor information and to tell the simulator which action/action pattern they decided to perform. This façade design pattern provides a temporal firewall between the simulator and the control logic. The decision units themselves are implemented in Java and are independent from the rest of the simulator.

A sequence of actions is called action pattern. Active entities provide a set of predefined action patterns. For example, the action pattern "flee" shown in Figure 2.27 is implemented using a state chart. Other implemented action patterns are: "Promenade", "attack", and "dance". They all have in common, that they are simple to describe, relatively short, and that they represent routines as described in Section 2.6.2. Other than the decision units — which are behind a temporal firewall — these action patterns have complete world knowledge (except the internal states of the agents). This "shortcut" allows focusing on the core topic within project ARS: Modeling of a framework according to psychoanalytical theories.

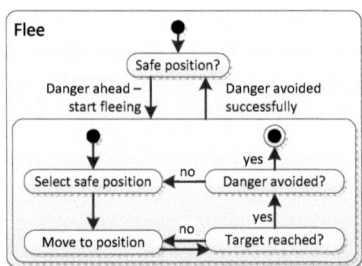

Figure 2.27: Simple flee pattern [DZLZ08, p. 1088]

As mentioned above, the reason for implementing an A-Life simulator is to provide a testbed for the decision model defined by project ARS. The three most important test cases which have been identified to support this task [DZLZ08, p. 998] are (cp. Figure 2.28):

Ask for a dance: Social interaction is a core issue in psychoanalysis. This should not be limited to aggressive tasks like fighting or hunting. Thus, dancing has been introduced. One agent decides that now would be the perfect time to dance with a team mate. It searches for one and asks if the other agent is willing to dance now. If yes, both have to move closer together and start the action pattern "dance" (which is turning left or right). Once successfully completed, both agents increase their believe of the other's social level. Thus, the binding between them is intensified. In times of need, it is more likely that agents with strong social bindings will help each other's on a benevolent level.

STATE OF THE ART

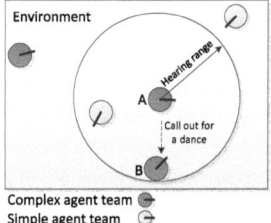
(a) Test case 1 'ask for a dance'

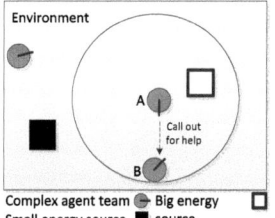
(b) Test case 2 'cooperation for food'

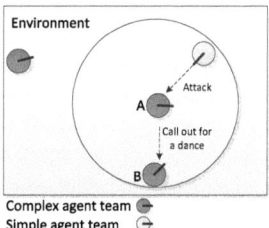
(c) Test case 3 'call for help'

Figure 2.28: Test cases [DZLZ08, p. 998]

Cooperation for food: Large energy sources cannot be consumed by one agent alone. A real world example would be stone-age hunters trying to slay a mammoth. The flow of this test case is comparable to "ask for a dance" with the difference that next to the increased social level, all participants have the possibility to eat.

Call for help: When attacked by several agents from another team, a Bubble has little other options than to flee. If this is not possible the only option left is to try to get help from team mates. Depending on the number of attackers and on its own social level team mates will decide to launch a counter-attack if such a call for help has been received. Other than with the first two test cases, this situation is potentially risky for the helpers. This makes it more unlikely that help will be granted. Thus, the sometimes "benevolently" performed help in the case of food or dancing might turn out to be of use in this situation.

Experiments have been performed in [DZL07, p. 999] and [Roe07, pp. 118–123]. The setup is rather simple: Two small energy sources, one large energy source, four agents with a simple rule-based decision unit, and four agents with a complex psychoanalytically inspired decision unit. The task is to survive as long as possible as a group. The survival rates for each group after 25 runs with 1000 simulation steps each are shown in Table 2.1.

Table 2.1: Survival rates for 25 runs [DZL07, p. 999]

	Simple Agent	Complex Agent
min	0.00	1.00
avg	2.79	3.44
max	4.00	4.00
std.dev	0.52	0.65

Although both types of agents have been able to survive to 1000 cycles as a whole (four agents alive), the complex agents outperform the simple ones. While the simple agents have an average survival rate of 65% the complex agents have 86%. Additionally, at least one agent of the complex type has survived each simulation run. Simulations with 500,

71

1000, and 2000 steps indicate that the probability to die for a complex agent decreases with time whereas simple agents have a constant rate. According to [Roe07, pp. 121–123], this performance gain is a result of the adaption ability.

Table 2.2 shows the utilization rates for the three test cases. Given is the amount of time a complex agent believes to be in this test case. An agent can be in more than one test case at any point in time.

Table 2.2: Utilization of test cases [Roe07, p. 123]

	Ask for dance	Cooperation for Food	Call for Help
min	48.1%	22.2%	0.0%
avg	76.1%	58.8%	6.0%
max	85.0%	95.0%	19.0%
std.dev	9.0%	21.0%	5.0%

The simplicity of the test case "ask for dance" together with the sufficient supply of energy makes it the most frequent one. More than 76% of its time an agent wants to perform this leisure activity. With only 6% of time, call for help is on the opposite side of the range. This is due to the rather peaceful configuration of the simple agents. Cooperation for food happens quite often with 59% of the time. The large standard deviation of 21% can be explained by simulation runs where at least two complex agents die early. In this case, an agent seeking help to consume a large energy source is very likely to wait a long period until its request is answered.

Overall, the test cases occurred in expected rates. Only the strong deviation in cooperation for food was unexpected. The social activity ask for dance has no direct influence on survival but the resulting stronger cohesiveness of the group seems to have positive influence on group survival [Roe07, p. 123].

All models are wrong, but some are useful.

George E. P. Box

3 Model

Based on the discussion of related work in the previous chapter, a technically feasible model is developed according to the concept sketched in the introduction. This is done by first discussing a conceptual architecture derived from psychoanalysis (Section 3.1). Applying a top-down modeling approach, the elements of the conceptual architecture is divided into several modules, leading to a more detailed description in Section 3.2. In the second iteration of the modeling process, new innovations are discussed in Section 3.3 before they are used in the next iteration. Finally, in Section 3.4 the final control architecture is discussed. It is generated by a second iteration of the top-down modeling process. This architecture consists of over 40 modules and 50 interfaces. The minimum subset of the model which still provides a functioning control architecture is shown in the last section. Its advantage is that it provides basic functionalities and keeps the system operational.

3.1 General Concept

Before a first version of the technically feasible psychoanalytically inspired model can be created, the foundational concepts from psychoanalysis have to be introduced. Step by step, these concepts are analyzed and transferred into technical terms. Afterwards, the first model plus its memory is sketched. Next, the view of psychoanalysis on embodiment is discussed. The design principles how to move on from the first model draft are introduced at the end of this section.

3.1.1 Psychoanalytical Theories Used

Usually the term psychoanalysis is associated with a therapy for mental illness. This is only one side to it. Psychoanalysis is a term which has three well-defined meanings:

> *Psycho-analysis is the name (1) of a procedure for the investigation of mental processes which are almost inaccessible in any other way, (2) of a method (based upon that investigation) for the treatment of neurotic disorders and (3)*

of a collection of psychological information obtained along those lines, which is gradually being accumulated into a new scientific discipline. [Fre23, p. 235]

The meaning important for this thesis is the third one: the scientific discipline. Neither the generation of knowledge for this discipline nor treatment are considered. A more precise definition of this scientific discipline which avoids ambiguity is called meta-psychology. It describes the theories introduced by Freud as a whole. Thus, when using *meta-psychology* the vast scientific field with partly contradicting models (see Section 1.2.3) is reduced to a single, more consistent subset of psychoanalysis. Definitions belonging to the first and the second meaning are left out.

I propose that when we have succeeded in describing a psychical process in its dynamic, topographical and economic aspects, we should speak of it as meta-psychological presentation. [Fre15b, p. 181]

Three concepts are introduced to describe psychic processes: dynamics, topography, and economy. Dynamic refers to the interaction of psychic entities like Id, Ego, or Superego. A topographic map of the entities and how they are interconnected is the second concept of metapsychology. The principle of economy introduces the concept of "energy[1]." Psychic energy regulates behavior — more psychic energy attached to a thought increases its relevance. Executed actions can reduce the amount of psychic energy by binding or discharge — rendering the thought less relevant (although the action thinking itself can result in a reduction). This results in a tendency of a psychic process to return to its idle position.

This thesis' topic is to translate parts of the description of the psychic apparatus into technically feasible terms. The psychic apparatus is the whole of psychic entities, functions, and activities. The used model describing the psychic apparatus in this thesis is Freud's second topographical model. As stated above, it consists of the three entities Id, Ego, and Superego which are depicted in Figure 3.1. From the interaction of these three entities emerge behavior, subjective experience as well as inner psychic conflicts. The conflict results from contradicting demands of different inner psychic entities. Demands in general can arise from three sources: Id, Superego, and the reality.

Id: This is the psychic entity which represents drives and affects. It works according to the pleasure principle. Thus, the psyche tries to satisfy all demands instantaneously. Mental contents are organized according to primary process principles and are thus unconscious. As a result, actions initialized by the Id are not necessarily accessible by deliberation.

---

[1] The term energy has a different meaning in psychoanalysis than in engineering. It refers to the relevance of representations [DFZB09, p. 421]. In Artificial Recognition System (ARS), a prefix — psychic — is used whenever the psychoanalytical definition of energy is used. To completely avoid this ambiguity, quota of affect is used instead of psychic energy wherever appropriate. This attempt to avoid the term psychic energy is in accordance with up-to-date psychoanalysis. The author of [MP08, p. 14] argues that the concept of quota of affect is more fitting than the one of psychic energy.

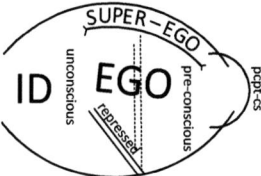

Figure 3.1: Second topographical model [Fre33, p. 77]

Ego: It synthesizes psychic processes and mediates demands forwarded by Ego, Superego, and reality. The reality principle — postponement or conversion of drive demands due to conditions in the outer world — is taking the place of the pleasure principle. Other important functions — next to mediation — are based on deliberation and focus of attention. In contrast to the Id, psychic contents are organized according to secondary process principles and are partly accessible by deliberation. The psychic contents processed in Ego are either preconscious or conscious. Some functions of the Ego are part of the primary processes (e.g. the defense mechanisms). These functions work with contents that are unconscious.

Superego: It contains restrictions, demands, and rewards. It operates as antagonist to the Id — "socially acceptable" behavior is its main objective. This is done according to internalized rules, most of them learned in childhood and adolescence. The resulting behavior is bound to these rules. Thus, the performed actions are not necessarily socially acceptable.

All mental contents are subject to cathexis. Thus, parts of the body (drives), objects as well as abstract contents like "sunset" are assigned a quantitative appraisal due to drive dynamics. Cathexis refers to this quantitative value as well as the process of appraisal. The affect is the consciously perceivable sensation of a drive tension reduction. Next to this perception, an affect has the additional function of representing the drive. The inner perception as represented by the affect can be repressed. Quota of affects describes the appraisal value which cathects primary and secondary organized mental contents. It originates from the drives and drive tensions. The afore described affects arise from discharging a quota of affect.

Drives are psychic representations of bodily needs:

> *Unter einem Trieb können wir zunächst nichts anderes verstehen als die psychische Repräsentanz einer kontinuierlich fließenden, innersomatischen Reizquelle, zum Unterschiede vom Reiz, der durch vereinzelte und von außen kommende Erregungen hergestellt wird. [Fre05a, p. 76]*

> *By a "drive [translation modified]" we can understand in the first place nothing but the psychic representative of a continually flowing internal somatic source of excitement, in contradistinction to the "stimulus" which is produced by isolated excitements coming from without. [Fre05b, p. 47]*

A drive aims at satisfaction of a bodily demand. This is done by the aim of the drive — a specific activity which ultimately results in dissolution of drive tension. Drive tension is caused by imbalances of the bodily homeostasis and is represented as psychic content by the quota of affect. The origin of the drive tension is the source of the drive — an organ or a somatic process. A drive as a whole is represented by its source of drive, object of drive, and its quota of affect. The object of the drive is the resource with which the drive tension — its quota of affect — can be reduced. What kind of object it is, is variable and situation dependent. It can be a person, a part-object, a fantasized object, or a real one. In ARS, the technical term drive content has been coined — it is the combination of drive object and drive source.

Based on the pleasure principle — maximal pleasure gain in combination with avoidance of unpleasure — the drive wish aims at fast satisfaction of the drive tension in respect of the drive content. This concept operates with what the psyche has already experienced and tries to re-experience situations where similar drive content has been successfully satisfied. This is primarily done by searching for fitting drive objects.

Self-preservation drives are representing demands which are linked to bodily functions. They are necessary to preserve the life of the individual. Sexual drive and self-preservation are tightly bound in the first years. Later, the sexual drive becomes autonomous. It is divided into partial drives — oral, anal, phallic, and genital. The sexual drive is an internal demand which searches for pleasure. The objects for satisfying sexual drives and therefore generating pleasure are highly variable. The drive tension of the sexual drive is called libido.

The sexual drive is represented in child development in different sources, the erogenous zones, which produce "partial drives". Psychoanalysis describes four phases of libido organization via erogenous zones: The first phase — oral phase — starts immediately after birth. It is connected with eating, sucking, and incorporation. People who remain fixed to this libido organization develop a so called "oral character." They tend to lust for meals and are interested in other persons. They are more dependent on other persons than this would usually be. Next is the anal phase — excretion and repression of excrements. An anal-fixed character is a person who tends towards greed, pedantry, and exaggerated sense of order. The third phase is called phallic, genitals come into focus. It results in behaviors like envy, rivalry, striving for power, and possession. The final phase is located between puberty and adulthood and is called genital phase. People with a genital character are said to be friendly, loving, and sociable.

Important Ego functions are the defense mechanisms. Their task is to decide if drive wishes can become Ego-contents and thus organized according to secondary process principles. If not, defense mechanisms can change them such that they have a higher chance to pass this barrier. The quota of affect can be split off from the actual drive contents. Using different mechanisms like repression the contents and affects are modified. Repression moves tabooed drives — e.g. drives associated with forbidden objects — back to functions of the Id which try to change them in such a way that these psychic contents can pass the defense mechanisms.

Primary and secondary processes define how Id-contents and Ego-contents are organized. Contents of the Id are always organized according to primary process principles. All of its mental contents are unconscious and thus are represented by thing presentations. From an economical/dynamic point of view, psychic energy is free floating — the assigned assessments can be moved from one mental content to another. This is different for data organized according to secondary process principles. All contents organized according to secondary processes are preconscious or conscious. Word presentations are used to represent them. Presentations are permanently linked with their quota of affects as opposed to the primary process where quota of affects can be detached from their thing presentations. Thus, mechanisms like drive deferral and thinking as acting-as-if take place instead. The basic idea of how word and thing presentations are connected is sketched in Figure 3.2.

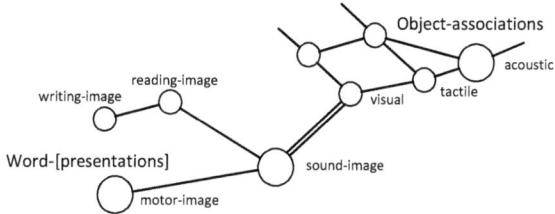

Figure 3.2: Psychological diagram of a word presentation [Fre15b, p. 214]
Originally, Freud called thing presentations object-associations.

Word presentations have to be aligned to the outside world constantly. Objects with the label "Apple" should be more or less the same for two people speaking the same language. Thing presentations are individual and different for each person.

In meta-psychology, four different basic types for data representation can be identified: thing presentation, word presentation, quota of affect, and association. Thing presentations can only be processed by primary processes. They refer to sensorial characteristics of an object. Only simple associations between thing presentations are possible. Temporal order like A has been observed before B cannot be represented. This can only be done with word presentations. They can represent an object using a set of symbols. In Figure 3.2 the lines between the circles represent associations. Thing presentations can be associated with other thing presentations. The same accounts for word presentations. Word presentations can be associations with several thing presentations. Similarly, a thing presentation can be associated to several word presentations. The process of generating permanent associations between word- and thing presentations is called symbolization[2].

3.1.2 Freud's 2nd Topographical Model

Psychoanalytic descriptions of the mental apparatus (see Section 3.1.1) have little in common with the minimum control loop of a control architecture as described in Section 2.1.1.

---
[2]Please note that symbolization in psychoanalysis has a different meaning than in engineering. In psychoanalysis symbolization refers to permanent associations between word- and thing presentations; in engineering it refers to the generation of symbols from raw data.

Model

The narrative descriptions given in meta-psychology offer a different view on the matter of subject than the model driven descriptions given by engineers. Thus, a step by step transformation is necessary.

To put the to be designed model into a larger context, Figure 3.3 shows how the decision unit is interconnected with the world and its body. Through the sensor interface information from the body and from the environment is passed through to the decision unit. The selected action commands are put to the actuator interface which forwards them to the body.

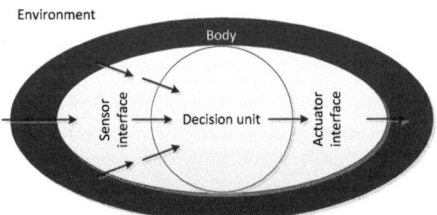

Figure 3.3: Information flow through the decision unit [Zei10, p. 62]

A first step is to transform Freud's second topographical model sketched in Figure 3.1 into a control loop. The three main elements of the model are Id, Superego, and Ego. To recapture the concept of this model sketched in the previous section, the core ideas of these three agencies are:

The Id is the demanding, driving part of the apparatus. It represents bodily needs by drives. The demands are generated regardless of time, space, availability, etc. Repressed contents are stored until they can reappear to the Ego. Drives as well as contents are attached with psychic energy. The higher the value of this psychic energy, the more demanding it is to process the content it is attached to.

The opponent of the Id is the Superego. While the Id demands without measure, the Superego provides restricting rules. They include restrictions, demands, and rewards. The Superego guides the agent how to act within a society.

To mediate between the two, possibly contradicting, agencies, a third — the Ego — is necessary. It perceives data from the world. Based on this information, demands generated by the Id which can be satisfied are selected. This list is reduced by removing Id demands which violate Superego demands. The removed entries may be repressed and pushed back to the Id. The remaining demands may be satisfied with what is available in the outside world.

Based on the definition of the Id, a fourth entity — the body — is introduced. It contains a homeostatic system, sensors, and actuators.

Figure 3.4(a) shows a control loop with the four agencies sketched above. External data is perceived via Interface 1 and processed by the Ego. Internal data — information about

Model

the internal state of the body — is retrieved and processed by the Id through Interface 2. Action commands generated by the Ego are transferred to the body (Interface 3). The current situation is passed from the Ego to the Superego (Interface 7). Fitting demands or rules are returned via Interface 6. Contents which are repressed are passed to the Id for storage (Interface 5). Two types of information are transported through Interface 4. First, bodily needs translated into psychic contents by the Id and second, repressed contents which are candidates to be processed again by the Ego.

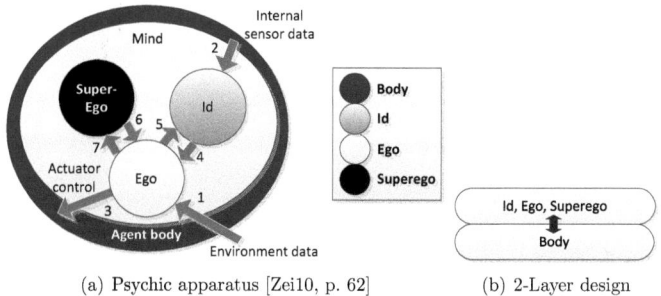

(a) Psychic apparatus [Zei10, p. 62]   (b) 2-Layer design

Figure 3.4: Technical view on Freud's second topographical model

At this stage of model development, only two layers can be identified: Mind — consisting of the psychic instances Id, Ego, and Superego — and body (see Figure 3.4(b)). Additional layers are added during the model-development progresses.

In comparison to the basic control loop depicted in Figure 2.2, the memories are missing. The three agencies of the psychic apparatus have all access to a common memory which is comparable to the episodic memory. A more precise view on this topic is given in the next section. The Ego — as the entity which controls the actuators — has access to procedural memory. Perception is divided between Ego and Id. The Ego perceives the external perception; the Id perceives the internal perception. Attention and action selection are parts of the Ego. The Superego has no direct equivalent in the foundational architecture; it can be attributed to the attention module.

Due to the design decision to create a functional model, memory access has to be treated differently. The modules themselves cannot have data storages. Thus, memory is realized using an information representation module which is described in the next section.

3.1.3 Memory

The term memory as used in context of this work refers to all information stored in the psyche. The typical memory related functions like storage and retrieval are done by the information representation module described below.

Works from Tulving [Tul72] and Baddeley [Bad97] suggest that memory is organized in several distinct entities. For example, episodic memory should be separated from semantic

Model

memory. Each memory operates as a "storehouse" (= a repository that stores information and events according to their type); an approach which fits engineers who are used to work with databases. This approach has been implemented in various Artificial Intelligence (AI) projects (see [HDN03] and [Tec05]). Also an implementation of episodic memory was used in an early version of the Bubble Family Game (BFG) [DGLV08].

This approach has been dropped in favor of an approach which is more suitable for embodied agents. See [PB07, pp. 300-302] for a detailed discussion on why not to use "storehouse" memories in general and [ZLM09, p. 25] why it is not appropriate for the architecture developed in ARS. The most important reason is that the memory is a result of the interaction of the embodied agent with the real world. This can only be partly modeled with the "storehouse" approach.

An embodied approach to memory developed by Bovet and Pfeifer [BP05] focuses on the connections of neurons based on incoming sensor signals. The emerging result is called memory. Thus, memory cannot be compiled from single functions. Extending this concept by internal system demands, an information representation for the ARS architecture is developed by Zeilinger in [ZLM09].

The basic concept of the information representation approach is shown in Figure 3.5(a). Modules from the reasoning unit are accessing information from the database by utilizing an information representation module. It is responsible for the technical realization of the functions searching, maintenance, storage, and retrieval. This concept ensures the distinction between the control flow in the functional model and the information flow [ZPK10, p. 710].

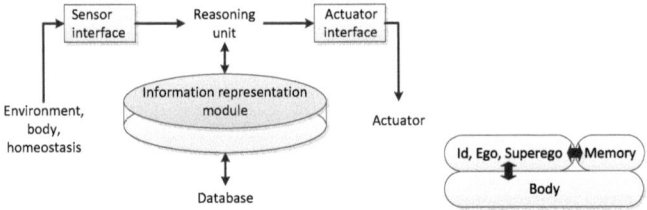

(a) Information representation module [ZPK10, p. 710] (b) 2-Layer plus memory module design

Figure 3.5: Information representation module

With the introduction of the information representation module an update of the two-layer design is necessary. The top layer is split horizontally into an Id, Ego, and Superego part and a memory part (see Figure 3.5(b)). Communication between the first and the second layer is done only between body and Id, Ego, and Superego. Memory can only be accessed by Id, Ego, and Superego. The necessity for this split will be explained in Section 3.2.

Before the perceived information can be integrated into the already stored knowledge, it has to be converted from raw sensor data into symbols in the sensor interface. This is done using a novel approach — neurosymbolization (see Section 2.6.1 and the work by Velik [Vel08]). The resulting symbols are equivalent to thing presentations as defined by psychoanalysis. This equivalence is not bi-directional. Thing presentations can also be motion sequences learned in early childhood like eating [ZLM09, p. 26]. Also situations can be modeled using thing presentations. A map consisting of several thing presentations which are temporally associated if grouped to thing presentation meshes. This accounts only for locally associated thing presentations — for example a green leaf on a tree. Temporally but not locally associated thing presentations form a template image [Zei10, p. 58]. A thing presentation can only be observed/worked with as a whole; decomposition into subparts — e.g. its corresponding sensor modalities — is not possible. The only part where thing presentations are decomposed is in the actuator interface but this is not part of the psychic apparatus anymore. Quota of affects — representing the drive demand's intensity generated in Id — are attached to thing presentations.

Thing presentations and quota of affects belong to the primary information layer (compare to primary processes in Section 3.1.1). The equivalent to the secondary processes — data structures of the secondary information layer — are the third type of information representation: Word presentations. A word presentation is associated with thing presentations. They define the meaning of this symbol by introducing logical and temporal relations. Word presentations are used for rational thoughts.

The temporal associations modeled with thing presentation meshes are simultaneously received sensor modalities. Temporal relations like before, after, or concurrently happening can only be defined between word presentations. Further, word presentations render it possible to make estimations on the duration of actions. Another difference between them is that word presentations can be aligned to reality — apples (the word) refers to apples (the objects) — whereas thing presentations cannot.

Figure 3.6 sketches how the above introduced concepts are interacting. In the primary information layer, thing presentation meshes are associated. Each mesh consists of thing presentations representing information from different sensory modalities. Further, one or more affects with their corresponding thing presentation can be attached to a mesh. The word presentations — located on the secondary information layer — are associated to thing presentations but they can contain richer information. Their associations include temporal relations and action relations. Thus, next to temporal order of the events, actions which have been applied to the object (which is represented by the word presentation) can be attached. Memories stored in this manner are called memory traces in psychoanalysis [ZDML08, p. 262].

Associations — temporal and attribute associations — between primary data structures are assigned a weight (see [Zei10, p. 52; pp. 56–57]) which defines the importance of the link. If a thing presentation is retrieved from memory — for example due to a (partly) match with incoming sensory information — its activation level increases. Further all associations are strengthened and — subsequently — all the activation levels of all connected thing presentations and affects are increased too[3]. However, the activation levels of the indirect activated

---

[3]The implementation ARS implementation number 10 (ARSi10) as described in [Zei10, pp. 102–109] does not contain this feature. It will be implemented in one of the future versions.

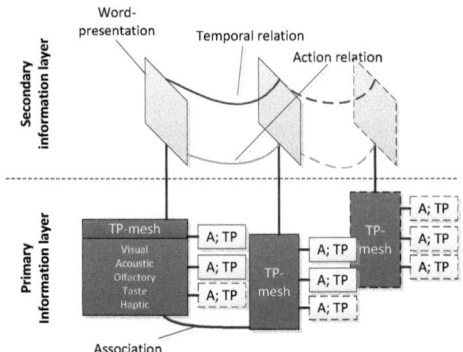

Figure 3.6: Information representation structure [ZPK10, p. 711]
A ... Quota of affect, TP ... Thing presentation

entities are exposed a lower rise than the ones which have been directly retrieved. The activation level of word presentations depends on its associated thing presentations.

With each retrieval, the activation level of each entry is lowered. Thus, activation levels of word presentations, thing presentations, affects, and associations which have not been accessed (directly or indirectly) for a long time converge to zero. Associations with activation levels close to zero can be removed. The other three entities will stay in the system even with very low activation levels.

The model from Section 3.1.2 extended by the memory approach described in this section form a good foundation for the task at hand (see Statement 1.1). Next, embodiment is discussed from a psychoanalytic point of view.

3.1.4 Embodiment in Psychoanalysis

In general, psychoanalysis views the connection between psyche and body as interplay between two entities. The psyche refers to the body and the body vice versa refers to the psyche. Thus, what is happening in the body has direct influence to the mental state, and mental states directly influence the body. It is not viewed as a cooperative task sharing as demanded by Pfeifer et al. in [PB07, pp. 95–96] (cp. Section 2.3).

The mental representation of bodily needs — the drive — refers to inner somatic sources of stimulations. It formulates tasks for the psyche: The reduction of tension which is created by these needs. Libido (cp. Section 3.3.3) is a motivational system with the body as its driving force. Various somatic sources and erogenous zones can operate as stimulation area for this system. In fact the whole body can be used as an erogenous zone. The body is immediately and fundamentally responsible for psychic ambition.

While the Id is responsible for broadcasting bodily needs to the psyche, the Ego is the reflection of the body. *"The ego is first and foremost a bodily ego; it is not merely a surface entity, but is itself the projection of a surface [Fre23, p. 25]."* Thus, the Ego is a mental projection of the body and is formed by the shape of the body. For example, if a human has no arms, he has a different mental image of his body too. This man without arms is not always aware that he is working without arms. His current constitution appears normal to him. The concept that the body is not a solid, atomic unit but that there are parts which can be detached (permanently) is experienced in childhood first (cp. [Fre17, p. 132]).

An important psychoanalytic concept regarding the interplay of body and psyche is conversion. The body is used as means of expression for psychic contents and is thus the communication medium of the psyche. It is well-known that the psyche has influence on the body (for affects and their manifestation as psychical and physical phenomena see [Sol96, p. 485] and for the conversion of excitation into something somatic cp. [Fre94, p. 48]). An example for this is the expression of "moods". Sometimes affects are so clearly visible that it appears that their essence is built solely of bodily expressions. Conversion reveals psychosomatic symptoms, next to everyday expressions like "moods." In case of an obsessional neurosis, there is almost no usage of conversion. Thus, the communication medium of the psyche is not used. The opposite — over usage of this medium — is called hysteria.

The central point in embodiment in psychoanalysis is that the body is the source of every action. The above described points are comparable to embodiment described in Section 2.3 with more focus on internal processes. It is important to point out that the Ego is a map of its body. Thus, a psychoanalytically inspired control system cannot be transferred from one agent to another if their bodies are different. Before continuing with generating a finer grained version of the model, design principles for it are explained in the next section.

3.1.5 Four Model Design-Principles

The overall approach used in the ARS project to modeling is sketched in Section 1.2.4. It describes the interdisciplinary modeling process — with focus on interdisciplinarity. What is not dealt with in detail is which design-principles are to be applied when following the top-down design approach.

These four principles guide the development process. They are listed to provide a better idea of how each iteration of the top-down design is done.

Top-Down Design: The first principle is the top-down design itself. The idea is to start with a crude concept of the to be designed system. In the first iteration, this crude concept is split into several — finer detailed — sub-concepts. The sum of the sub-concepts is identical with the crude concept with the only difference that the description is much more detailed. This principle is repeated with each consecutive iteration. The process is to be terminated if a sufficiently detailed level of description is reached. For example, if the sub-concepts can be implemented easily.
For the project at hand, the crude functional description of the human psyche given at the beginning of this chapter is split into smaller functions with each iteration.

Add Layer When Appropriate: Layers are introduced each time a distinct functionality can be applied to it. A new layer is dependent on the functionality provided by the existing layers and can provide functionality to future layers. A layer is built of a set of sub-functions. Each layer should be of comparable size regarding its functionality. Different functionalities should not be grouped to one layer. It is important to define the layers in a way that only few interfaces are needed between them.

Figure 3.5(b) and Figure 3.7(b) show this principle. In the first stage of the top-down modeling process, all psychic functions can be put into a single layer. There are only few functions available at this point. After the next iteration, two blocks of functions can be distinguished which need different types of data to work with. Thus, a new layer is introduced.

Top to Bottom: Another principle connected with Layers is top to bottom. Thus, when layer C is atop of layer B which resides atop of layer A, B is dependent on functionality provided by A and independent of layer C. Layer C accesses the interfaces provided by layer B. Layer A cannot be directly accessed by layer C.

This is the weakest principle. The project follows descriptions provided by metapsychology. Thus, it is not always possible to follow the top to bottom principle. As can be seen in the next section, the topmost layer has direct access to motility control and thereafter to the lowest layer—the layer in between is bypassed.

Back to Front: The forth principle deals with the definition of interfaces between the functions. They have to be created starting at the end and working into the opposite direction of the flow of control.

The next section describes the result of the first iteration of the top-down design and the above described principles.

3.2 Beyond a Shallow Model

The architecture sketched in Section 3.1.2 suffers the same problem as some of the related projects introduced in Section 2.4. It is built using shallow definitions for Ego, Superego, and Id. For example, the definitions used by Nitta et al. in [NTMI99] do not exceed the ones given in Section 3.1.2. Although, for the creation of this model it is necessary to clarify the interaction between the three agencies, the provided level of details is not sufficient to build a psychoanalytically inspired decision unit. To do this, a model reaching beyond the shallow definitions is needed.

First, a differentiation between primary and secondary processing modules is necessary. This differentiation results in different sets of data. Modules belonging to the first group can use thing presentations and quotas of affects only. This results in unorganized and partly contradicting data. Modules of the second type cannot operate with contradictions. The thing presentations are associated with word presentations. The advantage is that reasoning can be done using word presentations.

Due to the fact that the Ego cannot be assigned to one of these processing types exclusively, it has to be split up in submodules. The same is necessary for the Id. It has to fulfill several tasks which are more visible in the architecture if this is split up too. The two different outputs of the body (Interface 1 for external sensors and Interface 2 for internal sensors in Figure 3.4(a)) along with the processing of the output (Interface 3 for actuator control in Figure 3.4(a)) are hinting towards a split of the body into submodules.

Figure 3.7(a) shows an architecture with a finer granularity than the one developed in Section 3.1. The body is split into four, the Id into three, and the Ego into six submodules. The Superego is still one module; its task defined in the previous architecture does not make it necessary to split it at this granularity level.

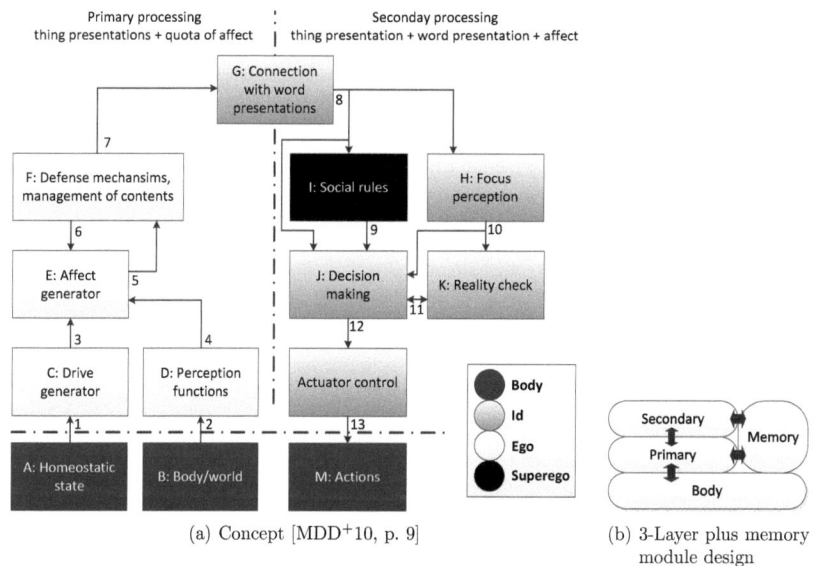

(a) Concept [MDD⁺10, p. 9]

(b) 3-Layer plus memory module design

Figure 3.7: Intermediate model

The body is split into three modules — two providing sensor information, one processing actuator commands. Module `Homeostatic state` (A) contains homeostatic body systems. If an organic state is out of balance — for example, the blood sugar-level — the difference is transmitted to the drive generator (Module `Drive generator` (C)) via Interface 1. There the values are converted into drive structures. The three-tuple source, aim, and object form such a structure. Additionally, death- and live-drive labels are attached.

Body and world information are provided by Module `Body/World` (B). Sensors like vision, tactile, or acoustics are used to gather data from the environment. Body information consists of data provided by sensors not involved in homeostasis. For example, the position of the elbow or a pain in the chest would qualify. Both types of information are passed on to Module `Perception functions` (D) through Interface 2. This module compares the perceived data with already known patterns. Missing information is complemented from memory.

The affect generator (Module `Affect generator (E)`) receives drive structures (Interface 3) and thing presentations (Interface 4). They are merged to a mental image which represents the current situation as perceived by the system. Affects are attached to the thing presentations. The result is put to the outgoing Interface 5 and is forwarded to the next module called defense mechanisms, management of contents (Module `Defense mechanisms, Management of contents (F)`). Repressed contents — passed from Module F via Interface 6 — may be merged with incoming contents to new sets of information.

Module F operates as a filter. Incoming data is matched against defense mechanisms using Superego rules. The three possible outcomes are: the information is passed to the outgoing Interface 7 without any changes, the contents have to be transposed but still are put to Interface 7, or they are repressed and sent back to the previous modules.

Until the contents have reached Module `Connection with word presentation (G)` they are manipulated by the primary processes only. Meaning that only the thing presentations and the quota of the affect are attended to; connected word presentations would have been ignored. This changes in Module G — the incoming mental contents are linked with word presentations. Now, they can be used for common logic decision making and they can map temporal orders of events. The information fed into Module D via Interface 2 are situations — a snapshot of the here and now. The outgoing Interface 8 distributes the resulting data structures to three modules (H, I, and J).

The Module `Social rules (I)` looks up information from the Superego rules. The current situation is compared to the existing rules and fitting rules are selected. This set is forwarded to decision making via Interface 9. The second module which receives data from G is `Focus perception (H)`. It generates a prioritized list of the secondary information. The order is determined by homeostatic demands and environmental information. The outgoing Interface 10 is connected to reality check and decision making.

Decision making (Module `Decision making (J)`) takes information from four modules — the whole list of current word presentations from G, the prioritized list from H, fitting social rules from I, and an assessment of the satisfiability of goals from `Reality check (K)`. The result is an action plan in form of word presentations. It is passed to actuator control via Interface 12.

The Module K has the task to check the satisfiability of goals. For this, two different sets of information are necessary. First, a prioritized list of demands is necessary. If at the moment a minor goal could be satisfied easily but this satisfaction would only be possibly by ignoring a major need — like energy is very low — it should be rejected (received via Interface 11). Second, the list of current goals is needed. The list is received from decision making and enriched by the assessment sent back through the same Interface 11.

Module `Actuator control (L)` disassembles the action plan into action commands processable by the last Module `Actions (M)`. The disassembled plan is transferred via Interface 13. Module M is situated within the body and can be compared to a low level motor control.

The modules which represent the three agencies Id, Ego, and Superego can be split into two groups: Modules which operate according to primary process principles and modules operating according to secondary process principles. To reflect this in the layer design, the Id, Ego, and Superego layer is split into two. Following the flow of information—from the body, through primary processes, up to secondary processes—the secondary process layer is atop of the primary process layer (see Figure 3.7(b)). The information representation module is accessed by both layers. It operates as a kind of cross-layer providing information to all other layers.

3.3 Drives—the Connection to the Body

Before the next iteration step of the top-down design process can be conducted, the drive system introduced by Lang et al. in [LKZD10] and Lang in [Lan10] has to be revised. First, only two drives have been defined (cp. [Lan10, p. 139]). Second, the function to split a drive into its aggressive and its libidinous components cannot be personalized (cp. [LKZD10, p. 719]). Third, and most important, only self-preservation drives are considered. The motivational system is left out. In psychoanalysis this system is called seeking system or sexual drives (see [ST02, p. 117]). Finally, the concept of primal repression is introduced which is necessary for categorization of thing presentations. The first two and the fourth one are improvements of the old model; the third one is a novel concept introduced.

3.3.1 Additional Drives

In the ARS project, psychoanalytically inspired models of drives have always been present (cp. [DLP+06, p. 114], [Roe07, p. 23], [Pal08, pp. 64–65], [Lan10, p. 59], and [LKZD10, p. 717]). The first approach described in Deutsch et al. [DLP+06, p. 4] was a simple one. Drives were seen as representation of homeostatic imbalances in the body. This is not wrong, but also not sufficient. Step by step, a more complete and finer grained model has been developed. The version this thesis builds upon is described by Lang et al. in [LKZD10, pp. 716–719] and Lang in [Lan10, pp. 59–61].

Freud describes a drive as *"[a] psychical representative of the stimuli originating from within the organism and reaching the mind, as a measure of the demand made upon the mind for work in consequence of its connection with the body [Fre15a, p. 152]."* In the same work, the four components which together form the concept of drive are formulated [Fre15a, pp. 152–153]:

Source of drive is the somatic source of the drive. Usually, an organ can be identified as the source. Its homeostatic imbalance is the force behind the drive.
Aim of drive is to remove the stimulation which causes the drive to be active. Although it might be unreachable, alternative aims can be selected—they ease the situation without ever clearing it.

MODEL

Object of drive is the thing with which or through which the imbalance is removed. It is the most variable component of a drive.

Affect is the driving force[4]. The quota of affect defines how urgent the satisfaction of the drive is.

Thus, a drive is the psychic representation of a bodily need and is defined by these four components. This is the definition of drive present in [Roe07, pp. 23–25] and [Pal08, pp. 65–66]. The main novelty added in [Lan10, LKZD10] is the differentiation between constructive and destructive drive components. A bodily need is always represented by a pair of opposites — a constructive and a destructive drive (cp. [Fre15a, p. 127]). This concept is known as life drive (or libidinous part) and death drive (the aggressive part) in psychoanalysis. All drives are either part of the life instinct or the death instinct. An example given in [LKZD10, p. 717] is in case of hunger the pair of opposite drives *nourish* and *bite*. *Nourish* is the constructive drive with a libidinous aim: Eating to satisfy the hunger. Its opposite is *bite*, a destructive drive with an aggressive aim: The destruction of the food. The first one is necessary in order to want something to eat and the second one enables the process of eating. Without the destruction of the food, it cannot be eaten. General examples for aggressive aims are: *bite, excrete, kill, regress, disintegrate, halt*, and *retreat*; for libidinous aims: *nourish, repress, sleep, breathe, relax*, and *reproduce* [LKZD10, p. 717].

Roesener has rendered a list of drives in [Roe07, pp. 24–25] based on the work of Panksepp [Pan98]. It contains four basic drive-specific systems: hunger, thirst, thermal balance, and sexual arousal. They are based on findings from neurology and not mapped to the drive concept defined above. Lang gives two examples in his work [Lan10, p. 135]: nourish and bite (hunger), repress and deposit (defecation). No complete list of drives or a description of their components could be found. Already in [Fre15a, p. . 123] Freud states that there are wide opportunities for arbitrary choices of drives. They are more to be seen as a working hypothesis which should be used as long as they proof useful. The list given in Table 3.1 is a first attempt to provide a structured overview. It represents drives for the ARS project which have been defined in interdisciplinary work. The table does not claim to be comprehensive. To generate such a list would be out of scope of this thesis and will have to be done in future by psychoanalysts.

The Table 3.1 gives a list of drive groups and their possible sources, aims, and objects. For example, a drive consists of the following triple (drive source, drive aim, and drive object): Blood sugar, nourish, and breast. These are all components existing in the drive group, thus, this drive is assigned to it. This is of interest for fusion of self-preservation drives. Now, pair-of-opposites can be built by combining drives from the same group. To form a pair of opposites one drive with a libidinous aim and one drive with an aggressive aim have to be created. The eight identified groups are labeled Eat, Consume, Defecate, Urinate, Genital sexuality, Sleep, Breathe, and Heat. Eat and Consume are connected to everything about things like food, nourishing, and drinking. Their difference is that

---

[4]In this context, the quota of affect is meant. In this model, affect and quota of affect are differentiated. Freud uses affect sometimes for both: affect and quota of affect.

Table 3.1: List of drives in ARS

Group	Source	Aim Libidinous	Aim Aggressive	Object
Eat	Blood sugar, stomach fill level	Nourish	Bite	Breast
Consume	Mouth, oral mucosa	Stimulation with object at source	Bite	Pacifier, cigarette
Defecate	Anus, rectal mucosa	Repression, retentive, to sort, to possess	Expulsion, elimination	Pile of feces; later, figuratively, money
Urinate	Urethral (bladder, ureter, urethra)	Retain warm, collect	Squirt out, to wet, flood	Urine
Genital sexuality	Genitals (gender-specific, related hormonal processes)	Male: to erect, to penetrate, to excite. Female: to absorb (to complete)	Male: amputate (projected to others). Female: to absorb (to suffocate, kill)	Opposite sex, own sex, own body (auto erotic)
Sleep	Metabolism, fatigue in general	Sleep, relax	Put to sleep	The own body
Breathe	Oxygen saturation, lung, trachea	Breathe	Annihilate	Air
Heat	Body temperature	To warm sth.	To heat (up) sth.	The own body

Eat belongs to self-preservation drives and Consume to sexual drives. It is preventing the agent from starving. The next group — Defecate — is at the opposite end of digestion. How, when, and where feces can be deposited is the topic of it. The group Urinate is connected to liquid disposals. Group Genital sexuality is containing erogenous zones and their stimulation. Regeneration and relaxation are the core components of group Sleep. The second to last group — Breathe — is responsible for keeping the oxygen saturation at its optimum. Finally, Heat deals with keeping the agent from freezing or overheating.

The current version of the implementation of the artificial life simulation (ARS implementation number 11 (ARSi11)) explained in the next chapter has no corresponding implementations of bodily processes to the drive groups Urinate, Genital sexuality, and Breathe. Thus, they are left out for the time being. In Chapter 5, the implementation of a pair of opposites from the group Sleep, one from the group Eat, and one from the group Defecate will be discussed.

3.3.2 Distribution of Drives

In psychoanalysis, drives are split into an aggressive and a libidinous component. These two are tightly coupled, showing two sides of the same thing. For example, if one is hungry and an apple should be used to ease this tension, two forces have to be present: a libidinous

MODEL

force which makes one want to devour it and an aggressive force which makes one want to bite into a piece of the apple. Without the aggressive component, it would not be possible to eat the apple. Thus, the somatic tension originating in the stomach is satisfied by the two drive contents. Both are described by the triple drive source, aim of drive, and object of drive. Their intensity is quantified by an attached quota of affect. The stronger the tension gets, the more aggressive is the resulting behavior. Once the most lustful point has been reached, the libidinous part decreases. For example, being hungry and waiting for the dinner to start is fine — a lustful reward for this behavior will be served soon. If one gets really hungry and dinner is canceled and there is no food available the next day too, the behavior will become very aggressive. A person who starves to death is not very likely to have a libidinous part at all. The resulting dissociations have influence on further decision making by rendering fitting contents more important than others.

An organ produces tension which has to be split into the two components described above. Meta-psychology defines only that such split occurs but does not describe the algorithm how the single value is divided. Lang et al. [LKZD10] propose a simplified approach — the tension is converted to an angle which points to a single point on a curve (see Figure 3.8(a)). The shape of the curve is an ellipse. The x-axis of this point is the libidinous part and the y-axis is the aggressive part. At 0°, both components are zero too. The maximum value for the libidinous part is reached at 26.6°, resulting in an aggressive quota of 50%. At 90°, the maximum value for the aggressive component is reached and the libidinous part is reduced to 0% again.

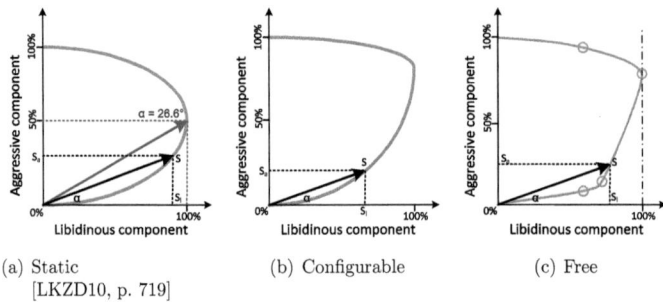

(a) Static
[LKZD10, p. 719]

(b) Configurable

(c) Free

Figure 3.8: Distribution of drives
S distribution vector; S_l libidinous component; S_a aggressive component; α angle proportional to drive tension

This approach realizes the above sketched demand that the libidinous component has to reach its climax before it returns to zero and the aggressive component has to reach its maximum after the libidinous one. Although this model does not claim to be psychoanalytical and is an oversimplification, the following three points of critique nevertheless have to be considered. First, it is not argued why the maximum libidinous value is at 26.6°. Second, the split function cannot be personalized. All agents using this model have the same proportion between aggressive and libidinous components for all their drives. Third, it is hard to determine the maximum value of tension a somatic source can produce. Thus, the normalization of this value between 0° and 90° can only be done if the maximum value is known.

The first and the second point can be approached by making the angular point configurable. As shown in Figure 3.8(b), the point where the maximum libidinous value is reached has been moved up on the y-axis, resulting in a different dissociation. A more advanced configuration possibility is to define the curve by tangential points (cp. Figure 3.8(c)). The small circles are the points which define the curve. A customizable curve which still can be used by this simplified model has to fulfill the following requirements:

- It has to start in the origin.
- At 90° the components have to be split to 100% aggressive and 0% libidinous quota.
- The angular point has to be at 100% libidinous component.
- The shape has to be concave—for each angle exists one and only one point on the curve.

The third point of critique—what is the maximum value of a somatic tension—can be approached with a different normalization function. Using a tangent-function, the angle values between 0° and 90° can be generated for all tension values ranging from zero to infinity. The problem is that 90° will never be reached—resulting in never reaching 100% aggressive component. This can be bypassed by making the scales customizable too. The current model and its implementation provide full knowledge about the maximum values for bodily tensions. Thus, this issue can be postponed until the model is used for a different application.

3.3.3 Seeking System

The drive system of the ARS-model as described by Lang et al. in [Lan10, LKZD10] discussed above is restricted to self-preservation drives. The concept of sexual drives is missing. The differences between the two are that the self-preservation drives are responsible for preservation of the agents' own existence. For example, to avoid starvation is such a drive. Its aim is to satisfy bodily needs. In contrast, sexual drives aim at pleasure gain. They operate similar to self-preservation drives with a few differences. Libido—the psychic energy—is constantly produced by an inner somatic source at an invariant rate. Within the body, no possibility exists to collect libido until an event discharges the psychic energy. In contrast to self-preservation drives which have an inner somatic counterpart to their tension, libido produced by sexual drives has to be collected within the psychic apparatus. The resulting tension is used as a basic motivational incentive for the agent to search for new sensory sensations. It is important to mention that sexuality in this context is not genital sexuality. The sexual drives are not reproduction drives.

According to Solms and Turnbull [ST02, p. 117], the sexual drives system as defined by psychoanalysis is comparable to Panksepp's seeking system described in [Pan98, pp. 144–163]. In an older version of the ARS-model, a seeking system was implemented according to

Panksepp's descriptions (see Section 2.6.2). Burgstaller et al. [BLPV07] and Burgstaller [Bur07, pp. 3–18] introduced the four components — seeking system, rage system, fear system, and panic system. Several reasons exist why the new model described in [DFZB09, pp. 53–64] did not include this implementation of the seeking system. The system described by Panksepp is a bodily one which operates on hormones. Further, it needs external perception to initiate seeking behavior and it is triggered by key stimuli which promise rewards. All these three points interfere with the psychic apparatus as described by Freud. If the seeking system uses hormones, it could be included in the overall architecture via the same functions as the self-preservation drives. This is in contradiction to the differences between the two types of drives sketched above. The next problem occurs with external perception — if its results are needed before the seeking system can operate, it would have to take place before perception can take place (which needs the results of the seeking system to be active). Finally, according to psychoanalysis, libido is constantly produced by an inner somatic source. This is in direct contradiction to reward promising key stimuli as source. They only produce libido if they are present and in different amounts. To conclude, there are similarities between the sexual drive system as defined by psychoanalysis and Panksepp's seeking system. As there are compatibility problems, only the basic idea of a motivational system is used in this thesis. To solve these problems would be out of scope of this thesis and should be done by psychologists and psychoanalysists.

Libido has an inner somatic source: "*[...] a continually flowing internal somatic source of excitement [...] [Fre05b, p. 47]*." It is not specified which organ this should be and how it communicates with the psyche. Again, to supplement this theory would be out of scope of this thesis. Instead the following two assumptions are taken: Some organ (or a set of organs) exists and it needs (physical) energy to operate. Communication with psychic processes is realized by a distinct channel.

As already mentioned, the body provides a continuous flow of libido at a very small rate. In Figure 3.9(a) is shown the constant values of libido provided by the body. The integration of tension of sexual drives has to be done in the mind. A buffer is needed which stores incoming libido until it can be discharged (Figure 3.9(b)). The value x at time t_n equals the tension produced by sexual drives at this moment. The reduction of the tension is coupled with external perception — external sensors like vision and body sensors like angular position of a joint. All perceptions are evaluated if they can be used. If yes, the buffered libido is reduced and the perceptions get a positive appraisal. In Figure 3.9(c) this happens at time t_m. At the very next step in time, buffered libido is increasing again. Thus, the tension produced by sexual drives can never be satisfied completely — the increasing of the buffer happens before a libido value of zero could have any influence.

Tension discharge can happen through among others sublimation, fantasy, or stimulation of erogenous zones. Sublimation is the concept of diverting psychic energy from its direct sexual aim to a more intellectual/cultural effort. The utility of stimulation of erogenous zones for technical systems is questionable and has to be researched in future work. Currently it is added to the model for the sake of completeness. Fantasy — some kind of behavior in rehearsal — can be used to experience sexual stimulation. Although all three have different origins, the discharge initiated by them can be modeled using the same functions. Unpleasure is proportional to buffered libido. Pleasure gain is realized by discharge of unpleasure.

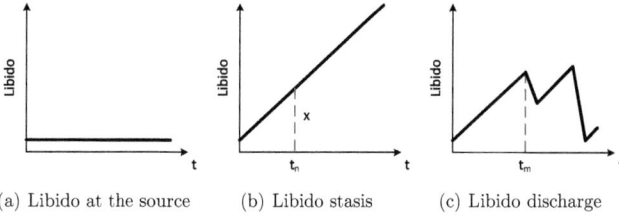

(a) Libido at the source (b) Libido stasis (c) Libido discharge

Figure 3.9: Libido and the seeking system

This is equivalent to unpleasure/pleasure for self-preservation drives. The components of sexual drives are equivalent to them as well. They are composed of aim of drive, drive object, drive source, and quota of affect. The sexual drives are split into a libidinous and an aggressive part with the approach described in the previous section.

A concept unique to sexual drives is the separation into the four partial-drives: oral, anal, genital, and phallic. As described in Section 3.1.1, partial-drives are developed in childhood. They have strong influence on the character (see [Fre08, p. 170]). Each partial-drive represents a group of distinct behaviors. Figure 3.10 shows how the libido tension is split. The sum of the four resulting tensions does not have to sum up to the original amount. Similar to splitting a drive into aggressive and libidinous parts, no further description of the separation formula is provided by meta-psychology. As a first solution, a straight forward multiplier based approach is used. For each partial-drive a factor is defined and applied independently of the three others. Usually, all partial-drives but the genital one have a low tension. Very high values in the other three may indicate fixations.

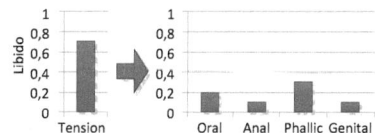

Figure 3.10: Separation into partial sexual drives

The seeking system provides a basic motivational source and a characterization by biasing the decision system towards certain behaviors (see Section 3.1.1). A further advantage gained is that if the current activity is liked, it is very likely to succeed better. This is due to the fact that more libido/psychic energy is available and therefor, more focus is set to it and more resources are made available.

3.3.4 Primal Repression

In very early childhood, the repression mechanisms are not present (cp. [Fre26, p. 93]). Nevertheless, infants have to deal with conflicts between their natural needs and limits posed by reality. Further, they learn to distinguish between controllable and uncontrollable aspects of reality. During this time primal repression is build. Experiences which are part of primal repression stay repressed and can never become conscious. Examples for contents of it are sexual desires towards a parent or the loss of mother's breast.

In the ARS model, the primal repressed thing presentations are organized to a scheme originating in partial-drives. They are categorized according to the concepts of oral, anal, phallic, and genital.

In the ARS model, when accessing memory to find matching thing presentations, several different parameters are used (cp. [ZPK10, pp. 84–86]). One of them is a categorization of the contents according to partial-drives and primal repression contents. The thing presentations which are generated either by external perception or by drives have to have such a categorization before they can be further processed. This is done by comparison of the thing presentations with primal repressed thing presentations. Of course, the search patterns used do not include the categorization. The results are four labels attached to the processed thing presentation which denote how much fitting content was found for this category.

This categorization functionality is not described in psychoanalytic literature. It is a technical feature introduced to enable further data processing inspired by psychoanalysis. The final model described in the next section will clarify the reason why this feature is necessary.

3.4 Final Functional Model

The model described in Section 3.2 is more detailed than the first one in this chapter. Nevertheless, more questions are raised than answered. New questions are for example regarding the affect generator. Are affects generated before or after merging perception and drive information? Another question is within perception functions: How are repressed contents attached? Interface 11 seems to open the possibility to send data between the two modules endlessly within one control loop. Can the recursion loop—interfaces 5 and 6—be resolved?

None of these questions and issues were present in the first approach. Thus, the creation of the intermediate model is useful—but only up to the extent of getting a deeper insight in the problems of the architecture. To answer these questions and issues, a third iteration of the top-down modeling process is necessary.

A first view on the final functional model is given in the first section. Next, Section 3.4.2 gives an overview on the innovations introduced to the previous version of the final model. A detailed explanation of the function modules and the interfaces between them is given in Section 3.4.3.

MODEL

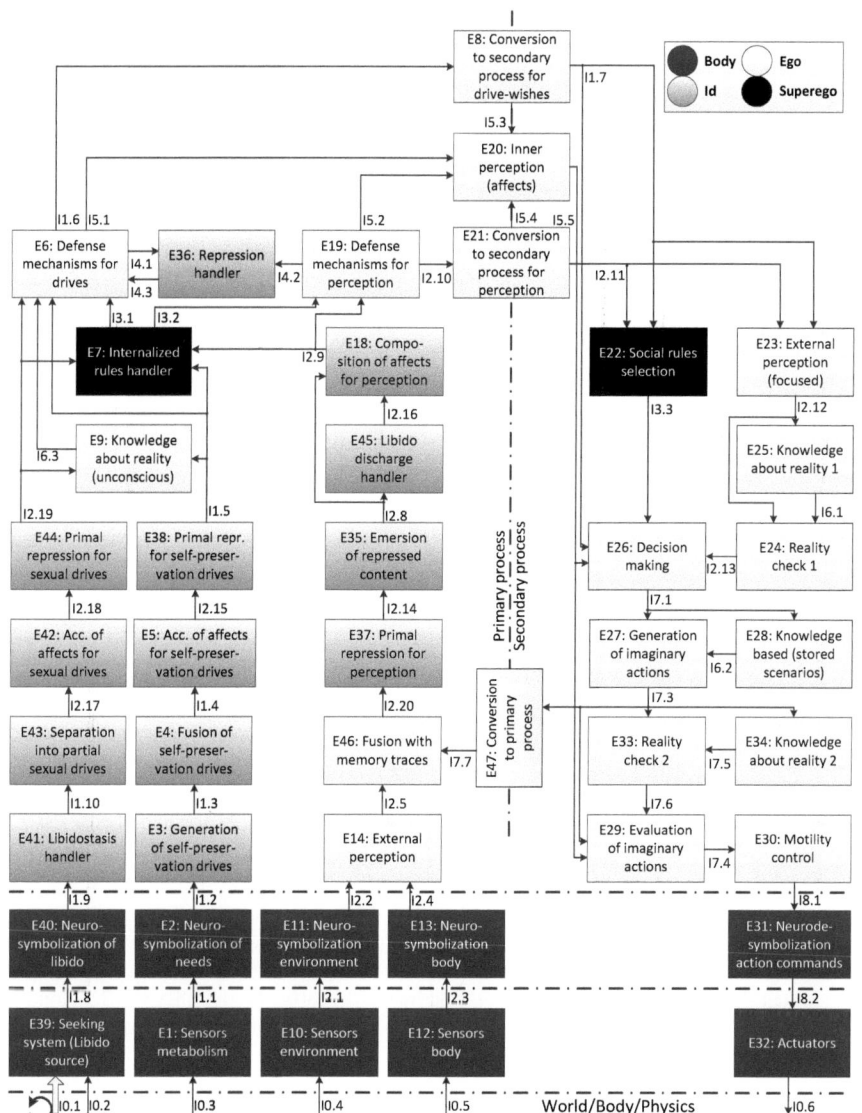

Figure 3.11: Final functional model

3.4.1 Complete Model

The final functional model depicted in Figure 3.11 is built of 44 function modules and 49 interfaces between them. It is roughly three to four times richer than the intermediate model (Figure 3.7(a)). Nevertheless, a mapping between the modules of the two can be made (see Section 3.4.3). The mapping to the main psychic entities — Id, Ego, and Superego — cannot be used one to one. On this finer granularity, defense mechanisms need a module which has to be assigned to the group of Superego functions. For most of the functions the mapping stays the same.

Each module is assigned to one or more categories which define general conditions within which it has to operate. The main category is the assignment to either the body or one of the three psychic entities. Next, a definition is given of the types of psychic contents the module can operate with. One or more of the following types can be assigned: thing presentation, word presentation, or affect. General memory access or access to special parts of it are is last category for each module. For example, Module E21 is assigned to Ego functions; it operates with all kind of psychic contents, and has general access to the memory infrastructure.

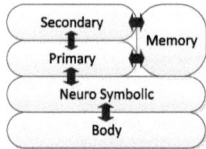

Figure 3.12: 4-Layers plus memory module design

In this new version of the model, the functional modules of the body are split into two distinct layers. The body layer contains modules like sensors and actuators. The conversion of the raw data these modules work with into a representation which can be processed by psychic functions is done in the other layer. It is the conversion of raw data into neuro-symbols and back again. Figure 3.12 shows the updated layer model with the new introduced neuro-symbolic layer.

The numbering of the modules and interfaces follows a strict concept. Labels for modules start with 'E' and are followed by a number which is increased with every new module. Numbers from removed modules are not reused. For example, Module E15 has been replaced by other modules (further below). Interfaces are labeled quite similar but not identical. They start with an 'I' and are followed by a category identifier which is followed by a dot. Each category uses its own running number. Labels from removed interfaces are not reused too (cp. missing Interface I7.2).

3.4.2 Innovations

The work presented in this thesis is embedded in project ARS. As sketched in Section 2.6, preliminary work has been created for the last ten years and new publications add innovations. This model is no exception. The first version of the functional model was created in spring 2008 and consisted of roughly 30 modules. Innovations introduced by this thesis are highlighted in Figure 3.13[5].

It is a pictogram of the final functional model. Modules filled with black are new (compare with [ZPK10, p. 79]); the gray ones are extended. Interfaces which companion new modules are not highlighted. The one interface highlighted is a feedback loop between modules E27 and E46 using E47 to convert the data back to thing presentations.

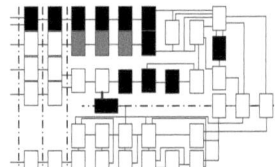

Fig. 3.13: Innovations

Most of the innovations are based on the argumentation given in Section 3.3. Modules E39, E40, E41, E42, E43, and E45 form the newly introduced seeking system/sexual drives. Interface I7.7 and the conversion module E47 enable the system to fantasize. E37, E38, and E44 are inserted to realize the primal repression as explained in Section 3.3.4.

Lang proposes splitting the module 'Management of Repressed Contents' into two independent functions in the implementation step (see [Lan10, pp. 103–105]). Following the modeling cycle described in Section 1.2.4, this result of the technical implementation was presented to the psychoanalytical research advisors. After evaluation of the proposed change, the model was adapted. The functionality of the replaced module is now represented by the modules E35 and E36.

The modules used for self-preservation drives — E3, E4, and E5 — stay unchanged in their basic functionality. The approach to split a drive into its aggressive and its libidinous components as well as the number of drives implemented have been reworked respectively extended.

The above listed modules are changes and additions to the model as proposed by this thesis. An in-depth explanation of all modules and their interfaces is given in the next section.

3.4.3 Function Modules

The modules of the intermediate model (cp. Section 3.2) are divided into submodules step by step. The result is a detailed functional model which can be implemented. In this section, the capital letters inside the brackets at the end of a header (e.g. **(C)**) refers to the corresponding module in the intermediate model.

Body Modules (A, B, and M)

In the intermediate model the body is represented by three modules: `Homeostatic state` (A), `Body/World` (B), and `Actions` (M) (see Figure 3.14). As they are all interface modules between psyche and body, they are treated in this part together.

---

[5]In this chapter, figures similar to Figure 3.13 are here to support the reader. They highlight which elements of the large and detailed Figure 3.11 are of interest in the current section.

MODEL

The true nature of the human body including its neural dynamics is of no interest for this thesis. Focus is on information processing and the functionality provided at a high abstract level. Four input channels and one output channel exist. Two input channels are used for the drives. The two different sources for the sensors — environment and body — are modeled. The body uses physical and chemical means of communication. These values have to be converted before they can become psychic contents. Thus, all four input channels operate in the same two-step manner: the body state is transformed into psychic processable data by a neurosymbolization. In the other direction — from psychic contents to motor control — a neurodesymbolization is used.

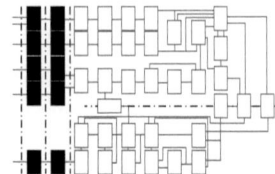

Fig. 3.14: Body modules

Modules: Two groups of modules can be identified: The somatic/neural sensor and actuator modules and the neurosymbolic translation modules. The four sensor and the one actuator modules are:

Seeking system (libido source) (E39): As described in Section 3.3.3, the seeking system is the basic motivational system. E39 is collecting information on libido produced by various inner somatic sources as well as by erogenous zones.
Homeostasis (E1): Sensors of Module E1 are collecting information on bodily functions like metabolism, blood pressure, heart beat, respiration. Thus the current state of the body and its needs is made available.
Sensors environment (E10): These sensors collect data of the environment. Typical sensors are the five senses: sight, hearing, smell, touch, and taste. Also non-human sensors like radar are part of this module.
Sensors body (E12): Although, modules E39 and E1 are collecting information on internal body values too, E12 focuses on sensors comparable to the one from Module E10 but which are directed inwardly. Thus, the sensors detect painful stimuli, tactile stimuli, balance and acceleration, body temperature and others.
Actuators (E32): How the body executes action commands is defined in this module. Various motor controls are operated from here.

The four neurosymbolization modules (Neurosymbolization of libido (E40), Neurosymbolization of needs (E2), Neurosymbolization environment (E11), and Neurosymbolization body (E13)) operate according to the same principles. The physical and chemical somatic raw data is converted into neurosymbols by the neurosymbolization algorithm described in Section 2.6.1. It is a multi-modal, three layer approach converting raw data to microsymbols/sub-modal symbols. These are condensed to unimodal symbols. Finally, all information is integrated into multi-modal neurosymbols. The modules Libidostasis handler (E41), Generation of self-preservation drives (E3), and External perception (E14) — which are next in line in the model — can process this type of information. Module `Neurodesymbolization action commands (E31)` operates the other way round. Psychic contents representing the selected actions are translated back into somatic/neural content and can be forwarded to the various motilities.

Interfaces: The group of the interfaces which names start with "I0." are not defined in detailed. They are denoting the connection of modules with the body and the transmitted data are pure electrophysical measures. Interfaces are explained upon first appearance in Figure 3.11.

I0.1: The inner somatic stimulation source which produces a constant flow of libido is represented by this interface. The circular loop in the figure defines that this source has a not identifiable bodily source and that the amount of libido produced cannot be influenced and stays constant. I0.1 connects the physical and chemical body with E39.
I0.2: The second incoming connection to E39 originates in the erogenous zones.
I0.3: This input connected to Module E1 represents the outputs of the sensors which measure the homeostasis.
I0.4: Environment sensors signals are fed into E10.
I0.5: The body sensors (see above) provide their information to E12 via this interface.
I0.6: Electrophysical signals are transmitted from E32 to the actuators.

The next group of interfaces transports data via neural networks. Interfaces I1.8, I1.1, I2.1, and I2.3 are connecting the sensors to their neurosymbolization modules. Interface I8.2 connects the neurodesymbolization of the actions to the actuators module.

The third group of interfaces related to the body functions is connecting the body with the psyche. They transport data in the form of neurosymbols.

I1.2: This interface transports the neurosymbolized bodily needs from E2 to E3.
I1.9: Neurosymbols representing libido are transmitted from E40 to E41.
I2.2: Neurosymbols derived from external sensors are transmitted from E11 to E14.
I2.4: Similar to I2.2, I2.4 transports neurosymbols to E14. This time, they originate from E12.
I8.1: Connects the last psychic module in the chain — namely `Motility control (E30)` — to the neurodesymbolization of the actions E31.

Drive Generator (C)

The Module `Drive generator (C)` of the intermediate model is split apart (Figure 3.15). The result is a chain of modules responsible for sexual drives and another one responsible for self-preservation drives.

Although sexual drives share common functionalities with self-preservation drives, they differ in important points (cp. Section 3.3). How they are generated and their inner somatic origin are the most important differences. To reflect this, the two chains of modules have been introduced.

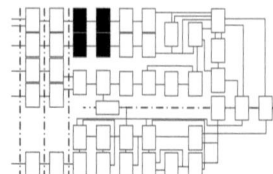

Fig. 3.15: Drive generator

Modules - Sexual Drives: Two modules are taking care of transforming the neurosymbols provided by E40 into memory traces[6] representing the sexual drives.

Libidostasis handler (E41): The constant flow of libido/psychic energy provided by the neurosymbols originating from E40 has to be buffered until the tension generated by the seeking system can be released. Module E41 adds the incoming libido to a libido buffer. The total amount of buffered libido is forwarded as total amount of tension. Further, the sexual drives are split into aggressive and libidinous components.

Separation into partial sexual drives (E43): As explained in Section 3.3.3, each sexual drive is split apart into four drives representing the four partial drives. Module E43 takes the aggressive and libidinous drives transmitted from E41 and splits them according to predefined but individual templates. The result set consists of eight sexual drives.

Modules - Self-preservation Drives: The self-preservation drives' tension has a direct mapping to inner somatic needs. If blood sugar is low, a corresponding drive is evoked — a buffer is not needed. The part which is more interesting in self-preservation drives than in sexual drives is the pair of opposites (cp. Section 3.3.2). Hence, these facts are represented in the model by different set of modules:

Generation of self-preservation drives (E3): The neurosymbolic representations of bodily needs are converted to memory traces representing the corresponding drives. At this stage, such a memory trace contains drive source, aim of drive, and drive object (cp. Section 3.3.1). The quota of affect will be added later. For each bodily need, two drives are generated: a libidinous and an aggressive one.

Fusion of self-preservation drives (E4): The libidinous and aggressive drives are combined to pair of opposites. For each bodily need, such a pair exists.

---

[6]In this model, memory traces are thing presentations which have no quota of affect attached.

Interfaces: All interfaces of this group transport memory-traces/thing presentations without attached quota of affect.

I1.3: Libidinous and aggressive drives represented by more or less complex associated thing presentations containing at least drive source, aim of drive, and drive object together with the tensions at the various drive sources are forwarded from E3 to E4.
I1.4: Pair of opposites in form of thing presentations and the tensions at the various drive sources are transmitted from E4 to Accumulation of affects for self-preservation drives (E5).
I1.10: The total amount of libido tension as well as the pair of opposites are transmitted from E41 to E43.
I2.17: The eight drives — the four partial sexual drives divided into libidinous and aggressive components — as well as the total amount of libido tension are transmitted from E43 to Accumulation of affects for sexual drives (E42).

Perception Functions (D)

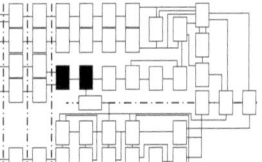

Fig. 3.16: Perception functions

Data provided by sensors of the environment and the body are processed by perception functions. The module Perception functions (D) of the intermediate model is split into two sub modules (see Figure 3.16). A new interface is added: Interface I7.7 feeds formerly secondary process contents of the last step back into the control loop. The conversion itself is done by Module Conversion to primary process (E47) which is described later on. The reason for this addition lies within the seeking system (cp. Section 3.3.3) — it enables fantasy which can be used to reduce libido tension by imagination.

Modules: The two submodules introduced in this group are: Generation of thing presentations of what is sensed and fusion of these presentations with contents of the memory.

External perception (E14): Neurosymbolic contents are transformed into thing presentations. Now, sensor sensations originating in body and environment sensors can be processed by the mental functions. The generated thing presentations are associated among each other according to their temporal and spatial vicinity and likeness.
Fusion with memory traces (E46): The thing presentations which represent the perception are associated with previously experienced and stored memory traces. This has two impacts: More information is added to the current perception and the perception is completed with previously stored information. Thus, if only parts of a well known object are visible, the other parts are added from memory. Next to information stored in memory, memory traces processed in secondary processes from the last step can be used.

Interfaces: The three interfaces which appear in this part of the model for the first time are:

- I2.5: Memory traces representing perceived environment and body information are forwarded to E46.
- I2.20: Similarly to I2.5, thing presentations are transported from E46 to `Primal repression for perception (E37)`. If quota of affects were retrieved from memory, these values are transported too.
- I7.7: Word presentations originating in `Generation of imaginary actions (E27)` are reduced to thing presentations in E47. These are forwarded together with their attached quota of affects to E46.

Affect Generator (E)

The module `Affect generator (E)` is divided into three types of modules: calculation of quota of affect, primal repression, and libido discharge (see Figure 3.17). The first two types are similar for all three lines of data (sexual drives, self-preservation drives, and perception). The third one is used for perception only. The gap in-between the three modules — E37 on the one side and `Composition of affects for perception (E18)` and `Libido discharge handler (E45)` on the other side — exists because `Emersion of repressed content (E35)` is part of the module `Defense mechanisms, Management of contents (F)` in the intermediate model. It is part of the loop generated by the interfaces 5 and 6 (see Figure 3.7(a)). With the new top-down modeling step, this loop can be removed by placing one sub module of the defense mechanisms between sub modules of affect generation.

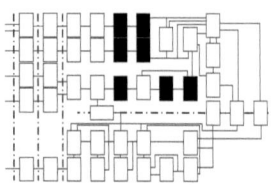

Fig. 3.17: Affect generator

Modules - Calculation of Quota of Affects: Three modules are responsible for determining the quantitative value of affects which are attached to thing presentations. `Primal repression for sexual drives (E44)` and `Primal repression for self-preservation drives (E38)` do this by translating the tension values provided by the body. For perceptions, no bodily tension source is available. Thus, E18 has to rely on memory for this task.

- `Accumulation of affects for sexual drives (E42)`: The amount of total stored libido which equals the tension of the sexual drives is attached to the memory traces. Now, thing presentations consisting of drive aim, drive source, drive object, and quota of affects exist and can be processed by the next modules.
- `Accumulation of affects for self-preservation drives (E5)`: Analogous to E42, E5 attaches quota of affects to the memory traces containing the drive contents. The difference is that the neurosymbols representing the drive tensions have been forwarded from E2 through E3 and E4. Thus, they are transferred into psychic processable form in this module.

Composition of affects for perception (E18): The value for the quota of affects for perception thing presentations is calculated by looking up all associated unpleasure and pleasure values retrieved from memory in E46 and E35. Pleasure gained in E45 is considered too.

Modules - Primal Repression: The second type of modules in this group is primal repression. As explained in Section 3.3.4, these functions are categorizing the thing presentations according to the four primary drives. The three modules — Primal repression for sexual drives (E44), Primal repression for self-preservation drives (E38), and Primal repression for perception (E37) — share the same functionality; they differ in data used. The result of them is that thing presentations have an additional value which can be used for further memory lookup to find similar entries.

Modules - Libido Discharge: This type is used for perception only. Libido discharge handler (E45) communicates with E41 via the libido buffer. Incoming perceptions are compared with memory to determine whether they qualify for libido discharge and thus for pleasure gain. If so, the value of the libido buffer is reduced (tension reduction is pleasure gain). The pleasure gain is forwarded to E18 as an additional value for the composition of the quota of affect.

Interfaces: Three types of interfaces exist for this group of modules: Thing presentations and thing presentations with quota of affects attached.

I1.5: Thing presentations and their quota of affects are transported from E38 to Defense mechanisms for drives (E6), Internalized rules handler (E7), and Knowledge about reality (unconscious) (E9).
I2.8: From E35, thing presentations and quotas of affects are transported to E18 and E45.
I2.9: Thing presentations of the perception (enriched with data from memory and feedback thing presentations) and their attached quota of affects are forwarded from E18 to E7 and Defense mechanisms for perception (E19).
I2.14: Thing presentations and their quota of affects are transported from E37 to E35.
I2.15: Self-preservation drives represented by thing presentations and their quota of affects are sent from E5 to E38.
I2.16: Quantified quotas of affect are transported from E45 to E18.
I2.18: Sexual drives in the form of thing presentations and their quota of affects are sent from E42 to E44.
I2.19: Thing presentations and their quota of affects are transported from E44 to E6, E7, and E9.

Defense Mechanisms, Management of Contents (F)

The description of this group in the intermediate model is very short. The concept of defense mechanisms and repression is important to psychoanalysis. To reflect this in the model, Module F has been split up into six submodules (cp. Figure 3.18) in the third iteration of the modeling process.

In Figure 3.7(a) module F is marked as part of Id. This is due to the fact that blocked/repressed contents are handled by the Id. But the defense mechanisms themselves are part of the Ego. Further, rules needed by the defense mechanisms belong to the Superego. Thus, the oversimplification — assigning this whole group of functionalities to the Id — has been abandoned in favor of a more diverse and precise view of the model.

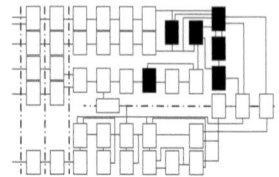

Fig. 3.18: Defense mechanisms, management of contents

Two main function blocks can be identified in this group. The first one consists of modules related to the defense mechanisms and the second one is related to handling blocked contents.

Modules - Defense Mechanisms: Defense mechanisms are guardians. They guarantee that only appropriate contents can become conscious. Inappropriate contents are either blocked or changed such that they become acceptable. The thing presentations provided by the two drive systems — sexual and self-preservation drives — are fed into a defense mechanism module. The perception has a different one. To perform their work, they are supported by two further modules: E7 and E9.

Knowledge about reality (unconscious) (E9): This module accesses knowledge which can be used to determine if a drive representation forwarded from E44 or E38 can be satisfied with a certain object. Not the reality/outer world is used as reference, instead the experiences how a special drive demand can be satisfied is used.

Internalized rules handler (E7): Rules which are only accessible to functions of the Superego are used to evaluate the incoming drive demands and perceptions. Three possible decisions can be made for each incoming information: they can be passed on without any changes, they can be passed forward but certain changes have to be made, and these contents are not allowed to pass at all. If the evaluated contents qualify for one of the latter two possibilities — a conflict occurs — defense mechanisms have to deal with them.

Defense mechanisms for drives (E6): Based on information provided by E7 and E9, this module decides which drive representations are allowed to become (pre-)conscious and if not, which defense mechanism is to be applied. These mechanisms can split the thing presentations from their quota of affect, change the thing presentations, repress the contents until later, attach them to other contents, and more. Examples for these mechanisms are repression, intellectualization, and sublimation (cp. [SSK97, pp. 51–62]). Next to evaluate newly incoming drive representations, the task of these modules is to re-evaluate repressed drive representations which are sent back by module Repression handler (E36).

Defense mechanisms for perception (E19): Analogous to E6, E19 evaluates incoming perceptions if they are allowed to become (pre-)conscious contents. Here, focus is on whether this "thought" is allowed or not. This is in opposition to defense mechanisms for drives where the focus is on the acceptability of satisfying a drive demand with a certain object. The mechanisms used for E6 are similar, but not identical to ones used for E19. A main difference is the available data: E6 has drive demands, internalized rules, and knowledge about its drives at hand; E19 has only internalized rules and the perception.

Modules - Repressed Contents: Although the two modules dealing with repressed contents are not connected via an interface, they share the same memory. Thus, contents repressed by the one module can be accessed by the other one. The two introduced modules replace Module --- (E15) from the previous version.

Repression handler (E36): Blocked contents — contents which could not pass defense mechanisms in E6 or E19 — are sent to this module for further processing. These contents are constantly tried to be send back to the defense mechanisms to test if they are able to pass them now. By using several tools, contents are changed and "disguised" to make the passing more likely. For drive representations these tools include that thing presentations and their quota of affects can be split apart and sent back individually to E6. Another possibility is to attach itself to other, more acceptable drive representations (e.g. ones with more acceptable drive objects). Thing presentations representing perceptions are stored in the repressed contents memory. They are processed by E35. It has to be mentioned that no content — thing presentations and/or quota of affects — can disappear. They are stored until it was possible to send them through the defense mechanisms.

Emersion of repressed content (E35): This module shares the same task as the second part of the tasks of E36. It is responsible for changing repressed contents such that they are more likely to pass the defense mechanisms. This is done by searching for fitting incoming thing presentations. If one is found, the repressed content is attached to it. All incoming thing presentations are forwarded to next modules, some of them with additional information attached.

Interfaces: In the previous groups, interfaces mainly connected one module with its successor. Almost all modules had only a single input and a single output. This is different for this module group. For example E6 has five inputs and three outputs. Of the total number of 15 interfaces which are utilized by this group, ten have not been introduced yet.

I1.6: Transports (unchanged or adapted) drive contents which passed the defense mechanisms from E6 to the conversion module **Conversion to secondary process for drive-wishes (E8)**.

I2.10: Transports (unchanged or adapted) perceptions which passed the defense mechanisms from E19 to the conversion module **Conversion to secondary process for perception (E21)**.

I3.1: Superego bans and rules are transported from E7 to E6.
I3.2: Superego bans and rules are transported from E7 to E19.
I4.1: Repressed or blocked drive representations are not forwarded to the conversion to secondary processes. Instead they are moved to the repression handler. Thing presentations and their attached quota of affects are transferred from E6 to E36.
I4.2: Similarly to I4.1, perception contents in the form of thing presentations and their attached quota of affects are sent from E19 to E36.
I4.3: Repressed drive contents and repressed quota of affects are sent back to the defense mechanisms. I4.3 connects E36 with E6.
I5.1: Transports quota of affects which have originally been attached to thing presentations representing drive contents from E6 to Inner perception (affects) (E20). The splitting apart is a result of the defense mechanisms.
I5.2: Analogous to I5.1, I5.2 transports quota of affects which have formerly been attached to thing presentations representing perceived contents. They are forwarded from E19 to E20.
I6.3: Knowledge about the possibilities to satisfy drive demands is transported from E9 to E6.

Connection with word presentation (G)

Figure 3.19 shows the four submodules, module Connection with word presentation (G) from the intermediate model has been split into. They are responsible for converting the data structures between the primary process and the secondary process area. Primary process functions operate with thing presentations whereas secondary process functions utilize word presentations (see Section 3.1.3).

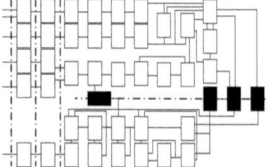

Fig. 3.19: Connection with word presentation

Modules: The first three modules (E8, E21, and E20) convert data from thing presentations into word presentations. The result of this conversion is a set of word presentations associated with the original list of thing presentations. In E8 and E20 the unordered contents of the primary processes are transformed into ordered contents of the secondary processes. They are ordered according to their temporal, spatial, hierarchical, etc. associations. They represent the functionality defined by module G in the intermediate model. The fourth module (E47) is introduced in this modeling step and enables the feedback of word presentations made necessary by the added seeking system (see Section 3.3.3).

Conversion to secondary process for drive-wishes (E8): For the incoming thing presentations fitting word presentations are selected from memory. The whole package — thing presentations, word presentations, and quota of affects — are now converted into a form which can be used by secondary process modules. The drive contents are now drive wishes.

Conversion to secondary process for perception (E21): This module does the same as E8 but with perceptions instead of drive representations. The thing presentations and quota of affects generated by incoming perceived neurosymbols are associated with the most fitting word presentations found in memory.

Inner perception (affects) (E20): Until now, only quota of affects attached to thing presentations were available. Although the value of these quota of affects has immediate and strong influence on decision making they cannot become conscious. The qualitative counterpart of the quota of affects in the primary processes is the affect in the secondary processes. The affect is represented by a word presentation and thus can become conscious. Two different groups of affects are generated. Based on the output of the defense mechanisms, a set of affects is built. For these no explanation on their origin is available; they cannot be grasped. The other set uses the output of E8 and E21. With the addition of word presentations "explaining" the contents attached to the quota of affects, the origin of the affect can be understood up to some extent. This results in more differentiated moods like unlust, fear, joy, sadness.

Conversion to primary process (E47): Contents of various action plans can be used to reduce libido tension in E45. Before they can be processed by primary process functions, they have to be converted back again. The preconscious parts of the contents — the word presentations — are removed by this module.

Interfaces: Three types of interfaces are attached to modules of this group. The first two are incoming or outgoing interfaces within the primary process area and within the secondary process area. Two interfaces transport information within modules of this group (I5.3 and I5.4). Although they are already transporting word presentations they are needed as input by another conversion module (module E20). Thus they cannot be assigned to either side solely and are viewed to be at the border between the two areas — similarly to the four conversion modules. The six interfaces which appear in this group for the first time are:

I1.7: This interface distributes the drive wishes produced by module E8 to the modules Social rules selection (E22), External perception (focused) (E23), and Decision making (E26).

I2.11: The perception contents consisting of word presentations, thing presentations, and affects are sent from E21 to E22 and E23 for further processing.

I5.3: Drive wishes are transported from E8 to E20. The contents are in the form of word presentations, thing presentations, and affects.

I5.4: Analogous to I5.3, this interface transports the perceptions in the form of word presentations, thing presentations, and affects from E21 to E20.

I5.5: Affects and differentiated experienced moods are transported from E20 to E26 and Evaluation of imaginary actions (E29).

I7.3: The various imagined action plans are distributed from E27 to E47, E29, Reality check 2 (E33), and Knowledge about reality 2 (E34).

MODEL

The modules of the intermediate model processed so far are either part of the body (modules A, B, and M) or part of the primary process (modules C, D, E, and F). After the introduction of the submodules the conversion module G has been split into, only modules belonging to secondary processes are remaining (modules Focus perception (H), Social rules (I), Decision making (J), Reality check (K), and Actuator control (L)).

Focus Perception (H)

The Module H from the intermediate model is one of the three modules which are not split into further submodules. The corresponding module in the final functional model is called External perception (focused) (E23) (see Figure 3.20). The task of it is to focus the external perception on "important" things. Thus, the word presentations originating from perception are ordered according to their importance to existing drive wishes. This could mean for example

Fig. 3.20: Focus perception

that an object is qualified to satisfy a bodily need. The resulting list — the package of word presentation, thing presentation, and drive wishes for each perception ordered descending by their importance — is forwarded by the interface I2.12 to Reality check 1 (E24) and Knowledge about reality 1 (E25). These two modules are part of reality check. The connection in the intermediate model between Module H and Module J is removed in this step of the modeling process. The loop between Module J and Module K is resolved by a two-step reality check — the first step is done by E24 and E25 and the second by E33 and E34.

Social Rules [I]

Like Module H, this Module (I) is not split further apart. The name of the corresponding module in the final functional model is Social rules selection (E22) (cp. Figure 3.21). Next to E7, E22 is the second module which is assigned to the top level module Superego. While the contents processed by E7 are unconscious and cannot become conscious at all, E22 processes social rules which are at least preconscious and can become conscious. These rules, com-

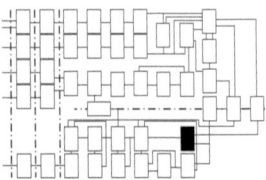

Fig. 3.21: Social rules

mands, and gratifications appear as word and thing presentations and influence decision making. Which rules are selected and forwarded is determined by comparing the drive wishes and the external perception with the stored trigger conditions. Interface I3.3 transports the rules from E22 to E26.

Decision Making (J)

The task of decision making is to take all information available, create action plans, and select the most promising one for execution. As shown in Figure 3.22, Module J is split apart into four submodules. As mentioned above, the loop with Module K is resolved by a two-step approach for the reality check. Decision making starts with the results from the first reality check and generates an intermediate set of imaginary actions.

These are fed into the second part of the reality check. Finally, the result of this check is used to select the most promising action.

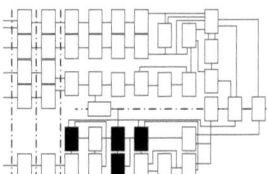

Modules: Module J's task is realized by a four step chain. First, decision making takes place; the result is given to a knowledge base. The output of these two is used by a module which created the imaginary actions. Finally, the fourth step selects the actions to be put to motility control.

Fig. 3.22: Decision making

Decision making (E26): Demands provided by reality, drives, and Superego are merged. The result is evaluated regarding which resulting wish can be used as motive for an action tendency. The list of produced motives is ordered according to their satisfiability.

Knowledge based (stored scenarios) (E28): Past experiences can be retrieved from memory by this module. It operates as some kind of episodic memory. The motives produced by E26 are used as search operator. The retrieved memory contents tell what happened previously when a motive has been tried to be satisfied with the objects currently available.

Generation of imaginary actions (E27): By combination of the motives provided by E26 and the experiences retrieved by E28, E27 generates a set of imaginary actions. Before actions are passed to E30 they are solely psychic contents and thus imaginary. An imaginary action (-plan) defines a more or less complex sequence of actions on how to satisfy a need based on actions taken in similar situations.

Evaluation of imaginary actions (E29): The imaginary actions are evaluated by this module based on the result of the second reality check. The result of this mental rating is a reduced list with the imaginary actions selected for execution.

Interfaces: The five interfaces which appear in this module group for the first time are:

I2.13: The results of the first reality check performed by module E24 is forwarded to E26.
I6.2: Contents of the "episodic" memory are transported from E28 to E27.
I7.1: Word and thing presentations representing the result of module E26 are distributed to E27 and E28.
I7.4: The final action plan is transported from E29 to E30.
I7.6: The result of the second reality check performed by module E33 is sent to E29.

As described above, the decision making is strongly interwoven with reality check. The first and the second stage of the realty check are described next.

Reality Check (K)

The reality check is split into a two stage, two-step solution. Thus, the module K is divided into 4 submodules (see Figure 3.23). Both stages are built of the same two steps: First incoming data is used to fetch knowledge from memory; next, the evaluation done by the reality check is performed. The memory accessed is not about ethical facts or episodic entries. It contains lexical knowledge about the world. This includes knowledge about function and attributes of objects —

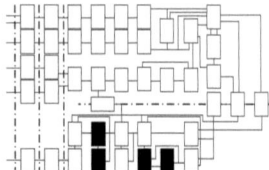

Fig. 3.23: Reality check

for example, raw potatoes can only be eaten after they have been cooked. This type of memory can be labeled as "semantic memory."

Modules: The tasks of the modules of one stage are: accessing the "semantic memory" and evaluating incoming information. This is the same for the two stages. They mainly differ in the data provided as input and their location in the final functional model.

Knowledge about reality 1 (E25), Knowledge about reality 2 (E34): Semantic knowledge is retrieved from memory for all word and thing presentations send to these functions.
Reality check 1 (E24): The external world is evaluated regarding the available possibilities for drive satisfaction and which requirements arise. This is done by utilization of semantic knowledge provided by E25 and incoming word and things presentations from E23. The result influences the generation of motives in E26.
Reality check 2 (E33): This module operates similarly to E24. The imaginary actions generated by E27 are evaluated regarding which action plan is possible and the resulting requirements. E34 provides the semantic knowledge necessary for this task. The result influences the final decision which action to choose in module E28.

Interfaces: The last two interfaces to be described in this section are I6.1 and I7.5. They both transport contents of the semantic memory in the form of word and thing presentations. I6.1 connects E25 with E24; I7.5 connects E34 with E33.

Actuator Control (L)

The last module of the intermediate model is Module L. Similarly to modules H and I, this module is not split into several submodules (see Figure 3.24). Its name changed from actuator control to Motility control (E30) in the final functional model.

Motoric movement can be controlled by psychic functions up to some extent. Drive inhibition — a mechanism necessary for the defense mechanisms — leads to the possibility to perform behavior in rehearsal. Module E30 uses this concept to evaluate how the submitted action plan can be realized best. The resulting action commands are forwarded to E31.

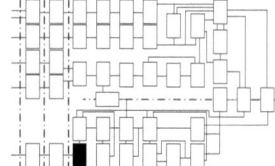

Fig. 3.24: Actuator control

Module E31 is a body function and has already been explained at the beginning of this section. Hence, the control loop is closed. The performed actions changed the world including the own body and the changed world/body is perceived by the sensors. The next loop of the final functional model can be processed. Next, which modules access the memory and special memories like the primary repression memory are discussed.

3.4.4 Memory Access

Until now, only the functionality of the modules has been described. What has been left out is how this information is stored and shared. Each module can have its own state and store information. This should be used only for things which are needed by this module only and will never be accessed by others. This applies especially to thing and word presentations which have associations with other presentations. If they are stored locally, updates to these connections would not be done and two inconsistent versions of the same piece of information would exist in the system. For the purpose of shared access to information, memory subsystems are introduced. The identified five different memory/storage systems are discussed in the following.

Standard Memory

In Section 3.1.3, the general memory subsystem is sketched. A module which retrieves or stores information to the memory accesses it through a façade object: The information representation module. As shown in Figure 3.25, not all modules need memory access.

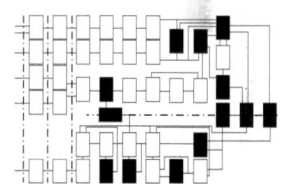

Fig. 3.25: Standard memory

All modules which provide knowledge about something are retrieving thing and word presentations from the standard memory. They are Knowledge about reality (unconscious) (E9), Knowledge about reality 1 (E25), Knowledge based (stored scenarios) (E28), and Knowledge about reality 2 (E34). Similarly, the two Superego related modules Internalized rules handler (E7) and Social rules selection (E22) are providing rules in the form of thing and word presentations fetched from the memory. Retrieved memory traces are forwarded by these modules to other modules for further processing.

111

MODEL

The second group of modules accessing the standard memory is the defense mechanisms: Defense mechanisms for drives (E6) and Defense mechanisms for perception (E19). Other than the six modules above, these two process the retrieved information by themselves. Thus, the fetched data is processed locally.

The conversion between primary and secondary processes modules needs access to this memory for local processing purposes too. The four modules are: Conversion to secondary process for drive-wishes (E8), Inner perception (affects) (E20), Conversion to secondary process for perception (E21), and Conversion to primary process (E47).

The last remaining module to have access is Fusion with memory traces (E46). It fetches memory traces to complement incoming external perceptions.

The modules belonging solely to the primary processes retrieve only thing presentations (E6, E7, E9, E19, and E46). All other modules operate with thing and word presentations.

Primal Repression Memory

The primal repression memory is a special section in the standard memory. It contains thing presentations which can never become conscious and can only be accessed by the special modules responsible for categorization of incoming thing presentation (see Section 3.3.3). Thus, the access is done using the information representation layer too. What is different to the standard access is that the four primary drives cannot be used as query parameter — they are available only after these modules have processed the data. The primal

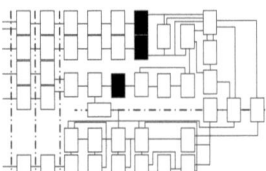

Fig. 3.26: Primal repression memory

repression modules with access to the primal repression memory are Primal repression for perception (E37), Primal repression for self-preservation drives (E38), and Primal repression for sexual drives (E44) (see Figure 3.26).

Repressed Content Memory

Module Repression handler (E36) retrieves blocked content from the defense mechanisms. This content tries to become unblocked again by emerging from E36 and Emersion of repressed content (E35) into the flow of the functional model. A special storage containing these blocked contents is necessary. The stored data is of type thing presentations with attached quota. Figure 3.28 shows that the two modules are connected to this special type of storage with read (D2.2 and D2.4) and write (D2.1 and D2.3) interfaces.

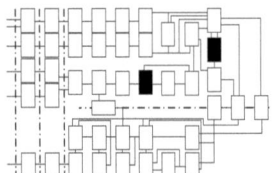

Fig. 3.27: Repressed content memory

MODEL

The two incoming interfaces into module E36 are I4.1 and I4.2. The first one transports blocked drives in the form of thing presentations plus attached quota of affects. The other one transports blocked thing presentations representing incoming perceptions in the same format. Both incoming information are stored into the memory via interface D2.3. Depending on future results of the functions of the module E36, drives pushed into this storage try to pass the defense mechanisms. Thus, drives in the form of thing presentations and attached quota of affects are sent via interface I4.3 back to E6.

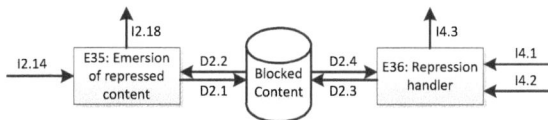

Figure 3.28: Repressed content memory connected with E35 and E36

The alternative possibility to reappear for blocked contents is module E35. Incoming perceptions in the form of thing presentations (transferred through interface I2.14) are compared with stored blocked content. If matching content is found it is attached to the incoming perception. The stored thing presentation plus attached quota of affects can be used as a whole or it can be split and only the thing presentation or the quota of affect is attached. The enriched thing presentation of the perception is forwarded via interface I2.15 to the next module.

Information for Thing Presentation Generation

To convert neurosymbols into thing presentations, additional information is needed. For example, the pair of opposites for the creation of drives has to be stored somewhere. The problem with storing this information in the standard memory lies within the data types of the database entries and the possible query arguments. The standard memory is specialized into storing memory traces and retrieving them by queries built of thing and word presentations. The result of the modules Generation of self-preservation drives (E3), Fusion of self-preservation drives (E4), and Libidostasis handler (E41) are thing presentations (see Figure 3.29). Thus, at the beginning of the conversion process, no thing presentations are present. A local storage which contains the necessary information is needed for each of the three modules. The concrete realization of these storages is not defined by psychoanalysis and thereafter an engineering task to be dealt with at the implementation phase.

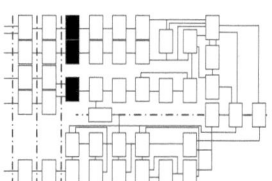

Fig. 3.29: Information for thing presentation generation

113

Model

Libido Buffer

The two modules which are communicating via the libido buffer are `E41` and `Libido discharge handler` (E45) (see Figure 3.30). Figure 3.9 depicts this interaction.

E41 is responsible of adding incoming libido to the buffer while E45 removes libido whenever possible. This results in a reduction of the libido tension and thus in pleasure gain. For this purpose a libido buffer is introduced. It is independent from the rest of the memory system. Figure 3.31 shows how this buffer is connected to the two modules. Each module is connected with two interfaces — read access (`D1.2`, `D1.4`) and write access (`D1.1`, `D1.3`).

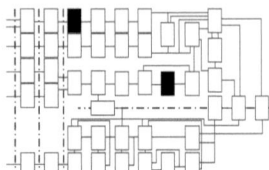

Fig. 3.30: Libido buffer

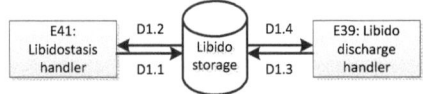

Figure 3.31: Libido buffer connects E41 and E45

The libido buffer stores a single quantitative value denoting the accumulated libido and its corresponding tension.

This concludes the description of the final functional model. The implementation of it and its memory is described in Section 4.5. This chapter is concluded with a technical view on the model and its critical implementation path.

3.5 The Id and Parts of the Ego

The developed final functional model consists of 34 modules (plus 10 which describe the necessary body functions). They are connected by 44 interfaces: 5 interfaces connect the body with the psychic functions and 11 are body internal interfaces. 21 of the psychic modules access the memory layer. Further, 2 feedback loops exist in the functional model. Not to be counted the feedback loops via the memory layer — for example between `Repression handler` (E36) and `Emersion of repressed content` (E35) — or via the real world closing the loop between the actuators and the sensors. This amount of modules, interfaces, and feedback loops makes it likely that system failures occur. Reasons for them may be design failures, implementation errors, data changes resulting in instable states, model intrinsic problems comparable to mental illnesses, problems arising from the systems complexity, and others. This list does not try to be comprehensive. It illustrates the motivation for examining the model at hand regarding its implementation.

The future target applications for the control system described are autonomous systems which interact with humans. Possible failures of the system should be limited such that no humans are harmed. In simple Heating, Ventilating, and Air Conditioning (HVAC) applications located in areas with mild climate, the control system can be turned off in case of malfunctions. The result is that the rooms will adapt to outside temperatures and it will be warmer or colder. As soon as the building with the HVAC system is transferred to more hostile environments—e.g. a polar station or an airplane—turning off the system is not an option. This accounts even more for more complex applications like the control system operates a fleet of large autonomous mobile robots to maintain the building. Thus, some kind of fall back system is necessary that guarantees—or at least tries to ensure— a minimum functionality in case of system failures.

Usual approaches are things like replication of elements or introduction of a watchdog function which restarts the system in case of failures. Replication of the elements is not applicable if the problem is intrinsic to the (complex) model. If a watchdog function detects a stalled module, the module or the whole system has to be restarted. This takes time during which all actuators of the system are possibly in an undefined state, resulting in a threat to humans in vicinity.

The questions derived from these points listed are: Are all 34 modules necessary from a technical point of view? Can a subset of the modules be identified that enables the system to provide a minimum functionality? What is the level of functionality that can be expected of this reduced model?

Using the Id alone is insufficient. Although the Id represents bodily needs to the psyche, it cannot perceive information from the outer world nor can it manipulate it. These two functionalities are performed by the Ego (cp. Figure 3.4(a)). Also the other way round— using functions from the Ego only—is not possible. Without the self-preservation drives and the seeking system, the system would not perform any action at all. The defense mechanisms and some basic functions of decision making (both part the Ego) are necessary to hold the drives at bay. Otherwise all drives would result in urgent needs which demand immediate satisfaction. This would result in the inability to act too. If the Superego is not present, socially not acceptable actions would be performed and decisions would be made which do not fit to the stored rules, demands, and gratifications. Nevertheless, in absence of the Superego the control loop defined in Section 2.1.1 can be realized.

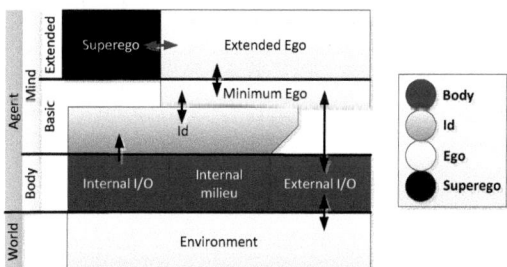

Figure 3.32: Basic and extended Ego [DTM+09, p. 380]

Model

Figure 3.32 depicts the selected subset at a high abstraction level. The body is identically to the one used in the final functional model. Rich internal system values (Internal Milieu) are perceived by the psyche via a different set of sensors (Internal I/O[7]) as information from the environment (External I/O). The whole functionality of the Id is necessary to process the incoming drive representations and to process the blocked drive demands. Only a subset of the Ego is necessary — mainly to interact with the environment and to hold the drives at bay. Thus, currently not important drive demands can be blocked by the defense mechanisms. An important information provided by Ego functions is the knowledge about how a drive demand can be satisfied. Additional functions from the Ego like the two-stepped reality check or defense mechanisms for perception are put into the extended system. The Superego is put into the extended system too.

Now the control system is divided into two parts — the minimal part and the extended part. The extended part can stall and be restarted without the need to turn off the whole system. The modules in the minimal part form a so called critical path. Special care has to be taken while implementing them.

Although the extended part can be turned off temporarily, the functionality provided by it is necessary for the system. The Superego is necessary for the development of the system — to learn what is wrong and what is right. Without the extended Ego functions decision making is reduced to a reactive approach. And without the two-stepped reality check, advanced planning is not possible.

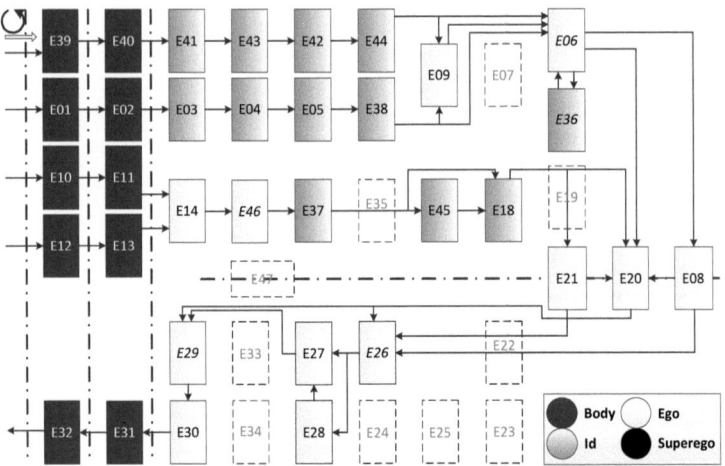

Figure 3.33: Minimal model

In Figure 3.33, the realization of the minimal part within the final functional model is shown. The following modules are moved to the extended part: Emersion of repressed

---
[7]I/O ... Input/Output

content (E35), Internalized rules handler (E7), Defense mechanisms for perception (E19), External perception (focused) (E23), Reality check 1 (E24), Knowledge about reality 1 (E25), Conversion to primary process (E47), Reality check 2 (E33), Knowledge about reality 2 (E34), and Social rules selection (E22). Although E35 is an Id function, is does not change incoming thing presentations in absence of the extended part. This is due to the absence of module E19 — no perceptions are blocked and moved to the repressed content memory (see Section 3.4.4). Thus, no blocked perceptions can be retrieved from it and attached to incoming perceptions. As stated above the Superego related modules are removed (E7 and E22) as well as the reality check related modules (E24, E25, E33, and E34). The focused perception (E23) is primarily needed for the first part of reality check and for extended decision making and is thus moved to the extended part. Finally, the back-conversion module from secondary process related data structures to primary process ones (E47) is removed because the feedback loop enabling the system to fantasize is defined not to be part of the minimum implementation.

With the reduction of the model by removal of nine modules, the following five modules have reduced functionality. **Repression handler (E36)** needs only to process blocked drive demands. Thus, all functions dealing with perceptions can be turned off. Next, **Defense mechanisms for drives (E6)** does not need to process Superego rules next to the incoming drive demands. Similarly, **Decision making (E26)** does not get additional information from the knowledge base, the focus of attention, or the social rules. This module can only process data provided by the three data conversion modules **Conversion to secondary process for drive-wishes (E8)**, **Inner perception (affects) (E20)**, and **Conversion to secondary process for perception (E21)**. Module **Evaluation of imaginary actions (E29)** has no additional information at hand to assess the chance of success of the incoming action plans. With the removal of the conversion module E47, Module **Fusion with memory traces (E46)** does not need to merge incoming perceptions with action plans generated in the previous step.

Although the modules E19, E22, and E35 are either moved to the extended part or will not change incoming data at all, they need to forward the incoming thing and word presentations to the outgoing interfaces. Thus, a dummy implementation of these three modules is necessary which performs the forwarding in case the extended part is not available.

From the original 34 modules belonging to psychic functions, ten have been removed and another five are reduced in their functionality. Thus, roughly a third of the modules are moved to the extended part. The remaining functions form the minimal part and the critical path which should be treated with special care during implementation. They should not fail or at least fail later than modules belonging to the extended part.

The result of this division into two parts is a control system which ensures up to some extent a minimal functionality. The amount of the resulting behavior could be loosely approximated to a four or five year old child who has developed an Ego and a Superego — the Superego is necessary for development but not for the minimal operation. The child can distinguish between important and less important drives which enables it to delay drive discharge demands. It is important to mention that this division into two parts is a technical discussion of the produced model. With the removal of the Superego and important Ego functions the remaining model cannot be seen as psychoanalytically inspired as described in Chapter 1. How the critical part should be treated and what special measures should be taken is out of scope of this thesis. Nevertheless, the principal functionality of the model consisting of the Id and parts of the Ego is shown in Section 5.5.

In this chapter, a step by step development of the psychoanalytically inspired final functional model has been done. Starting from plain psychoanalytical descriptions, a technically feasible model is generated. In the next chapter, the implementation of an agent equipped with a psychoanalytically inspired control architecture is described.

> "And your field, Mr. Hall, is stim - stimulative
> – ?" "Simulectronics." "How fascinating! I
> understand that when you and Mr. Siskin get
> your machine – I may call it a machine, mayn't
> I? –" "It's a total environment simulator. We've
> got the bugs out at last – third try. We call it
> Simulacron-3."
>
> Daniel F. Galouye, Simulacron-3 (1964)

4 Platform, Framework, and Decision Unit Implementation

For the development and evaluation of the psychoanalytically inspired control system an artificial life simulation is needed (see Section 1.5 and Section 2.1.3). It provides a platform for comparing different models. An implementation of a model is assigned to virtual, embodied agents. To enable a simple exchange ability and thus easier comparison between different implementations, a framework for implementing control systems within this implementation is defined.

In the first section the requirements for such an artificial life simulation are discussed. Based on these requirements and the model developed in the previous chapter, use-cases for evaluation and comparison purposes are defined. Next, the design of the simulation — the platform — is described. This includes all types of objects the simulation can contain — from stones and cans to plants, to animals and finally to agents. In the next section the interface between the embodied agents and their control system — the framework — is introduced. This chapter is concluded with the description of the implementation of the psychoanalytically inspired decision unit based on the model developed in the previous chapter.

4.1 Requirements Analysis

The purpose of the simulator ARSIN World is to provide a testbed for different control systems. The main focus lies on Artificial General Intelligence (AGI) related projects but the use of simpler approaches like implementations of the subsumption architecture [Bro86] should also be possible. The test consists of a description of a situation (available resources, shape of the world, involved agents, etc.) and one or more desired behaviors the agents should show. The agents are exposed to this setup having neither knowledge about the desired behaviors for this test nor knowledge about which test they are exposed to. At the end of the simulation it should be possible to evaluate the shown behaviors. This is usually to be done by a human observer. For simpler setups, values like survived agents or maximum age of agents can be used for automatic evaluation.

As stated above, the simulation should not only be used to evaluate a single implementation of a control system. Moreover, it should be possible to use the simulation as a platform to compare different implementations of different models. From this analysis the first requirement statement can be extracted:

Statement 4.1. *An interface between the body of an agent and its control unit is necessary. It should provide standardized access to the available sensors and actuators.*

This leads to the next necessity: Predefined setups and situations have to be present for such a comparison. A set of such "use-cases" serves two purposes: First, the comparison and evaluation is standardized. Second, the design of the shape and contents of the artificial life simulation is driven by the needs of the comparison. Without this set, the comparison would be made according to what is possible and not to what is meaningful. Thus, the next requirement statement is:

Statement 4.2. *A set of use-cases defining situations and pre-requisites along with desirable resulting behaviors of the agents has to be defined.*

An artificial life simulation is used to study (software) agents roaming in a predefined environment. The world and its inhabitants can have any shape, granularity, "reality", etc. The definition of which kind of physics and time model can be freely chosen. The idea behind the work in this thesis is to use the human psyche as described by Freudian metapsychology. Humans have evolved in a real world with real physics and real time. Every action taken needs time and energy; every observation changes the world (cp. Section 2.3.3). A simulation of the real world is not feasible. First, if no simplifications and abstractions are allowed, the real world could be used as test platform instead of a to be developed simulation. Second, for evaluation of the designed model a controllable and thus in its complexity reduced environment is needed. The resulting statement is:

Statement 4.3. *The simulation has to consist of a "simple" world inspired by the real world.*

This thesis focuses on the Id and its interaction with the body. The body provides the sources for the drives and the resulting tension. Further, the psyche consisting of Id, Ego, and Superego can only interact with the world through sensors and actuators provided by a body. Thus, the next statement is:

Statement 4.4. *The agent which is equipped with the psychoanalytically inspired control system has to have a body which provides internal and external sensors and actuators as well as rich internal systems which operate as motivational sources.*

The different bodily needs have to have counterparts in the artificial environment. The stomach needs different types of nutrition, some nutrition might be poisonous. Other things which should be provided by the simulation are threats which lead to avoidance of pain or even death, search for pleasure like a nice view or a delicious apple. Also "tools" make the world more interesting—for example, using a stone to convert a cactus from a dangerous item into edible flesh. Resulting, the next requirement statement is:

Statement 4.5. *The world has to be equipped with things like different types of nutrition, with dangerous or interesting objects, with hunters and with prey.*

Psychoanalysis deals with interaction of humans. For example, the generation of Superego rules during childhood is forced by rules, bans and rewards given by the parents or others. To evaluate functionalities related to Ego and Superego, interaction with other agents beyond a simple hunter/prey schema or aggression vs. ignorance towards an agent of a different team is needed. This leads to the following statement:

Statement 4.6. *Social interaction is necessary for evaluation of a psychoanalytically inspired control system.*

A bodily need combined with social interaction is reproduction. The agents need to have the possibility to have some kind of mating procedure which results in the production of offspring. This provides three advantages: First, sexual arousal generated by stimulation of erogenous zones can be released (see Section 3.3.1 for a discussion of sexual drives). Second, raising infants and learning through childhood can be performed. This is necessary to test and evaluate learning — especially learning of social Superego rules. Third, by variation of personality parameters of the parents, the adaptability of the agent generations to larger changes in the environment can be assessed. The resulting statement is:

Statement 4.7. *The artificial life simulation has to provide possibilities for reproduction of the agents.*

A technical requirement is the maintainability of the simulator. The use-cases lead the design of the artificial life simulation. They can be adapted to new needs and insights or extended to new fields that have to be tested too. Thus, an intrinsic demand for the platform is that it can be extended:

Statement 4.8. *The software design of the artificial life simulation has to be done with expandability and scalability in mind.*

The first requirement (Statement 4.1) is met by the introduction of a framework described below in Section 4.4. The use-cases demanded by Statement 4.2 and defined in Section 4.2 guide the design of the simulation platform. It is designed as an artificial life simulation inspired by the projects listed in Section 2.5.2 (Statement 4.3). The agent body described in Section 4.3.3 deals with the requirements formulated by Statement 4.4 and 4.5 (see also Section 2.3). The ARSIN simulation platform provides all means necessary to fulfill the two requirements Statement 4.6 and Statement 4.7 (details are given below). The implementation of the ARSIN simulation is based on the Java multi agent development framework Multi-Agent Simulator of Neighborhoods ... or Networks ... or something ... (MASON) (see Section 2.5.1). Its modular design helps in satisfaction of the requirement by Statement 4.8.

After this short overview about how the various requirements are met, a more in depth explanation of the use-cases, the platform — the ARSIN simulation — and the framework — the body-mind interface — and an overview on the implementation of the Artificial Recognition System (ARS) model are given in the rest of this chapter.

4.2 Use-Cases

As already discussed in Section 2.1.3, evaluation and comparison of AGI architectures is difficult and no standardized test is available. Usual methods for this consist of manual comparison of the models at hand and implementation of a model into a simulation environment which is designed only for this purpose. Deutsch et al. defined three use-cases and the fitting simulator in [DZL07, DZLZ08] — see also preliminary work in Section 2.6.3. These use-cases are described very similar to use-cases in software engineering. There, a use-case is a sequence of interactions between two entities which result in a certain behavior. For example the legacy use-case "call for help" is described as one agent calls for help in case of danger, and if another agent of the same team answers the call this use-case qualifies as fulfilled. This is a possible approach for small, isolated tasks. But with increased complexity more than one possibility exists to solve the task at hand. Based on the work by Kohlhauser [Koh08, pp. 40–41] a more fitting definition of use-case is derived:

Definition 4.1. A use-case *is a textual description of a desired observable behavior given defined preconditions. It consists of the following parts:* Description ... *a narrative definition of what this use-case is about.* Actors ... *the involved autonomous agents.* Precondition ... *required state of the world.* Course of Action ... *a narrative description of which actions are most likely to happen. Optional, alternative actions can be defined as well.* Results ... *expected results. They can be mandatory, optional and contradicting.*

The important part of this use-case definition is that resulting use-cases guide the development process. If an agent fails to produce the predefined course of actions or the experiment ends in a result not listed it does not necessarily mean that the agent has failed the use-case. Rather, analysis of the shown behavior and the internal states of the agent should lead to new insights on the model. Thus, these use-cases cannot be used for automatic testing. Defining a framework within a decision unit enables it to be evaluated or compared with others.

With the redesign of the artificial life simulation — the step from the old Bubble Family Game (BFG) to the new ARSIN World — a list of new use-cases which this world should provide is generated. The topics covered by them range from simple setups with only one agent and plenty of food to complex setups enforcing social interaction.

Use-Case 0 — The Lonely Life of a Hungry ARSIN

This use-case is the most simple one regarding actors, preconditions, actions, and results. Its purpose is to provide a test-bed for bodily demands and basic sensing capabilities. Only one agent — an ARSIN — roams in a small world filled with various food sources and stones. No harmful food or potentially dangerous other agents are present.

The three bodily demands which are put to test are hunger, expulsion, and exhaustion. The first demand defines that the agent should eat when it is hungry. Pro-active behavior — like eating in advance because the agent knows that soon there will be a food shortage — is not considered in this use-case. The next one is the opposite of eating. The different food sources provide different qualities regarding their nutritional value per unit. The remainder of each unit is non-digestible. To make room for new food, the agent has to expulse it. This should not happen next to fresh food. The third bodily demand is to avoid exhaustion. Thus, the agent should not move at maximum velocity all the time.

The external sensors needed for this scenario are vision and the information that a certain food source is close enough to be consumed. Needed sensors of body internal values are stomach fill level (how much potential energy is available), amount of stored non-digestible units, and the agent's stamina level.

The actions are simple: If hungry eat the closest food source. If not hungry, search until close to a food source. In case of the need to deposit excrements, move away from all nearby food sources.

The expected results are autonomous agents which are able to feed themselves and to differentiate between food and non-food. Further, a basic resource management which on the one hand avoids exhaustion but on the other hand guarantees that the agent does not starve, is expected as well.

Use-Case 1 — Collecting and Taking Food Home

This use-case consists of a single agent again. In contrast to the previous use-case, food sources are limited resources. Additionally, they appear clustered for a short time. Staying at a single position and consuming the available food would lead to starvation. The agent cannot eat all available food at once. Thus, the agent has to search for the next occurrence. Due to the fact that the agent cannot predict where and when it will appear, a harvesting and storing behavior has to be developed by the agent. The food source can be picked up and carried home. Only within a small radius around its home food does not vanish after a while. With the collected pile of food at home the agent can roam the world to find additional food and carry it home.

This use-case forces the agent to have at least limited deliberation capabilities. Planning, pro-active behavior and knowledge about the world are necessary. For example, the agent has to have the possibility to repress the demand to eat while it harvests food. Otherwise, it would eat all food instantaneously and nothing is brought back for storage purposes.

The needed sensors are similar to the ones defined in the previous use-case. The vision sensors need to be able to differentiate between the special storage area, the home, and the rest of the world. Additionally, the information where the home base is located might be added by a special sensor. This enables to focus on the development of the pro-active behavior without the need of dealing with localization, map-building, and orientation. Next to the ability to eat a food source, actions to pick it up, carry it, and lay it down are necessary.

Use-Case 2 — Confronted with Different, potentially Dangerous, Energy Sources

The first two use-cases confronted the ARSIN Agent with energy/food sources which had only positive effects. Although the sources might appear and disappear and have different nutrition values, no harmful energy source has been introduced yet. Until now the agent could consume everything without the danger of any type of damage. The analogy for already introduced energy sources is plant. Thus, they are stationary and (re-)grow. This use-case adds animals to the list.

Energy source can be dangerous in different ways. Common to all sources is that they could be poisonous. This can range from necessary nutrition in combination with slightly poisonous nutrition leading to a trade-off between pain and necessity to deadly poisonous sources. Another threat is the "surface" of the source. Plants with stings or bone-plated animals need special treatment before they can be eaten. If done otherwise, pain and damage of body parts are the result. The possibilities restricted to animals are: If prey is eaten before it is killed, it is very likely that the hunter gets hurt by it. And, not all edible animals are peaceful prey they could be hunters too (more dangerous to kill). And, to make things worse, the ARSIN agent could be the primary prey of such a hunter.

The abilities an ARSIN Agent needs to perform this use-case are basic sensing, movement, and consuming. Additionally, actions for killing or application of special treatment are needed. The agent has to be able to identify different types of plants and animals. Further, sensors to get information on pain generated by the current activity as well as some kind of measurement of the body integrity are needed.

The agent should show a hunting behavior. Further, experience gained by interaction with the various energy sources should influence made decisions.

With the realization of this use-case an environment which can induce pleasure, pain, curiosity, and fear is provided. The agent has to have extended external sensors as well as internal measures. The decision unit has to support concepts like affects, conscious planning, acting-as-if, and experience.

Use-Case 3 — Searching for Type of Energy Source

A variation of the use-cases "collecting and taking food home" and "confronted with different, potentially dangerous, energy source" is the searching for special types of energy sources. All abilities from both use-cases are needed. The difference is that plenty of energy sources are available but not all are useful — some are poisonous, others are dangerous. The agent has to learn which energy sources can be easily consumed. Further, some nutrition types needed by the agent's digestion system are provided by harmful sources only. Thus, the ARSIN agent has to make a plan about his preferred diet.

In addition to the results produced by the two original use-cases, this use-case adds more deliberation capabilities to the system. The agent has to learn through positive and negative feedback which energy sources to eat and to generate a plan of what to eat when and how.

Use-Case 4 — Location Identification

The use-case "collecting and taking food home" bypassed the orientation problem by introduction of a beacon signal which is received by a special sensor. It tells the agent in which direction home is. While this is sufficient for the previous use-case — focus of it lies within handling energy sources — it is a bypass which cannot exist in reality. Thus, this use-case adds the demand that the ARSIN agent has to be able to localize itself and to generate a map of the world.

To make orientation possible, additional objects have to be added to the world. Until now, only uniformly shaped stones are used in the first use-case. A location can be identified by two approaches: First, a unique landmark is present and second, several (non-unique) objects form a shape in the world which is unique.

With the possibility to generate a map of the world and to find its own location within it, the agent can now search more efficiently for food and take it home. Different to the previous use-case where neither the location nor the time of the appearance of an energy source was of importance, now an energy source at a special position should not disappear. Like an apple tree, it should be visible that this is an energy source and that currently there are apples or no apples available. Removed apples regrow after a while.

No additional abilities of the agent's body are needed. The decision unit of the agent has to be able to detect chronological aspects (regrowth of apples after a period) and to store information about locations in its memory.

Use-Case 5 — Planting Energy Sources

This use-case is another variation of "collecting and taking food home." Next to the abilities to search, collect energy sources and to bring them back home, planting them again is introduced. Now the agent does not have to rely on finding food in time. Fitting energy sources can be relocated to a place closer to home. There they continue to grow and thus provide a constant supply of energy.

The ARSIN agent has to be able to perform an additional action: Planting. This action can only be performed on fitting plants. Two "insights" have to be possible for the decision unit. First, planting and waiting can lead to another, yet unknown energy source. And second, a delay of drive demands might be advantageous. Instead of eating the energy source or storing it for consumption, the next time, the energy source is planted and the gratification for this behavior is delayed for a much longer time.

The result of this use-case's implementation is an agent which can do long term planning and acting-as-if.

Use-Case 6 — Transforming of Energy Sources (Cooking)

A variation of the previous use-case "planting energy sources" is cooking them. Instead of a long term planning, combinatorial analysis of the energy sources at hand is needed.

By application of the transformation action, one or more energy sources are combined and changed into a new energy source with different nutrition values. For example, previously poisonous food is now harmless and the needed nutrition can be eaten. This use-case focuses more on the agent's knowledge about the world than on its ability to delay drive demands for a long period.

Use-Case 7 — Body Integrity

As already hinted in the use-case "Confronted with Different, potentially Dangerous, Energy Sources" it should be possible that the agents can be hurt and injured. Badly wounded agents may die. It is in the self-interest of an autonomous embodied agent to avoid damage of its body.

Dangerous objects, painful surfaces, hunting animals, or other aggressive agents are the sources of pain and injuries which should be avoided. The world has to be designed such that the agent cannot avoid the dangers totally. A balance between dying due to starvation and exposure to these risks has to be found by the agent's deliberation system.

This use-case trains a behavior needed for interaction with human operators: accomplish the task at hand with minimum damage to the system (which is sometimes inevitable).

Use-Case 8 — Barter Trade

In all previous use-cases social interaction is non-existing. Although ARSIN agents can harm and kill other ARSIN agents too, it is not really a social interaction. Until now, the other ARSIN agents were exchangeable with animals without a change in the use-case. This use-case introduces social interaction in the form of barter trade. Based on the abilities trained in use-cases "collecting and taking food home" and "searching for type of energy source," ARSIN agents can try to get missing nutrition by trading food with other ARSIN agents.

At least two ARSIN agents, two home bases, and two areas where to store energy sources are needed for this use-case. A hand-over action is needed to enable an agent to give a carried energy source to another agent. Further, the agents have to have some form of communication channel. At least an exchange of simple symbols without grammar is needed. Each symbol represents one idea like "I need apples."

Required capabilities of the decision unit are: Knowing which one is its own home base and which home bases belong to others. The concept of ownership is necessary to understand that the objects close to its own home base should not be taken by others. Further needed knowledge is that other ARSIN agents might have what is needed at the moment.

The agents can adapt different strategies like exchanging pieces one to one. Or — a more complex set up — figuring out which resources are limited and looking especially for them and asking for a different exchange ratio. Alternatively, a benevolent behavior between the agents could evolve. The symbol system has to be mighty enough to cover these alternative behaviors.

With this use-case the step from a simulation with several agents to a multi-agent simulation is taken. Now ARSIN agents can communicate which allows evolving more complex interactions.

Two further strategies which could be developed by the agents in this use-case are stealing and protecting. If needed goods are found unprotected at someone else's home base, stealing could be an option.

Use-Case 9 — Dancing

In case of benevolent behavior some kind of social currency is introduced: If you help me now, I will try to help you in the future. This use-case introduces the social interaction dancing as a possibility to tighten the relationship in absence of any need to trade at the moment. Thus, agents who danced together a lot in the past are more likely to help each other by trading or defending against enemies.

The action dancing should only be possible together with another agent. By experiencing dancing as something joyful, the agents should try to re-experience it as often as possible. Nevertheless, the agent should not forget to search and consume energy sources. Thus, a learning process has to be initiated, training the agent not to search for pleasure too much.

Next to strong social ties due to the experienced collaborative joy, this use-case enforces the decision unit to deal with the trade-off between joy and survival (in contrast to the trade-off between pain and survival from the use-cases above).

Use-Case 10 — Reproduction

Another type of interaction between two agents is reproduction. By introduction of the action mating, they can generate offspring. While the motivation for an ARSIN agent to reproduce is based in its sexual drives (see Section 3.3), the implications for the agent can be modeled in different ways.

If the research interest is within large groups and their evolvement — comparable to genetic programming — the task for the individual agents is completed after the offspring is produced. Another possibility is to simulate upbringing. Thus, the offspring cannot survive on its own. The parents have to provide food and shelter. An extension of this scenario is to introduce education. Now, the parents have to teach and enforce social rules.

The eleven use-cases described above are defining the features which the artificial life simulator has to have implemented. Due to the fact that each feature is more or less dependent on the previous ones, the list also gives a development road map.

As the focus of this thesis lies within the interaction between the body and the psychic instances Id and Ego, only use-case 0 and parts of use-case 2 are of interest. Although the simulation platform described in the next section is designed with all eleven use-cases in mind, not every part is implemented in the current ARSIN World implementation ARS implementation number 11 (ARSi11). However, the important parts for the experiments described in Chapter 5 are implemented.

4.3 Platform ARSIN World

A platform is a software framework which makes it possible to execute a piece of software. In the context of this work, the platform is an Artificial Life (A-Life) simulator where different control architectures can be tested. The definition of A-Life coined by Langton is:

> *Artificial Life is a field of study devoted to understanding life by attempting to abstract the fundamental dynamical principles underlying biological phenomena, and recreating these dynamics in other physical media — such as computers — making them accessible to new kinds of experimental manipulation and testing [Lan92, p. xiv].*

While this definition focuses on biological phenomena and emergence (cp. [Sip95, p. 5]), A-Life simulations are used for agent based models and evaluation of control architectures as well (see Section 2.5.2). Based on the principles listed in the definition, the testbed for the use-cases defined above is described in detail below.

4.3.1 Concept

The basic idea for this simulator is to create a world in which a special type of agents is put to test by exposing them to special setups. For this, the world has to offer an environment consisting of different objects and other agents. The objects range from pure obstacles and landmarks like a special pole or a wall to small stones which could be used as tools. A special type of object is energy source. Inspired by food like grass or bushes, these sources provide nutrition for the agents and can be removed from the world by consuming them. Some of them regrow, providing a constant source of food. The agents resemble something like animals. Equipped with more or less complex control architectures, they provide nutrition, are things to play with (like a pet), sources of danger (in case they are fearsome hunters), and other interaction possibilities. The special type of agents — named ARSIN[1] — is used for the control architectures which should be evaluated. Their body consists of various sensors, actuators, and internal mechanisms.

The implementation of the simulator is based on the development toolkit MASON version 13 [13] (see Section 2.5.1). The world is two-dimensional and projected onto the surface of a torus. Thus, the x-axis end points are connected, as well as the y-axis end points. This results in a ring-shaped world enabling the agents to move unbounded. As all objects and agents within the world are two-dimensional, a fully featured physics engine like ODE [14] cannot be used. These types of physics engines require a three-dimensional world. Thus, a simpler, 2D rigid body physics engine [15] developed for MASON is used.

---

[1] A single agent is called ARSIN, the plural of it is ARSINI. ARSINO refers to a single male agent and ARSINA to a single female agent.

Platform, Framework, and Decision Unit Implementation

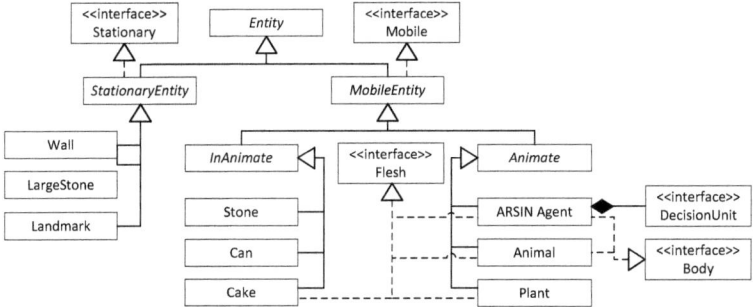

Figure 4.1: Entity hierarchy in UML

As shown in Figure 4.1[2], every object, animal, or agent is designed to be a specialization of the *Entity* class. The rigid body physics engine knows two types of objects: stationary and mobile ones. This is modeled by the first specializations of class *Entity*: *MobileEntity* and *StationaryEntity*. Each of them implements one of the two interfaces to the physics engine (<<interface>> Stationary, respectively <<interface>> Mobile). Stationary entities like Landmark, Wall, and LargeStone are of infinite weight and can never be moved throughout the whole simulation. This is different for mobile entities, their weight is limited and they have a friction coefficient. Objects of type *InAnimate* can be moved around, but they can never set any action. Objects of this group are not only things like Stone or Can. Additionally, energy sources which are removed from the world after they have been consumed like Cake belong to it. Although objects of type Plant cannot move by themselves nor can they be moved by others, they are a sub-class of *Animate*. The reasons for this design decision are that plants can regrow and are thus not inanimate, and that plants can be picked up and carried around which makes them mobile. If a plant can be carried depends on its weight and the abilities of the agent trying to perform this action. Thus, it makes no difference if very large — in fact stationary — entities like huge trees are part of mobile or stationary entities. The class Animal as well as the class ARSIN Agent implement the interface Body which is used to instantiate more or less rich bodies for the agents. Additionally, class ARSIN Agent implements the interface DecisionUnit. This provides the framework to use different control architectures for this entity. All entities which are consumable — independent of the consequence for the agent eating them — have to implement the <<interface>> Flesh.

Neither entities of type Plant nor of type Animal are modeled to be close to their counterparts in nature. Moreover, they are rough concepts used to guide further development. Plants refer to stationary objects which have a growth life cycle and can usually be consumed. Animals refer to mobile objects which move around, might need to consume food, and have a simple control attached.

---

[2] Details of all UML diagrams in this chapter are omitted to not occlude the diagrams. The used UML notations are explained in Appendix A.

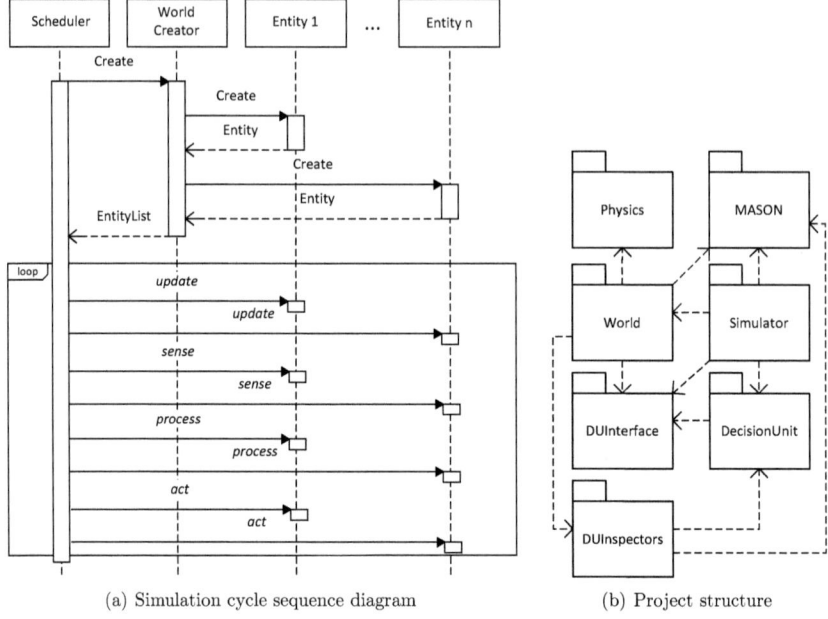

(a) Simulation cycle sequence diagram   (b) Project structure

Figure 4.2: UML diagrams of the ARSIN world simulator

Each specialization of class `Entity` has to implement the following four public methods: *update*, *sense*, *process*, and *act*. Within each simulation step, all four methods are called such that all entities do one of these sub-steps at the same time. The diagram shown in Figure 4.2(a)[3] depicts this control sequence. Before the first simulation cycle can be performed, the world and all its entities have to be created. The class `WorldCreator` is responsible for this act. Each entity has access to the list of all existing entities. This is necessary to perform the sensing step. Within the simulation step loop, the first action performed by the entities is *update*: Plants update their growth cycle information, animals "digest" consumed nutrition, and `ARSIN Agents` update their rich internal system. The next sub-step is execution of the method *sense*. All entities which have sensors update their world information by accessing data of entities which are within range of their various sensors. After sensing, all entities execute their *process* method which calls their control algorithms to decide which actions should be selected for execution. Finally, by calling the method *act*, all agents execute their actions and thereafter change the state of the world. The reason for dividing the simulation step into these four sub-steps is to ensure that all agents base their decisions on the same world state. This approach avoids favoritism of the agent which is first in the list of entities. Now, a conflict occurs when two agents decide

---

[3]The calls of the entity functions *update*, *sense*, *process*, and *act* are shown simplified.

to consume the same energy source at the same time. Without the sub-steps, the first in the list would consume it and the other one would be punished for trying to consume a non-existing source. This has negative impact for example in case of negative feedback learning. Another advantage of this approach is that within one sub-step, the method calls can be parallelized. For the entities, three of the four sub-steps take zero time. Only the last sub-step — acting — is perceived by the entities to take time as it alters the state of the world. Many of the entity types do not need any of the four methods. A stone has no internal states, no sensors, no actuators, and definitely no control architecture. The reason for the design decision to force all entities to implement these methods is to enable some programmable behavior for all entities. For example, a lighthouse added as a special type of landmark could turn its light on and off by implementing the code into method *process*.

The whole project is divided into seven sub-projects (see Figure 4.2(b)[4]). The reason for this design decision is to keep the various sub-projects as independent from each other as possible. The control architectures which are part of sub-project `DecisionUnit` are totally independent from the multi-agent framework in sub-project `MASON`. The main sub-project is `Simulator`. It is responsible for world creation and contains the scheduler described above. Each entity is created with its optional decision unit. How an entity is defined in detail is implemented in sub-project `World`. It contains things like the sensors, the bodies, interaction possibilities, and utilizes the two interfaces to the physics engine provided by `Physics`. In sub-project `DUInterface`, common classes needed for the decision unit framework are implemented. MASON provides several inspectors to view internal states of the agents. Body and entity related inspectors are stored in `World`. The ones necessary to view internal states of a decision unit are stored in `DUInspectors`. With this design, all three main parts of the simulation — the multi-agent simulation framework, the ARSIN world, and the decision units — can be exchange without the need of changing much in the other sub-projects.

Each parameter of an entity and all other parameters of the simulation can be configured using external config files. This enables to generate different setups for the use-cases and to test the influence of various parameters on the personality of the `ARSIN Agents`.

After this rough overview of the ARSIN world simulation, the three types of mobile and animate entities are described in more detail in the next two subsections.

4.3.2 Animals, Plants, and Energy Sources

Alternatively to the categorization of the entities given by the class hierarchy depicted in Figure 4.1, the entities can be divided into "part of food cycle" and "not part of it." Stones, landmarks, and cans are definitely not edible and thus part of the latter group. All entities which implement the `Flesh` interface are part of the first group.

Animate entities like animals and plants as well as inanimate entities like cakes can be consumed. The reason why food is used equivalent with energy source in this work is in

---

[4]Details are omitted not to occlude the diagram. The sub-project at the origin of an arrow accesses classes which are contained by the sub-project the arrow points at.

the nature of keeping the A-Life simulation as open as possible. Thus, an electric power recharge station would be modeled similarly to a plant. A special nutrition type would have to be added which is only available at this station. All this is done by implementing the `Flesh` interface. It contains one method which returns two values: First, a list of the different nutrition fractions per unit the flesh is made of. Second, the amount of flesh withdrawn from the entity is returned. Thus if entity A tries to consume entity B, "flesh" or nutrition is removed from B and added to the "stomach" of A. If the retrieved nutrition is nourishing or poisonous has to be decided by the internal systems of entity A.

The fate of entity B in case all of its flesh is removed has to be decided by the controller of entity B. Within the update phase of a simulation step, entities can define what happens to their "flesh." In case of animals, the "wound" generated by the missing "flesh" could heal; plants could regrow their "flesh." Another possibility could be that they "die."

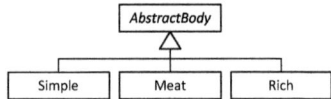

Figure 4.3: Different bodies for entities in UML

The entity types `Animal` and `ARSIN Agent` implement the interface `Body`. Figure 4.3 shows the list of available bodies which can be used with this interface. All three are specializations of the abstract class ***AbstractBody***. The body of type `Meat` consists only of "flesh." It is used for special purpose entities which do not need any further sensors and actuators or bypass the regular interfaces to the MASON framework. The `Simple` body contains some sensors and actuators to enable animals to interact with the environment. The internal systems available with the third body type are bypassed by a very simple energy system. If fitting food is consumed, energy is increased. If not or if injured, energy is reduced. In case the energy level reaches zero, the entity dies. The third type—class `Rich`—consists of an internal system as well as sensors and actuators for the internal system and the environment. This body is explained in the next section in more detail.

The simple body is capable of performing five actions, has five external, and two internal sensors. The external sensors are:

Acoustic: Sounds emitted by entities within a predefined distance are perceived by this sensor. Additionally, depending on the distance details can be omitted. For example, far away sounds cannot be deciphered, only the information that a noise occurred is perceived.

Bump: The force and the body part which has been hit by another entity are perceived.

Eatable Area: Right in front of the agent is a small area. Entities which are within it can be eaten. This sensor returns a list of entities within its borders.

Olfactoric: An entity can smell the presence of other entities. The closer they are, the more intense they smell. Odors of one type are added to a single value. Thus, depending on the result of the olfactory sensor alone the exact number of nearby entities of one type cannot be determined.

Vision: This sensor returns information on all entities which are within the field-of-view. At the current stage of implementation, no difference between hidden and non-hidden entities is made. Similarly to the acoustic sensor, the amount of information received decreases with the distance of the observed entity.

The second group of sensors perceives information from inner body processes like available energy. The simple body contains two internal sensors:

Energy: The available energy of the entity is returned by this sensor.
Energy Consumption: Returns the rate at which the energy is reduced by the performed actions.

Every action performed costs energy. Even if no action is executed, "life" itself has a need for energy. Each action can be executed at different intensities resulting in different energy demands. A detailed explanation of the action command system in the simulator can be found at [Doe09]. The five actions which can be executed by the simple body are:

Move: Move forward or backward with a given force. The stronger the force, the faster the entity moves. The resulting speed depends on the floor friction and on the entities' own weight. As long as the applied force is stronger than the counter force defined by the friction and the weight, the entity moves. If no or not enough force is applied, the entity stops after a while. The energy demand is directly proportional to the applied force.
Turn: This actuator operates similarly to the move actuator. As long as enough force is applied, the entity turns left or right. Again, the energy demand is directly proportional to the applied force.
Eat: Consume an energy source which is located within the range defined by the eatable area sensor. The eat action's energy demand is a constant value withdrawn from the available energy as long as it is performed.
Attack Bite: This is the first of the two aggressive actions available. Before a prey can be consumed it has to be hunted down. Or, nearby enemies can be bitten to either drive them off or to even kill them. To bite an entity it has to be within the eatable area. In the current implementation, the bite action's energy demand is constant for each bite performed.
Attack Lightning: This is a long-range weapon. It can be used to attack prey or enemies that are within sight. Other than the bite attack, the strength of a lightning attack can be controlled. The energy demand is directly proportional to the strength of the emitted lightning strike.

Next the ARSIN agent is described. It differs from the entities already introduced as so far that more sensors and actuators are available and that the body contains rich internal systems.

4.3.3 ARSIN Agent

The ARSIN Agent is an entity which offers the most internal systems, sensors, and actuators in ARSIN world. It resembles the "vehicle" to test various AGI control architectures in this simulator. Figure 4.4 shows the four internal components which are introduced with the rich body: IntraBodySystem, ReflexSystem, InterBodyWorldSystem, and InternalSystem. The ReflexSystem is executed during *process* phase, while the other three are executed during *update* phase. Functionality provided by InterBodyWorldSystem is invoked by external functions asynchronously.

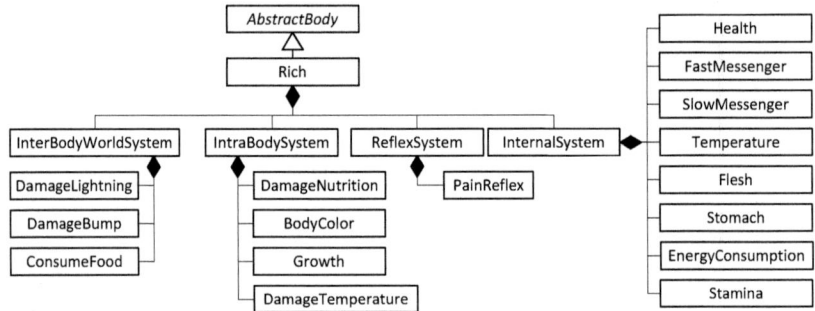

Figure 4.4: Components of the rich body in UML

The ReflexSystem deals with instant, bodily reactions to sensor stimuli. For example, if the agent is bumped and the force inflicted is strong enough to be perceived as painful, a sound meaning "ouch" could be emitted (implemented in class PainReflex).

Class InternalSystem operates as façade for all systems which deal with body internal concepts like digestion, communication between internal systems, and health. Stomach processes consumed food and calculates the potentially available energy. From this potential energy, EnergyConsumption withdraws the amount of energy needed to perform all actions and to operate all internal systems. Analogous to the energy demand of the actuators described in the previous subsection, internal systems need energy to operate too. All these elements register their current energy demand in EnergyConsumption. A second type of energy resource is stamina. Each action which withdraws energy needs also stamina. Class Stamina processes these demands. As long as sufficient stamina is available, all actions can be executed. Otherwise, the agent has to rest. Stamina restores itself at a configurable rate. Usually, stamina is much faster exhausted and refilled than energy. Flesh defines which nutrition the agent is built of and its basic weight. The total weight is the sum of nutrition units stored undigested in the stomach and the weight of the flesh. The agent has a body temperature which is controlled by Temperature. Depending on the outer temperature, the activity rate, and the health condition, the temperature is lowered or raised. Two different types of communication channels are implemented in the rich agent's body: SlowMessenger and FastMessenger. The channel SlowMessenger is inspired by hormones. Several sources can emit a hormone which results in an increased aim value. The measurable value of the slow messenger is increased to this value fast. A slow decay rate lets the value converge towards zero. The resulting behavior is that for example several internal systems can emit the slow messenger signal A and the internal sensor receives the current value. Thus, the control architecture cannot tell which source has emitted how much of this messenger and the effect of the emitting is present for some time. This is different with messages generated by the `FastMessenger` channel. It is inspired by the human nervous system. A distinct channel connects the emitter directly with the receiver. The emitted value exists as long as the source produces it. `Health` stores the information on the body integrity of the agent. In its simplest implementation, `Health` consists of a single value where *1* equals full health and *0* equals death. The health of the agent is influenced by external causes like being bumped or attacked as well as internal causes like poisonous food or a too high temperature.

These intra body interactions between different internal systems and the causes of external events like being attacked are processed by `IntraBodySystem`. In case of poisonous food, class `DamageNutrition` determines the severity of the poisoning. Possible results range from higher body temperature, color change, pain originating in the stomach to reduction of health. Another body related cause for health problems is a too high or too low body temperature. This is done by `DamageTemperature`. The task of `BodyColor` is to adapt the skin color of the agent to various internal states like health, temperature, and activity. In case the agent should have the ability to grow with time, this is done by `Growth`. It withdraws energy and nutrition from `Stomach` and adds them to `Flesh` and updates the MASON shape of the agent.

The last of the four systems introduced is `InterBodyWorldSystem`. It consists of the three components `DamageBite`, `DamageLightning`, and `ConsumeFood`. The first two respond to attacks by other entities and reduce health and add pain messages to the fast message system. The third one is invoked by another entity (entity A) in case it tries to eat this agent (entity B). If successful, the weight stored in B's `Flesh` is reduced and the agent A's stomach is increased by the corresponding amount. If B is still alive, pain and health reduction is performed similarly to the other two damage functions.

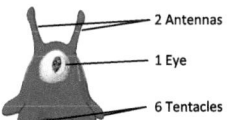

Figure 4.5: ARSIN agent

Figure 4.5 shows the shape of the ARSIN agent. This alien form has been chosen deliberately. As explained in Section 1.5, the body of the agent is only loosely inspired by nature and the human body. To avoid the trap of trying to emulate the human body as precisely as possible — which is not the aim of this research — a body shape not existing in nature has been chosen. It consists of a torso with six tentacles attached. They can be used for movement and for object manipulation. Further, the body consists of two antennas and a single eye. Every other aspect like ears or internal systems is not visible from the outside.

Additionally to the sensors and actuators of the simple body described previously, the rich body introduces several new internal and external sensors as well as possible actions. The eight added internal sensors are:

Health: This sensor returns a value denoting the state of health the agent is in.

Fast Messenger: It generates a list of all currently emitted fast messenger signals. Each entry consists of the signal's source and its intensity. Not active sources have no corresponding entry in this list.

Slow Messenger: The list generated by this sensor contains all defined slow messenger types independent of their current value. For each type only its measured amount is listed.

Stamina: It returns a value corresponding to the available stamina as stored in the `Stamina` system.

Heart Beat: This one is linked to the `Stamina` system too. Other than the stamina sensor, this sensor returns a representation of the stamina reduction in the last step. Thus, in case of high activity of the agent and the resulting fast reduction of the available stamina, a high heart beat value is returned.

Stomach: This sensor returns the aggregated value of the available potential energy resembled by the various nutrition types and their amount stored in the stomach. The non-availability of an important nutrition has an above average impact on the resulting value.

Stomach Tension: It returns the normalized amount of nutrition units stored in the stomach. If a lot of units are in the stomach a high tension value is returned. This is independent of the case that a particular nutrition type is missing.

Temperature: A representation of the current body temperature is returned by this sensor.

Three additional external sensors are introduced. They enable feedback on the movement commands and add the sensing abilities needed for the below added manipulation actions.

Acceleration: This sensor returns the direction and the forces of the last position change.

Manipulateable Area: Analogous to the eatable area sensor, this sensor is needed for the agent to detect which objects can be manipulated.

Tactile: The surface condition of the floor and of entities within the manipulation area can be perceived with this sensor.

Next to the five basic actions which allow the agent to roam the world and survive in it, several interactions are introduced with the rich body. Two different types of interaction groups exist: interaction with entities and interaction with other agents. Three actions related to the introduced internal systems are added too.

Say: This action enables the agent to transmit symbols to other agents in the vicinity. Each symbol equals a concept like "I need help against an enemy." Thus, this concept bypasses language with its syntax and grammar. The energy consumed by execution of this action is proportional to the loudness used. Nevertheless, the resulting amount is still very low compared to the energy demand by the action move.

Kiss: A social interaction between two ARSIN agents. A small fraction of energy is needed for the execution of this action.

Sleep: Sets the agent to rest mode. Sensor sensitivity is turned down and no other actions are executed. This results in a low energy demand and can be used to regain stamina. Thus, execution of this action does not need additional energy. Although, internal systems like the stomach still need energy during sleep.

Excrete: Gets rid of indigestible nutrition stored in the stomach and produces a corresponding entity in the world. Execution of this action needs a small amount of energy.

Body Color: Change the color of the agent's skin. The values for red, green, and blue can be changed independently. This action needs no energy to be performed.

Facial Expression: Change the facial expression of the agent. The parts which can be changed by this action are the positions of the antennas, the size of the eye's pupil, and the shape of the pupil. To change the facial expression, only a small fraction of energy is needed.

Pick Up: This action allows the agent to manipulate entities. Depending on the weight of the entity and the strength of the agent, all mobile entities can be carried. Only objects within the manipulateable area can be picked up and only one object can be carried. The necessary energy to perform this action depends on the weight of the to be lifted entity. Once an entity is carried, additional energy to keep it is necessary each step.

Drop: This is the inversion action of "pick up." This action does not need any energy to be performed.

To Inventory: If the agent is equipped with an inventory, currently picked up entities can be moved to it (if there is still room left). The action itself does not consume any energy, and once an object is within the inventory less energy is needed to carry it.

From Inventory: This is the inversion action of "to inventory." It can be executed only if no other object is carried. This action does not need any energy to be performed. However, more energy is needed to carry the object retrieved from the inventory.

Cultivate: Currently carried plants can be cultivated. This special version of drop attaches the plant with the surface and — if everything worked as planned — the plant starts to grow. As this action is more complicated than just putting an object to the ground, it needs some energy to execute it.

The result of the introduction of the above listed internal systems, additional sensors, and more possible actions is an agent platform capable of acting within complex and social environments. The system is designed to be open to additional components. Thus, additional components can be added to the A-Life simulation to meet new requirements in case the focus is put to one of the later use-cases described in Section 4.2. The tools to measure and observe the internal components are introduced in the next subsection.

4.3.4 Inspectors

MASON offers a variety of inspectors to probe the internal states of the agent of interest. These inspectors can be used to view vital relevant information on each agent/entity during a simulation run. In combination with the graph drawing tool JGraphx [16], the following set of probes for bodily states have been implemented into the ARSIN world simulator:

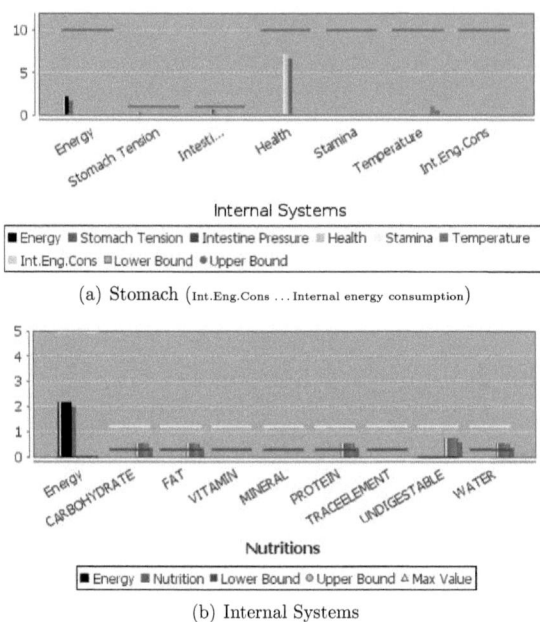

(a) Stomach (Int.Eng.Cons ... Internal energy consumption)

(b) Internal Systems

Figure 4.6: Body Inspectors

Attributes: This probe displays body attributes like facial expression and body color.
Fast Messengers: It displays the list of the currently active fast message entries. Each entry consists of the triple: Source, destination, and intensity.
Flesh: The current composition of the agent's flesh as described above.
Internal Energy Consumption: This one displays a detailed list of the total energy consumption and the energy consumption for each component. The last ten steps are listed in full detail. Older steps are grouped and their average value is shown. This is an important tool to balance the energy demand of the various components.
Slow Messengers: It displays a time line graph containing the values for all existing slow messengers.
Stomach: This inspector displays the various nutrition types the agent can process. A screenshot of this inspector is shown in Figure 4.6(a). All other nutrition types are

grouped to the column undigestible. The column on the left side depicts the potential energy available.

Internal Systems: If the state of an internal system like stomach, health, or stamina can be represented by a single value, it is shown in the internal systems inspector (see Figure 4.6(b)).

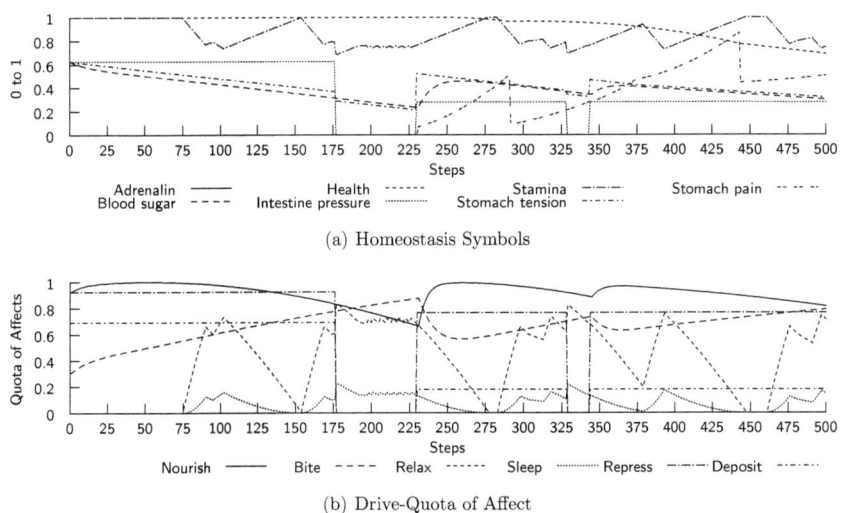

Figure 4.7: Decision Unit Inspectors

Next to these body state inspectors, special inspectors exist to probe the state of the various modules of the decision unit. They range from displaying the incoming sensor information, to the memory meshes processed in the current step, to the active wishes, and to a list of the last selected actions. The body state sensors are located in the project World, whereas the decision unit inspectors are located in the project DUInspectors.

Two decision unit related inspectors are shown exemplarily. The inspector for Neurosymbolization of needs (E2) is shown in Figure 4.7(a). This chart displays the change of the internal measures after they have been converted into processable symbols by the neurosymbolization. The y-axis is labeled with 0 to 1. All homeostatic values represent something different. Thus, a more detailed label would occlude the graph. Nevertheless, the intensity value of each symbol is normalized to the range 0 to 1 by E2.

The second inspector shown (Figure 4.7(b)) displays the results of Module Accumulation of affects for self-preservation drives (E5) for the simulation steps 0 to 500. In each step, the results from E2 are processed by the modules Generation of self-preservation drives (E3), Fusion of self-preservation drives (E4), and E5. After

E5, the homeostatic symbols have been converted to drives represented by their pairs of opposites plus the attached quota of affects.

The data shown in Figure 4.7(b) and Figure 4.7(a) is explained and discussed in the sections 5.3 and 5.4.

4.4 Decision Unit Framework

While the ARSIN world is the platform for the use-cases, the decision unit framework is the interface to the different control architectures which should be evaluated by these use-cases. This framework provides an abstraction of the whole ARSIN world and the body the decision unit should control. The sensor data and the actuator commands are passed through a temporal firewall. Thus, it is not possible to access anything else than the provided data from the decision unit. For example, direct access to objects from the simulator is prohibited. This eases the task of implementing several control architectures for the same setup by providing a well-defined interface with no side effects.

The decision unit framework is divided into two projects (cp. Figure 4.2(b)): DUInterface and Decision Unit. The first project resembles the temporal firewall and the interface between the body and the control architecture. The second project contains the implementations of the various control architectures.

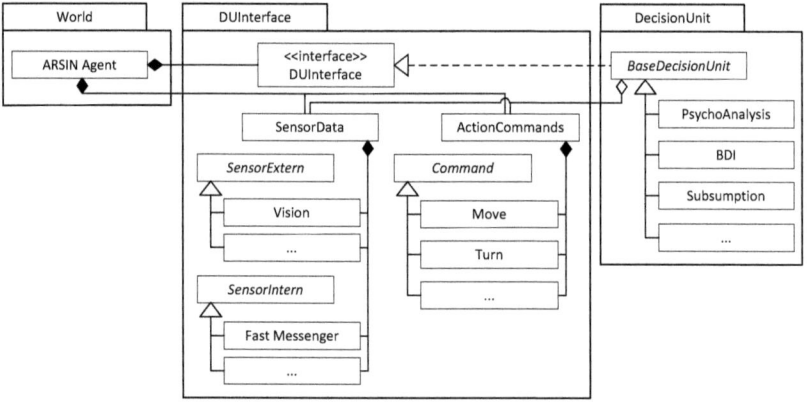

Figure 4.8: Decision unit framework

Figure 4.8 depicts the UML class diagram of the main classes and interfaces involved in the framework. The project frames are added to show the assignment of the classes to different projects. The abstract class *BaseDecisionUnit* needs two lists: the current sensor data and current actions. The first one is update by ARSIN Agent during the *sense* phase. The latter is updated at the end of the *process* phase. The actions in this list are then executed by ARSIN Agent during the *execute* phase. ARSIN Agent creates the instances of `SensorData` and `ActionCommands` and passes the references to *BaseDecisionUnit* through the interface `DUInterface`. Now both objects (`ARSIN Agent` and *BaseDecisionUnit*) work with the same instances of the above described lists. The specializations of the classes *SensorExtern*, *SensorIntern*, and *Commands* correspond with listed abilities of the simple and the rich bodies in Section 4.3.

The interface `DUInterface` provides two public methods: *update* and *process*. The first one tells the decision unit that the update of the sensor data has been finished. The second one starts the current iteration of the control loop — the processing of the sensor data and generation of the next actuator commands.

The three classes `PsychoAnalysis`, `BDI`, and `Subsumption` are implementations of the abstract class *BaseDecisionUnit*. Class `PsychoAnalysis` is the implementation of the model described in the previous chapter and will be explained in the next chapter. The other two are sample and reference implementations of existing Artificial Intelligence (AI) architectures. One is based on Brook's subsumption architecture [Bro86] and the other one is based on the Believe-Desire-Intention (BDI) model described by Bratman in [Bra87].

The setup chosen for the subsumption architecture is based on Toda's Fungus-Eater (cp. Section 2.5.2). The implementation of the `ARSIN Agent` is changed to fit the description of the Fungus Eater. They can sense and collect fungi and have a special sensor which shows them the direction to the base station. The control architecture is consisting of several layers as described by the subsumption architecture.

The BDI implementation utilizes the Jadex framework (see [PBL03]). In Jadex, the believes, desires, and intentions are stored in Extensible Markup Language (XML) based files and in Java code. A BDI interpreter applies them to the currently incoming sensor data and returns the resulting action commands. Thus, the class `BDI` is a wrapper which instantiates and operates the Jadex framework. The setup for testing and developing BDI related control architectures is a hunter/prey situation. Hunter and prey agents are equipped with BDI based controllers and have to survive as long as possible.

For the time being, no AGI reference implementation exists (see Section 2.1). To identify which model to choose and to produce a working implementation of it, is a project on its own and would exceed limitations of this thesis. In the next section, the implementation of the psychoanalytically inspired decision unit as described in Chapter 3 is discussed.

4.5 Psychoanalytically Inspired Decision Unit

The design for the framework implementation ARSi11 is straight forward. Each module in the final functional model (cp. Figure 3.11) has its corresponding class. Only one container that creates and processes the class instances exists. In the previous version — ARS implementation number 10 (ARSi10) — a hierarchical approach was used. Analogous to the top-down design, several layers of containers were introduced. For example, the psychic apparatus contained an instance of the class Id — which contained instances of several other classes again. This leads to an overloaded design. In the implementation the abstraction levels served only two purposes: Creating the sub levels and passing the data between the instances. These tasks can be served by a single container class without any loss of functionality. Moreover, the reduction of classes and interfaces involved adds clarity to the design.

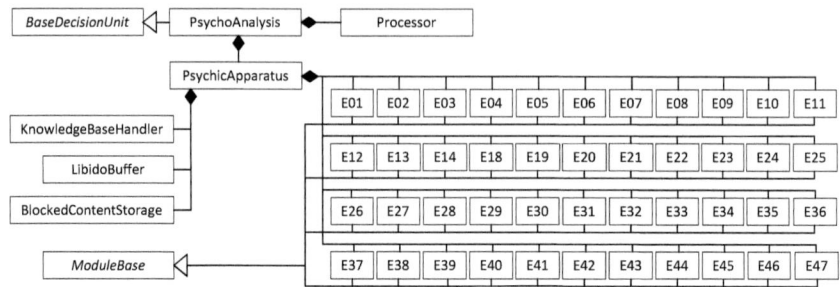

Figure 4.9: Design of the final functional model implementation in UML

Figure 4.9 sketches the principal design. Class `Psychoanalysis` — a specialization of the abstract class *BaseDecisionUnit* — has four purposes. First, the communication with the body via the decision unit interfaces is done before and after the data has been processed. Second, the class `PsychicApparatus` is created and with it all modules and memory related instances. Third, a processor is instantiated. Its task is to process all modules in the appropriate sequence. Finally, different versions of the psychoanalytically inspired decision unit can be instantiated by this class. Currently, ARSi10 and ARSi11 exist and can be used.

The information storage class `KnowledgeBaseHandler` is a façade class to the implementation of the psychoanalytically inspired memory described by Zeilinger in [ZPK10, pp. 88–109]. The class `LibidoBuffer` provides access to the libido buffer as described in Section 3.4.4. Analogous, `BlockedContentStorage` provides access to the special purpose memory which stores memory contents blocked by the defense mechanisms (see Section 3.4.4).

The 44 classes representing the functional modules (E01–E47[5]) are all derived from the abstract base class *ModuleBase*. It provides a structure which all module classes should implement. Each module class has to implement interfaces for sending and receiving data as defined by the interfaces in the final functional model. The methods for receiving data have to make a deep copy of the incoming objects and lists to avoid side effects. Each module class has to implement three different process methods: A dummy implementation which forwards the incoming data where appropriate. An empty data package is forwarded otherwise. A development version which is used during implementation and testing has to be added. The third process method contains the final version. If this method is present, its functionality is equivalent to its definition in Section 3.4. Using a configuration file, each class can be configured to use any of these three versions. This design decision helps for example examining changes of the model. Finally, sending is

---

[5]The full names of the classes are reduced to their unique identifier prefix to not occlude the diagram.

centralized by class *ModuleBase*. A module class has to implement all sending methods according to the included interfaces. These methods are called by send method which is triggered by the processor class described above. Upon creation, each module class is given reference pointers to the various data base classes (e.g. BlockedContentStorage or KnowlegdeBaseHandler) as necessary.

An important design decision is to add all functional modules to the composition list of Class PsychicApparatus. Although it can be argued that the classes representing modules assigned to the body — E01, E02, E10, E11, E12, E13, E31, E32, E39, and E40 — are not part of the psychic apparatus, they are deliberately included into it in ARSi11. As the simulator provides high-level symbolic information on the environment and the bodily systems and accepts high-level commands for actuator control, these classes are added for the sake of completeness in this implementation. For this reason, and to avoid unnecessary added levels of classes in the implementation, the body related classes are not put into a separate container class.

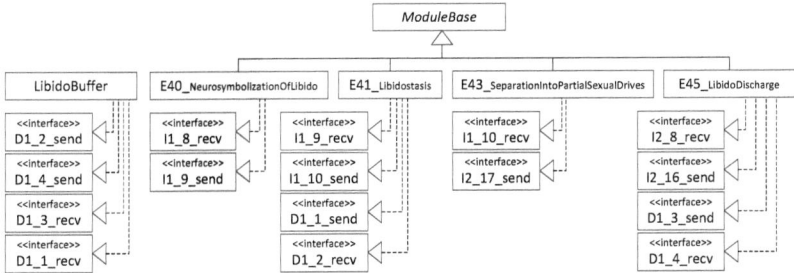

Figure 4.10: Selected seeking system related modules and their interfaces in UML

All module classes have been drawn without their interfaces in Figure 4.9. Due to the large number of classes and interfaces, the UML would be occluded by details and not be readable any more. In Figure 4.10, a subset of the module classes and their interfaces are shown. The shown concept is the same for all 44 classes. In Section 3.4.3, the Module Neurosymbolization of libido (E40) gets its data from Seeking system (libido source) (E39) via Interface I1.8 and sends the processed data to Module Libidostasis handler (E41) via Interface I1.9. The class corresponding to Module E40 — E40_NeurosymbolizationOfLibido — implements two interfaces: *I1_8_recv* and *I1_9_send*. According to the definition of Interface *I1_9_send*, a member method called *send_I1_9* has to be implemented. The task of this function is to call its counterpart — Method *recv_I1_9* in Class E41_Libidostasis as defined by the Interface *I1_9_recv* — and to pass on the data. As described above, the task of Method *recv_I1_9* is to make a deep copy of the incoming data and to store it until the Method *process* of Class E41_Libidostasis is called the next time. Analogous, the communication between Class E41_Libidostasis and E43_SeparationIntoPartialSexualDrives via Interface I1.10 is implemented. The same design is used to communicate between classes which control a buffer (e.g. Class LibidoBuffer) and the classes corresponding to functional modules (e.g. E41_Libidostasis and E45_LibidoDischarge).

143

Sequence 4.1 Processor sequence

Sensing
1. E01_SensorsMetabolism
2. E02_NeurosymbolizationOfNeeds
3. E10_SensorsEnvironment
4. E11_NeuroSymbolizationEnvironment
5. E12_SensorsBody
6. E13_NeuroSymbolizationBody
7. E39_SeekingSystem_LibidoSource
8. E40_NeurosymbolizationOfLibido

Self-preservation drive generation
9. E03_GenerationOfSelfPreservationDrives
10. E04_FusionOfSelfPreservationDrives
11. E05_AccumulationOfAffectsForSelfPreservationDrives
12. E38_PrimalRepressionForSelfPreservationDrives

Libido generation
13. E41_LibidostasisHandler
14. E43_SeparationIntoPartialSexualDrives
15. E42_AccumulationOfAffectsForSexualDrives
16. E44_PrimalRepressionForSexualDrives

Perception to memory and repression
17. E14_ExternalPerception
18. E46_FusionWithMemoryTraces
19. E37_PrimalRepressionForPerception
20. E35_EmersionOfRepressedContent
21. E45_LibidoDischargeHandler
22. E18_CompositionOfAffectsForPerception

Defense mechanisms
23. E07_InternalizedRulesHandler
24. E09_KnowledgeAboutReality_unconscious
25. E06_DefenseMechanismsForDrives
26. E19_DefenseMechanismsForPerception
27. E36_RepressionHandler

Primary to secondary process conversion
28. E08_ConversionToSecondaryProcessForDriveWishes
29. E21_ConversionToSecondaryProcessForPerception
30. E20_InnerPerception_Affects

External perception
31. E23_ExternalPerception_focused
32. E25_KnowledgeAboutReality_1
33. E24_RealityCheck_1

Decision making
34. E22_SocialRulesSelection
35. E26_DecisionMaking
36. E28_KnowledgeBase_StoredScenarios
37. E27_GenerationOfImaginaryActions

Secondary to primary process conversion
38. E47_ConversionToPrimaryProcess

Evaluation and pre-execution
39. E34_KnowledgeAboutReality_2
40. E33_RealityCheck_2
41. E29_EvaluationOfImaginaryActions
42. E30_MotilityControl

Acting
43. E31_NeuroDeSymbolizationActionCommands
44. E32_Actuators

The task of the class Processor is to call the classes E01 to E47 in a pre-defined order. In Sequence 4.1, this order is listed. Each entry represents a class and the call of its Method *process*. The steps of this execution sequence are arranged in eleven groups. Each group represents a part of the final functional model. For example, the five classes E6, E7, E9, E19, and E36 are forming the cluster "Defense mechanisms." The formed groups follow more or less the partition of the intermediate model (cp. Section 3.2). It differs in the modules which were introduced in the step from the intermediate to the final model.

The presented simulation platform ARSIN world with its ARSIN agent together with the framework to use different control architectures meets the requirements defined at the beginning of this chapter. Although not all parts are fully implemented yet — for example, reproduction and communication are missing — they provide an environment to evaluate the presented model with focus on the newly introduced functionalities as defined in Chapter 3. In the next chapter, the evaluation of the concepts with this simulator is executed.

> I believe there is no philosophical high-road in science, with epistemological signposts. No, we are in a jungle and find our way by trial and error, building our road behind us as we proceed.
>
> Max Born

5 Results

In Chapter 3, the final functional model is developed and discussed based on psychoanalysis in general and drive related concepts in particular. This is followed by an introduction of the approach to evaluate all aspects of the final functional model (see Chapter 4). This broad view is narrowed down to focus on the interplay of the Id with its body in this chapter. The concepts introduced and discussed in Section 3.3 have to be evaluated. Due to the basic research character of this work and its focus on the theoretical concepts, this evaluation has to be done using a proof-of-concept approach. Step by step, the function of each module of interest is analyzed and the impact on the whole model is discussed based on use-case 0. The other use-cases introduced in the previous chapter cannot be used currently. Defense mechanisms and the modules of the secondary processes are available in a basic development stage only. Thus, the performance of the model and the implementation on the other ten use-cases is of little significance for the time being. Next to the use-case related evaluation, the minimal model implementation based on Section 3.5 is analyzed. Finally, the implemented model is successfully integrated into a real robot and first impressions are discussed.

5.1 Environment Setup

Figure 5.1 shows the setup used for the experiments described. Elements present are an ARSIN agent, three carrots, two cakes, two stones, and two plants. The world is surrounded by a solid impenetrable wall.

Wall: A wall is a stationary entity that is an implementation of the abstract class *StationaryEntity* (cp. Figure 4.1). Thus, it cannot be moved and no interaction with the wall is possible. If an agent moves into the wall, it is reflected. Additionally, the health of the agent might be reduced and the accident might be experienced as a painful event by the agent.

Stone: Other than a wall, a stone is mobile and thus a descendant of the abstract class *MobileEntity*. A stone is an inanimate entity — reflected by its parent class

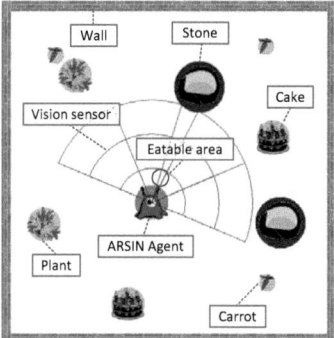

Figure 5.1: Simulation setup

InAnimate — and cannot be consumed. Any attempt to bite or swallow a stone results in pain and injury. If the act of moving into a stone results in pain and injury too, depends on the weight ratio between agent and stone (next to the impact speed).

Cake: The first edible entity in this list is the cake. Similar to the stone, it is an inanimate entity but the class representing a cake implements `<<interface>> Flesh` next to being a descendant of `MobileEntity`. This interface provides methods to eat the cake bite by bite. When the cake is totally consumed, it is removed from the simulation. The nutrition types the flesh of a cake is built of are: Fat, carbohydrate, water, protein, and undigestible[1].

Plant: A plant is of type `Animate` and implements `<<interface>> Flesh`. The plant designed for this work consists mainly of water and of undigestible parts. Minor fractions of the nutrition types fat, carbohydrate, and vitamin are present too. In principle, a plant can be designed to grow or even regrow but this entity is configured to behave similar to a cake. As soon as it has been consumed totally, it is removed from the simulation.

Carrot: This is a special type of plant that regrows. After all of its flesh has been consumed the state of the carrot changes. Instead of orange, it is colored gray and cannot be consumed for a while. After this regrow phase, the color changes back to orange and the flesh of the carrot can be eaten again. The nutrition types provided by a carrot are fat, carbohydrate, water, and undigestable.

ARSIN agent: This is the implementation of the ARSIN agent described in Section 4.3.3. The applied decision unit is the one described in Section 4.5. Thus, it is an embodied autonomous agent equipped with a decision unit inspired by psychoanalysis. It plays the active part in the experiments and is the object of interest. All presented charts, internal states, or interpretations refer to the performance of this agent. Two external

---

[1] Please note that the current implementation of ARSIN world does not assign any special attributes to the nutrition types. Instead of using names like fat or water, abstract labels like A or B could have been used. Nevertheless, to support readability of the text and the results, labels existing in a real body have been used.

sensors are used in the experiments:

Vision sensor: The halved circles represent the three different ranges the vision sensor can differentiate (near, medium, and far). The tangential rays show the differentiation of the vision sensor in objects located at the center, near left, near right, far left, and far right. Thus, all objects within the range of this vision sensor are grouped to fifteen locations. For example, the stone that touches the largest arc is assigned to the location center/far.

Eatable area: *Iff* there is a single, eatable entity within this circle, the agent can decide to eat it.

From the list of actions described in the sections 4.3.2 and 4.3.3 the following subset is utilized: Move forward, turn left, turn right, eat, sleep, and excrete. The body of the ARSIN agent has flesh too. The nutrition types it consists of are: fat, water, carbohydrate, protein, vitamin, and undigestable. If more than one ARSIN agent is present, cannibalism would be possible (see the results section in [Zei10]).

Each entity has a wide range of customizable properties. In Table 5.1, a basic set of these properties is given. The first three attributes can be perceived by the vision sensor. When the agent has for example a wall in range, the information that a black wall of rectangular shape with a width of ten pixels is returned. All size measures are given in pixel in the ARSIN world simulator. The length depends on the actual length of the wall. The weight influences the movement characteristics like how much energy is needed for moving at a certain velocity. Weight is measured in units; no real world equivalent exists. The body types as well as mobile and stationary are explained in the previous chapter. The specialty refers to configurable things like "regrow after being consumed" or "which type of decision unit is used."

Table 5.1: Properties of the entities
px ... pixel

	Color	Shape	Size	Weight	Body	Mobile	Specialty
Wall	Black	Rectangle	Width: 10 px	∞	Simple	No	—
Stone	Gray	Circle	ø15 px	500 units	Simple	Yes	—
Cake	Pink	Circle	ø10 px	100 units	Meat	Yes	—
Plant	Orange	Circle	ø10 px	200 units	Meat	Yes	—
Carrot	Orange	Circle	ø5 px	50 units	Meat	Yes	Regrows
ARSIN	Green	Circle	ø10 px	150 units	Complex	Yes	Psychoanalytical inspired decision unit

The ARSIN agent is equipped with a stomach that can process different types of nutrition. The five types that contribute to the potentially available energy are: Water, fat, carbohydrate, protein, and vitamin. As simplification, all five are of equal importance and contribute with the same amount to the energy conversion process. All nutrition types which are not in this list are attributed to the undigestable type. As the nutrition type undigestable is not used for digestion, the stored amount of it has to be deposited time after time. If not, the overfilled intestines are perceived as being painful.

Table 5.2: Nutrition types provided by edible entities per bite

	Undigestable	Water	Fat	Carbohydrate	Protein	Vitamin
Cake	11.1%	5.6%	27.8%	27.8%	27.8%	0.0%
Plant	70.4%	14.1%	7.0%	7.0%	0.7%	0.7%
Carrot	11.1%	55.6%	0.0%	11.1%	0.0%	22.2%
ARSIN	16.0%	40.0%	20.0%	20.0%	2.0%	2.0%

The nutrition type distribution for a bite of an edible entity is given in Table 5.2. Each time the ARSIN agents bites a bit of a cake, a plant, a carrot, or another ARSIN agent, it retrieves ten units of flesh. In case of a cake, this chunk of flesh consists of 11.1% undigestible parts, 5.6% water, 27.8% fat, 27.8% carbohydrate, and 27.8% protein. The cake contains no vitamins. As the ARSIN agent's stomach needs vitamins too, this nutrition has to be supplemented by eating for example a carrot. It provides a lot of water and vitamins, some carbohydrate, and no fat or protein. Two entities provide the full range of nutrition types: Plant and ARSIN agent. The plant is easy to consume but provides only small amounts of proteins and vitamins. A further problem of eating a plant is the high fraction of undigestable parts. Thus, when eating a lot of plants, the agent has to find a place to deposit its excrements. The flesh of the ARSIN agent provides a better distribution of the nutrition types. Nevertheless, killing and eating another agent is dangerous and might be socially inacceptable.

Of the many internal systems of an ARSIN agent described in Section 4.3.3 the following three are of special interest for the performed experiments:

Stamina: This internal system defines how much activity an agent can show in one time step. Each action performed does not only consume energy which is provided by digestion of the stomach content but also stamina. Stamina is depleted much faster than the stomach contents. It is refilled at a constant rate each step. Thus, in times of high activity, stamina is reduced; in times of low activity stamina is regained. In case of no stamina available, no action is executed.

Slow messenger blood sugar: The available energy is communicated through the slow messenger blood sugar. The value of this messenger is direct proportional to the average amount of stored nutrition types in the stomach. Other than with stamina, blood sugar decreases in case of no activity too. Living and thinking do need energy but not stamina. Thus, resting too much can cause the agent to starve to death — not enough energy causes the agent's health to decrease. Even if the agent is not dying due to energy shortage, actions cannot be performed if no energy is left. To prevent this case to happen too often, the corresponding drive should be very strong at an early point in time.

Fast messenger intestine pressure: As explained above, eating undigestable food leads to an overfilled stomach. The intestine pressure is a measure indirect proportional to the available space. The agent can reduce this tension by depositing its excrements. Different to stamina and blood sugar, too high intestine pressure does not result in death or not being able to perform an action. Nevertheless, it is perceived as a painful experience by the decision unit.

The configuration file storing all possible tuning parameters of the ARSIN agent's body consists of roughly 400 entries. As an example, the parameters for the stamina system are shown:

```
body.internal.stamina.change=0.005
body.internal.stamina.content=1
body.internal.stamina.maxcontent=1
```

The first line defines that the stamina is regained at a rate of 0.005 per step. The next line defines that the agent's start value for its stamina is 1. This is according to the third line (maxcontent=1) the maximum value possible. If a value greater than 1 is set, it is reset to 1.

Other customizable body parameters include all internal systems like which nutrition can be used by the stomach, what are the slow messengers and what are their decay rates. Further, all sensors can be turned off and on and their parameters can be set as well. The same accounts for the actuators.

The psychoanalytically inspired decision unit has much less parameter lines in its configuration file. It consists of tunable personality parameters. For example, the drive splitter discussed in Section 3.3.2 can be customized for each pair of opposites. The contents of the memory are defined in a separate file (see [Zei10, pp. 97–102]). It is created with the ontology editor protégé [17]. A detailed discussion of the stored memory entries and existing rules and bans would exceed the scope of this work and is for the shown proof-of-concept experiments unnecessary. Most of the stored entries are related to Ego and Superego functionalities, while the discussed parts of the model belong to the Id. Whenever necessary, the used data from the knowledge base is introduced.

The described body and world fulfill the statements defined in Section 4.1. Hence, the described setup is suitable for the use-cases defined in Section 4.2.

5.2 Use-Case 0 Revisited

In Section 4.2 a list of eleven use-cases is given. As argued at the end of this section, only use-case 0 and use-case 2 are of potential interest for this evaluation. Both deal with Id functions and the reaction of the body to consumed food. The main difference is that use-case 2 has a higher demand regarding deliberation capabilities than use-case 0. The current version of the model implementation offers limited deliberation capabilities only. The creation of more powerful secondary process modules has to be delegated to future theses. For the time being, only the demands of use-case 0 are met. Thereafter, use-case 0 "The lonely life of a hungry ARSIN" is used in the following sections.

The use-case 0 defines that the world has to be populated by one ARSIN agent and different types of food (cp. Figure 5.1). The tested abilities are that hunger should be satisfied whenever necessary, the bowels should be emptied only if no food is close by, and that the agent should rest in case of exhaustion.

To support the evaluation of these three abilities, basic decision making abilities are provided by the secondary process module E26. The types of decision that can be made are: Consume a certain piece of food that is within sensor range, excrete at the current position, rest at the current position, seek the world for better positions for excretion, and seek for food. Module **Generation of imaginary actions (E27)** creates an action plan for the selected decision. For example, if a carrot is visible in the far left/medium segment of the vision sensor, the plan would consist of the steps: Turn left, move forward, and eat carrot. Module **Motility control (E30)** executes the action plan.

For this setup, the perception has been configured to work without errors and all entities that populate the world are well known. Thus, all entities that are within sensor range are perceived correctly and no false positives are added. The output of Module E35 is an unbiased list of the current perception.

What is to be shown is that the self-preservation drive representations are generated according to the model. The output of **Primal repression for self-preservation drives (E38)** has to be justified in relation of the incoming homeostatic values in Module **Homeostasis (E1)**. The drive representations and their attached quota of affects have to influence decision making such that the most urgent drive is most likely to be the one selected for fulfillment.

The second part that has to be shown is the proof-of-concept of the libido system. This requires a two-folded approach. First, the generation of libido and the corresponding drive representations has to be shown. Second, the interplay between integration of libido in Module E39 and discharge of libido in Module **Libido discharge handler (E45)** has to be shown.

The evaluation of these three sub-systems has to be done in a step by step approach. For a given input set, for all involved modules, the resulting outputs should be shown and discussed.

Finally, the impacts of the three sub-systems on decision making and their interplay should be discussed. The questions to be answered are: Has libido discharge influence on the decisions made by Module E26? Can a very intense drive demand change decisions usually made? How does the system react in case of exhaustion?

This proof-of-concept has succeeded if the three step by step analyses and the overall model impact analysis showed that the resulting behavior can be explained by the model.

5.3 Step by Step

The three main innovations in this work are to be found in the self-preservation drive generation, in the sexual drive generation, and in the introduction of libido (cp. Section 3.3 and Section 3.4.2). In the following these three subsystems are discussed step by step. It provides insights in how the modules are connected and how the result is influenced by them.

5.3.1 Self-Preservation System

The task of the self-preservation system is to transform bodily demands into drive representations which bias decision making towards the satisfaction of these bodily needs. In Figure 5.2, the involved modules and their interfaces are shown. The six modules are Homeostasis (E1), Neurosymbolization of needs (E2), Generation of self-preservation drives (E3), Fusion of self-preservation drives (E4), Accumulation of affects for self-preservation drives (E5), and Primal repression for self-preservation drives (E38). The first five modules existed in the previous version of the model, while the sixth one is new. In the following, each module's function is described with the help of the incoming and outgoing data. This process is started with an arbitrary set of values incoming to Module E1.

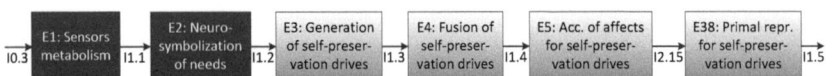

Figure 5.2: Excerpt of the final functional model — the self-preservation system

Module E1 receives the following list of raw data from the body via Interface I0.3: Blood sugar 64.8%, health 99.9%, intestine pressure 68.1%, stamina 76.0%, and stomach tension 68.1%. The values can range from 0% to 100%. Blood sugar 64.8% means that the current level of blood sugar is 0.658 of the maximum blood sugar value possible. The same accounts for the other four values. Blood sugar is a measure for the total available energy. Health defines the body integrity. If at 100%, the agent's body is at full health and unharmed. The lower the value drops, the more the body is injured and malfunctioning. A health of 0% equals death. Intestine pressure measures how much undigestible nutrition is stored. Currently, with 68.1% of the maximum amount the storage of undigestable nutrition is filled well but not full. Stamina is the measure how much activity the agent can develop in the next few steps (see explanation in Section 5.1). With more than 75% of stamina available, the agent is not limited in its activity at present. Stomach tension operates similarly to intestine pressure. It gives the total amount of stored nutrition in respect of the maximum amount. Thus, undigestable nutrition is part of this measure too. Health and stomach tension are listed to show that the complex body provides several different internal systems. They are not needed for use-case 0. Hence, they are left out further on.

The data flow over time of the values described above is shown in Figure 5.3(a). At step 0, the agent is at full health and rested (health=1 and stamina=1). Blood sugar defines

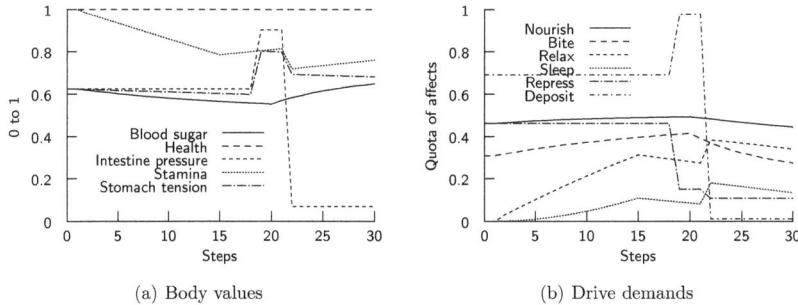

(a) Body values (b) Drive demands

Figure 5.3: Data flow over time (steps 0 to 30)

that the stomach is filled more than 60%. The same accounts for the undigestible nutrition storage. In this example, a cake is placed in front of the agent. With nothing else to do, the agent moves slowly towards the cake which results in stamina reduction between step 1 and 15. Movement and life itself need energy which is withdrawn from the stomach. Thus, the blood sugar level drops. With "digestion" of some of the nutrition stored, the content of the stomach is reduced which leads to a reduced stomach tension. After 20 steps, the blood sugar level drops below a threshold and the agent consequently eats a piece of the cake. The immediate results of this action are increased stomach tension and increased intestine pressure. "Digestion" takes some time. Thereafter, blood sugar starts to increase one step later and reaches its peak value twelve steps after eating the cake. In step 21, the most urging demand is the intestine pressure. Thus, the agent decides to empty its intestines. As result, the intestine pressure drops down to below 10%. The stomach contains several type of nutrition with undigestable being only one of them. Hence, stomach tension drops too but at a much lower rate. During the remaining eight steps, the agent is resting or moving slowly around.

The list of these normalized values is forwarded to Module E2 via Interface I1.1. The task of this module is to convert the raw data from Module E1 into symbols that can be processed by the following modules. For the time being, a simple, straight forward approach is sufficient. Each symbol consists of a label denoting the type (e.g. blood sugar) and a numeric value equal to the one received. This may change in future versions of the implementation.

The next module in line is Module E3. The list of symbols received via Interface I1.2 is used to generate drive representations in the next modules. This module creates a memory trace for each drive and defines the drive demand each bodily source produces. Based on the drive demand, the fitting quota of affects will be calculated in one of the following modules. For the following three homeostatic values six drive representations/three pairs of opposites (see Section 3.3.1) are generated:

Blood sugar: The drive demand is the inversion of the incoming value. The lower the value of blood sugar gets, the higher is the need to find something to eat. The created pair of opposites is *nourish–bite*.

Stamina: Similarly to blood sugar, the drive demand representing the need to take a break is the inversion of the incoming value. For stamina, the created pair of opposites is *relax–sleep*.

Intestine pressure: This drive demand is identical to the received value from E2. Its pair of opposites is *repress–deposit*.

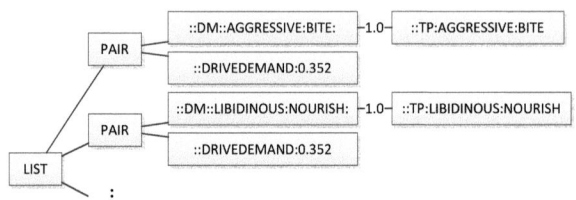

Figure 5.4: Structure of the data transferred via Interface I1.3
DM ... drive mesh; TP ... thing presentation

The result of Module E3 is sketched in Figure 5.4. Interface I1.3 takes a list of pairs. Each pair stores one drive representation and the corresponding drive demand. The drive representation is a mesh consisting of only one element at the moment. This element is a thing presentation defining which drive is represented. In Figure 5.4, the top entry is the aggressive component of the blood sugar related pair of opposites: Bite. The other values that resemble a drive demand — quota of affect and primal repression based categorization — will be filled in, in the next modules. The second part of the pair is the demand with a value of 0.352. The next pair in the list is the libidinous component: Nourish. As it has the same drive source as bite, it has the same drive demand value attached. The other four drives (relax, sleep, repress, and deposit) are created similarly. Resulting, a list with six entries is forwarded to the next module (Interface I1.3).

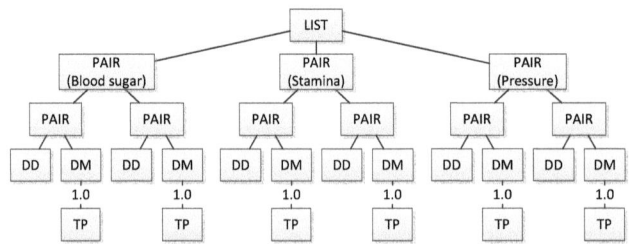

Figure 5.5: Data structure of drive representations with pairs of opposites
DM ... drive mesh; TP ... thing presentation; DD ... drive demands

In Module E4, the single drives are paired to the pair of opposites in the data structure. This is important for the next module which creates the quota of affects based on the pairs of opposites and the drive demands. Figure 5.5 depicts the new data structure. The list contains three pairs of opposites. The two entries for each pair equal the corresponding entries of the previous list. Thus, the pair for the bodily source blood sugar consists of the two drive representations nourish and bite. The list is forwarded via Interface I1.4.

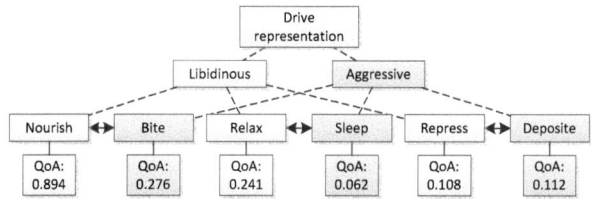

Figure 5.6: Current drive representations in Module E5
QoA ... quota of affect

Finally, the drive demands are converted into quota of affects in Module E5. Based on the distribution of drive demands introduced in Section 3.3.2, the attached value is split into a libidinous and an aggressive component. For example, starting from the blood sugar level of 0.681, a drive demand of 0.352 is calculated in Module E3. The libidinous part is calculated using the formula $sin(\pi\alpha)$; the aggressive part with the formula $(1-cos(\pi\alpha))/2$. The drive demand is inserted in these formulas as α. The resulting values for the corresponding quota of affects are 0.894 for nourish and 0.276 for bite. Thus, the quota of affect for nourish is very high and most likely to be the dominant influence on decision making.

The drive representation is almost completed with the quota of affects attached. Figure 5.6 shows the drive representations with their quotas of affects attached. The dashed lines define a membership to a category. Starting from the top-most category drive representations, two different sub-categories are defined: Libidinous and aggressive drive representations. To each of the two belong three of the generated drive representations. Nourish, relax, and repress belong to the libidinous category; bite, sleep, and deposit belong to the aggressive component. The two-headed arrow defines a pair of opposite relationship. The single solid line marks an association. For example, the drive nourish is associated with a quota of affect with the value of 0.894. This is the highest value of all drive representations in the current example.

Analogous to Figure 5.3(a), the corresponding data flow of the quotas of affects is shown in Figure 5.3(b). For each of the six drive representations, a line denotes the change of values from step 0 to step 30. The values for the pairs *nourish–bite* and *relax–sleep* are relatively low for the whole period and do not much influence decision making. This is different for the pair *repress–deposit*. At step 19, the stomach gets filled with undigestable nutrition so much that the intestine pressures value gets higher than 0.9. For high values, the drive distribution formulas transform the drive demand into a very high aggressive and a low libidinous part. The stomach is filled with undigestable nutrition so much that it dominates decision making. After execution of the command deposit, the intestine pressure drops and so do the corresponding quotas of affects.

After execution of the drive demand distribution and attachment of the quotas of affects, the strong connection between the pair of opposites is not needed any more (from an

RESULTS

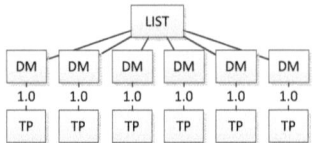

Figure 5.7: Structure of the data transmitted via Interface I2.15 and I1.5

implementational point of view). The drive representations are processed independently from now on. Thus, Interface I2.15 accepts a list of drive representations only. The pairs of opposites and the attached drive demands are removed.

The last module belonging to the self-preservation system is Module E38. It assigns the drive representations to the four primal repression categories oral, anal, phallic, and genital (see Section 3.3.4). In the current ARS implementation number 11 (ARSi11), a predefined categorization is stored for each drive. Primal repression is character related. Its values are learned and stored in early infancy and cannot be changed later on. This and the fact that there is a limited number of possible drives makes this approach valid.

The result of Module E38 is put to Interface I1.5, which accepts the same data structure like Interface I2.15. The recipients of the list of drive representations are the modules Defense mechanisms for drives (E6), Internalized rules handler (E7), and Knowledge about reality (unconscious) (E9). Drive representations are the base for decision making in the secondary processes. If they are able to pass the defense mechanisms they have great influence on which plan to choose.

5.3.2 Seeking System

The second system to be analyzed is the seeking sub-system (see Section 3.3.3). The setup for creating the test data for the step by step discussion of this sub-system is created by a single ARSIN agent with no other entities in range. As shown in Figure 5.8, this system consists of the following modules: Seeking system (libido source) (E39), Neurosymbolization of libido (E40), Libidostasis handler (E41), Separation into partial sexual drives (E43), Accumulation of affects for sexual drives (E42), and Primal repression for sexual drives (E44).

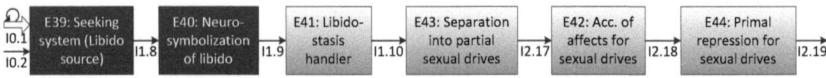

Figure 5.8: Excerpt of the final functional model — the seeking system

From the two interfaces transmitting raw data to Module E39 only Interface I0.1 is used. Interface I0.2 needs external interaction with the ARSIN agent to produce an input value greater than zero. The only difference for the task at hand — discussion of the seeking system — would be that a variable amount of libido is incoming. The functionality and the impact of the other modules is not influenced (it would have influence on modules later on). Hence, it is set to zero deliberately. Each step, 0.1 libido[2] is perceived via Interface I0.1. Similarly to the self-preservation system, this value denotes that the incoming value is equivalent to 10% of the maximum libido the system can handle. The single value of the sum of the two incoming libido sources is forwarded to the next module via Interface I1.8. In this case, the value is 0.1.

Module E40 transforms the numeric value into a symbol. Again, this symbolization is done in a simple, straight forward approach. The symbol contains a single numeric value with the range of 0 to 1. This single symbol is sent to Module E41 through the Interface I1.9.

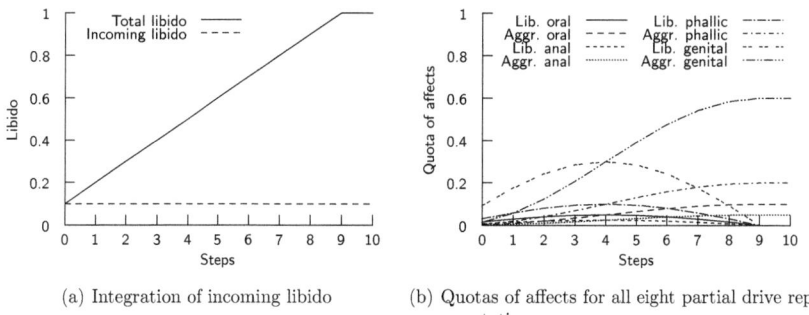

(a) Integration of incoming libido

(b) Quotas of affects for all eight partial drive representations

Figure 5.9: Libido and quotas of affects of the seeking system

The two tasks of Module E41 are to integrate incoming libido and to generate a pair of opposites of drive representations. Figure 5.9(a) shows for each step of the first eleven steps the value of the incoming libido and the resulting libido that is stored in the libido buffer (described in Section 3.4.4). After ten steps, the libido buffer is filled with the maximum value of 1. Any further incoming libido is discarded (an event unlikely to happen with the usual amount of incoming libido). Analogous to Module E3, two drive representations are created: Libidinous and aggressive. Along with the attached drive demand, which is equivalent to the stored libido, the two drive representations are transferred to the next module via Interface I1.10.

In Module E43, the incoming drive representations are split into the four partial drives: Anal, oral, phallic, and genital. Thus, the two incoming drive representations are split into eight. Again, like for the self-preservation drives, the pairs of opposites are grouped in the data structure (cp. Figure 5.5). Each newly generated partial drive representation gets its own drive demand value attached. It is calculated by multiplication of the incoming drive demand with a personality factor for this particular partial drive. As described in Section 3.3.3, the sum of these factors does not have to sum up to 1. Similarly to the parameters of the primal repression of self-preservation drives described above, these factors are hard-coded and not subject to change. The values used for this experiment are: Oral 0.1, anal

---

[2]The value is increased to 0.1 for this example to tighten the time line. Usually, it is set to 0.01.

Results

0.05, phallic 0.2, and genital 0.6. For example, the drive demand attached to the two genital drive representations at step five has the value 0.36. The resulting list of four pairs is sent to Module E42 via Interface I2.17.

Using the same approach as in Module E5, Module E42 distributes the drive demands to the eight drive representations. The drive demands are distributed using above described formulas and result in the data flow over time depicted in Figure 5.9(b). The different quotas of affects increase and decrease with time based on the available libido, the distribution function, and the previously defined factor. In this example, the genital partial drives are dominant as shown in this figure. Further, step four is the point from which on the aggressive drive representations are more important than the libidinous ones. At step ten, the maximum libido is reached in the buffer. At this point, the aggressive genital part is most important. Thus, thing and word presentations that are associated with this drive representation have stronger influence than for example presentations associated with the libidinous genital drive representation. This has influence on the data used for decision making. Alike after Module E5, the strong binding of the pairs of opposites is no longer necessary. Thereafter, a list containing all eight drive representations is sent to the next module via Interface I2.18.

Finally, Module E44 performs the categorization according to the four primal repression categories: Oral, anal, phallic, and genital. Similar to E38, the values for this categorization are hard-coded. After this module, the drive representation generation is completed. The resulting list is forwarded to the follow-up modules E6, E7, and E9.

The described behavior of the implemented sub-system suits the model description in Chapter 3. The result of this system on the one hand influences the defense mechanisms and on the other hand tries to pass them. If successful, they impact decision making in the secondary processes.

5.3.3 Libido Buffer

Different to the first two sub-systems discussed, this sub-system connects two different parts of the model with a buffer to exchange the stored libido. Next to the libido storage (cp. Figure 5.10), the system consists of the following modules: Emersion of repressed content (E35), Libido discharge handler (E45), Composition of affects for perception (E18), and Libidostasis handler (E41). The last one is part of the seeking sub-system and discussed above. The first three are part of perception (cp. Section 3.4.3).

Different to the other two scenarios, this analysis provides no entity within range for the first twelve steps. At step twelve, two entities are placed within the vision sensors' range: A cake to the far right and a carrot to the far left.

Module E41 fills the libido buffer with incoming libido. The integrated result is stored in the libido storage. Figure 5.11(a) shows three graphs: The incoming libido from the bodily source, the integrated total amount of available libido in the system, and the amount of libido discharge in each step. Module E41 interacts with the libido storage with the two

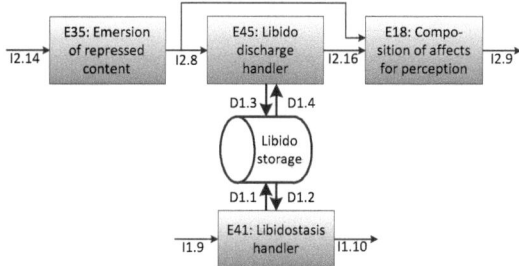

Figure 5.10: Excerpt of the final functional model — the libido buffer system

interfaces D1.1 and D1.2. D1.1 is used to add the incoming libido to the stored libido. D1.2 returns the total amount stored. As already stated above, the total amount is delimited with the upper bound of 1.0.

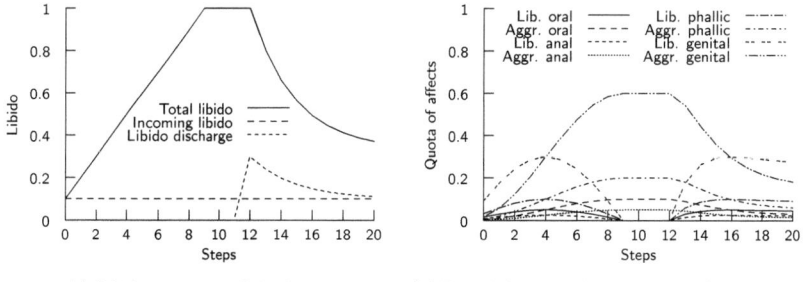

(a) Libido storage and discharge

(b) Partial drives with increasing and decreasing libido

Figure 5.11: Interaction of the libido buffer with the partial drives

In context of the libido buffer system, the only task of Module E35 is to provide a list of thing presentations containing the current perception. This list is forwarded to the modules E45 and E18 via Interface I2.8. In the current example this list is empty for the first twelve steps and contains the representations of a cake and of a carrot from step twelve on.

In Module E45, the incoming perceptions in form of thing presentations are used to search the knowledge base if this entity was already successfully used for libido discharge. Found entries provide a value that is equivalent to the experienced suitability of the entity for discharge. In the current knowledge base definition, the carrot's suitability is set to 0.5 and the cake's suitability is set to the maximum value of 1.0. Hence, the cake is very well suitable for libido discharge while the carrot is only at an average level. The result of a libido discharge is pleasure gain. Thus, the ARSIN agent tries to re-experience this pleasure gain. A part of this re-experience is that the perception of such an object alone is a pleasureful experience. The algorithm in Module E45 withdraws for each fitting perception a pre-defined fraction from the libido storage, multiplies it with the suitability factor and assigns the resulting pleasure gain to the perception. For example, if the pre-defined fraction is set to 0.2, the pleasure gain for the carrot is $0.2 \cdot 0.5 \cdot 1.0 = 0.1$ at step twelve (pre-defined fraction=0.2, suitability=0.5, and total libido=1.0). The cake has a suitability value of 1.0. The resulting pleasure gain is 0.2. The sum of 0.3 libido is withdrawn from the libido buffer after all pleasure gains have been calculated for this step. In case that more libido is converted into pleasure gain than is actually stored in the libido storage results in recalculation of all pleasure gains to meet the available libido. At each step, the stored libido is increased by 0.1. Thus, the net reduction of libido from step 12 to step 13 is 0.2. In step 20, the total libido is decreased to 0.4. The conversion of libido to pleasure gain is now at the same rate as the increasing of the stored libido. Thus, from step 20 onward, the pleasure gain is at a constant value until the perception changes or the agent performs an action.

Figure 5.11(b) depicts the interplay of the libido discharge in Module E45 and the generation of quota of affects for sexual drives in Module E42. With the reduction of stored libido from step 13 onward, the intensity of the quota of affects of aggressive drive representations decreases. At step 16, the tension produced by the stored libido is sufficiently reduced to allow again the libidinous drive representations to be more important than their aggressive counterparts.

With Interface I2.16, the pleasure gains per perception are forwarded from Module E45 to Module E18. The task of Module E18 is to integrate these values to the overall appraisal of each perception entry. This is done by changing the attached quota of affect by adding the pleasure gain value calculated in Module E45. This change of appraisal influences decision making and has direct impact on the order of action plans in Module E26. This is discussed in more detail in the next section.

5.4 Impact

Until now, the innovations to the model have been discussed isolated. The step by step analysis in the previous section highlighted the functionality of each single module. To give a broader perspective on the influence of these modules and what behavior emerges from their interplay, a more global point of view is taken in this section. The first experiment deals with the influence of the libido buffer on decision making. Next, an experiment regarding the influence of bodily demands on Superego rules is performed.

The initial setup of the first experiment is identical to the one conducted in Section 5.3.3. In front of the ARSIN agent a cake and a carrot are placed just out of sight (see Figure 5.12(a)). The development of the drive demands is equal to the one depicted in Figure 5.3(b) for the first 15 steps. After the ninth step, the libido storage is filled with the maximum value (cp. Figure 5.9(a)). The knowledge base is configured such that a carrot is slightly preferred to a cake.

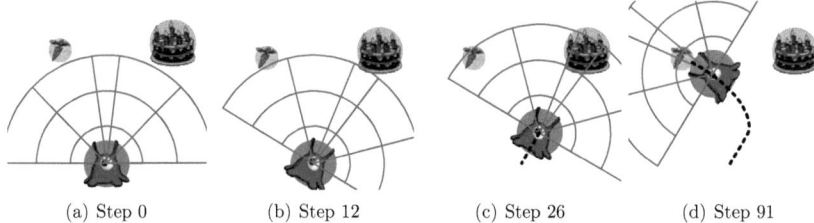

(a) Step 0   (b) Step 12   (c) Step 26   (d) Step 91

Figure 5.12: Steps 0 to 91

During the first eleven steps the ARSIN agent moves slowly ahead. At step eleven the two entities come into sight (see Figure 5.12(b)). With the stored libido at its maximum, the cake is perceived as very pleasureful (cp. Section 5.3.3). The agent selects the cake as the preferred food. Until step 26, the agent moves directly towards the cake (Figure 5.12(c)). At each step, the stored libido is reduced by the pleasure gain the sight of the cake produces. As can be seen in Figure 5.13, the buffered libido has dropped to 0.338 by then. At this level, the pleasureful appraisal of the cake drops below the original appraisal of the carrot. Hence, the carrot is selected as the preferred food from now on. The current implementation of the decision making does not take into account the length of an action plan and has not implemented goal persistency. This results in a re-creation of action plans at each step and in this case of changing the plan from the cake towards the carrot.

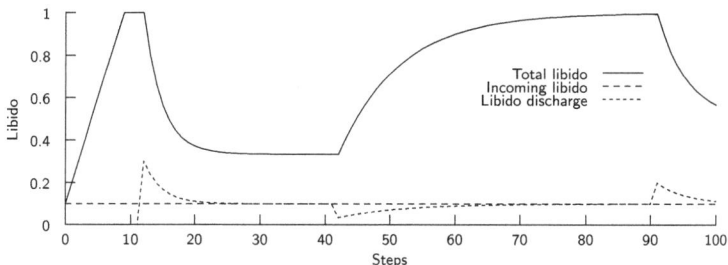

Figure 5.13: Libido buffer fill level for the steps 0 to 100

The cake is visible until step 41. From step 42 to step 90, the carrot is the only object within sensor range that is suitable for pleasure gain. Due to its lower suitability as in comparison to the cake, the stored libido is rebuilt and reaches its maximum in step 88. From step 91 on, the carrot is within the eatable area (see Figure 5.12(d)). Next to sights of carrots and cakes, also the positioning of one of them within this area qualifies for pleasure gain. Thus, next to the pleasure gained by reduction of blood sugar related drive tension by eating the carrot, pleasure is gained by sensing food within the eatable area too.

The first third of the distance from the agent's position at step 12 towards the cake took eleven steps of continuous movement. For the distance from position at step 26 to the carrot took the agent 65 steps. This is almost twice as long as the projected time for this distance. It is roughly the same distance the agent would have to move to get to the cake. The reason for this delay is the depleted stamina reserves. Between steps 26 and 91 the agent alternates between the action move forward and sleep. Each movement action depletes the stamina again and the agent is not able to perform any other activity than to rest.

It was possible to show that the introduction of the libido system positively affects the decision making process and biases the agent towards entities that have been experienced to provide some kind of tension relieve and thus pleasure gain. To take full advantage of this feature, future versions of the implementation of secondary process modules have to have some kind of goal persistence.

The second experiment highlights the impact of self-preservation drives on decision making. In general, these self-preservation drives form the base upon which decisions are made. Each of these drives has a more or less high tension that has to be relieved as soon as possible. The Superego provides rules that overrule these demands. In this example, the ARSIN agent is applied with a rule that as long as there is food visible the action deposit is banned. The setup is simple: A single ARSIN agent and a carrot position within the eatable area of the agent. The agent is configured to have a high intestine pressure right from start.

Two types of variations are defined: The strictness of the Superego rule and the parameter for the drive demand distribution of the pair of opposites *nourish–bite*. The two levels of strictness for the rule are very high and high. To be overruled by a drive demand, the tension of the drive has to be greater than the corresponding Superego rule. This is impossible for the case of very high strictness as very high is the highest level possible. Thus, overruling should only be possible in the second case. The first case is added as a control group. By application of a factor f to the input value α of the formulas for the drive distribution introduced above, the result of the value can be biased towards either the aggressive component or the libidinous component of the pair of opposites. For this analysis two configurations for the distribution are used: the default distribution as used above and a distribution which biases slightly towards the aggressive drive representation.

The experiment is repeated four times with the described two by two parameters varied. As expected, the cases with very high rule strictness resulted in not performing the action deposit. The configuration of the drive demand distribution had no influence. The case with a high Superego rule and the normal distribution configuration the agent did not overrule the ban in the first step. If the blood sugar level is reduced to a low level initially, the agent performs the action eat in the first step. In the next step, the tension inflicted by the intestine pressure is high enough to overrule the ban and action deposit is performed in the second step. With the slightly shifted drive demand distributor the agent overrules the ban already in the first step. The tension is sufficiently unpleasant from the start.

This experiment shows that the customizable personality parameters like the various drive demand distributors can influence decision making. Further, Superego rules guide the decision making as long as possible. If the bodily demands get too pressing, the rules and bans might be overruled by the drive demands. This fact has to be considered in the design of the next version of the implementation. By pro-active planning, the ARSIN agent can avoid these unpleasant and unwanted situations when Superego bans are overruled.

5.5 Minimal Model

In Section 3.5 a minimal model is introduced. It is a subset of the final functional model that is still able to perform basic actions. Six secondary process modules (E22, E23, E24, E25, E33, and E34), three primary process modules (E7, E19, and E35), and one conversion module (E47) are removed from the full set. In the current implementation ARSi11, the modules E7, E23, E24, E25, E33, E34, and E47 provide no functionality — the detailed specification of functionality and their implementation has to be done by future theses. Hence, their presence is for an operational minimal set not of relevance. The remaining three modules have some functionality implemented and their removal has impact on the system's overall performance.

The setup of the experiment to compare the minimal subset with the full model consists of five cakes that are placed at arbitrary positions. The first cake is placed right in front of the ARSIN agent. The bodily demands are set to the same values as in the first experiment described above. The corresponding drive demands for blood sugar and intestine pressure have a resulting value of 0.6 at step 0. The Superego rule of the second experiment in the previous section — do not perform action deposit if food is visible — is activated with a high strictness. Thus, in case of too much intestine pressure, this rule can be ignored. The first 300 steps of each simulation run (one with minimal subset and one with the full set) are analyzed.

In case of the full implementation, the agent moves around and searches the environment. At step 174, the action deposit is performed at a location that suits the Superego rule. The only time a piece of a cake is consumed is at step 267. Before that the agent did not have the need to eat one. Except for the short period from step 174 to step 182 at least one cake was always within sensor range. Concluding, in this setup the agent equipped with the full implementation moved through the world and needed to perform the actions deposit and eat only once.

The second run is performed with the minimal subset activated. The main difference is the lack of Superego rules provided by Module **Social rules selection (E22)**. In the current configuration of the knowledge base, the modules **Defense mechanisms for perception (E19)** and **Emersion of repressed content (E35)** only influence is a small adaption of the appraisal of incoming perceptions. The resulting behavior developed by the ARSIN agent is to stay close to a cake and perform the actions deposit, eat, and sleep alternating. With no Superego rule present, the agent's primary objective is to immediately satisfy the bodily demands. While consuming the first cake, action deposit was executed twice. After step 5, the agent rested for 75 steps until the low blood sugar level drove the agent to search for the next cake. It appeared in the distance at step 100. Being exhausted made the agent perform the alternating sleep and move pattern observed in first example in the previous section too. Thus, it took the agent until step 155 to get there. The same behavior was executed as shown in the beginning of this simulation run: Eating and depositing. After the cake was consumed, the agent started to search for a cake again. It took almost 100 steps to get the next cake within sensor range.

The interesting aspect in this comparison is that the agent equipped with the full implementation needed to eat and deposit less often and had a cake almost always within vision range. The minimal subset agent performed eating and as a consequence depositing much more often and had no information on the location of a cake for 186 out of 300 steps (as compared to 8 out 300 steps for the full implementation). The differences in the shown behaviors between the minimal subset and the full implementation will increase with the progressing development of the model and the implementation. Nevertheless, this experiment has shown that the minimal subset implementation is sufficient for basic activities.

5.6 ARS Goes NAO

A complete different type of experiment is performed in this section. For the first time ever, the Artificial Recognition System (ARS) model is implemented into a real world system [DBZ+11]. In this case the platform used is the humanoid robot NAO developed by Aldebaran Robotics [18]. The aim of this experiment is to analyze the applicability of the model to a robot and to evaluate if the robot's body can provide the bodily needs as discussed in Section 3.1.4.

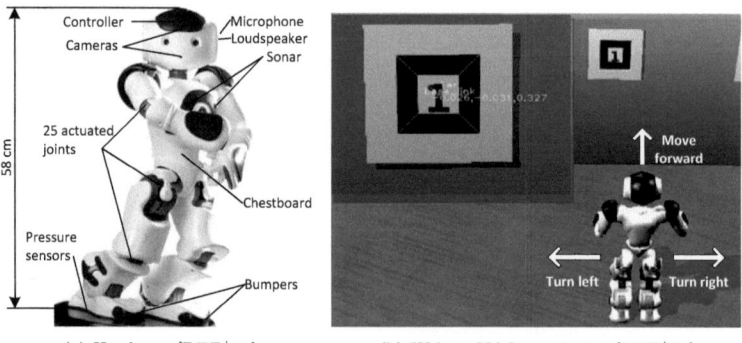

(a) Hardware [DBZ+11]   (b) Webots NAO simulation [DBZ+11]

Figure 5.14: Robot NAO

Figure 5.14(a) shows the rough configuration of the robot. Two on board computer exist: The chestboard is the interface to the actuators and sensors and the controller. The controller runs high level control architecture like the one developed in this thesis. NAO has 25 actuated joints. Each joint provides its position and the temperature of the motor as sensor values. Additional internal sensors provide the battery level and the current charge/discharge rate. Five different types of external sensors exist: Cameras, microphones, sonar, bumpers, and pressure sensors.

To control the robot a framework called NAOQi is provided. It provides high level access like walk five steps ahead or the position of the left arm. Further, direct access to all joints and single sensors is possible. For development purposes a simulation environment called Webots is used (see Figure 5.14(b)). Three different markers are used to bypass the object recognition problem. One of these markers is shown in the upper left corner of Figure 5.14(b) — the white square with a "1" inside a thick lined black box. The other two are similar but with other symbols than "1".

The system is configured to search for pleasureful symbols — comparable to the example with carrots and cakes in Section 5.4. As expected, the robot showed a similar behavior as described in the carrots and cakes example.

The important part in this experiment lies within the lessons learned from preparing it. Although the NAO robot provides data from over 50 internal sensors, the rich internal systems demanded are not present. Further, the well-crafted framework NAOQi bypasses many of the functional modules defined. Especially the body related modules are not needed. For a full integration of the ARS model, no such framework can be used. The model's implementation has to start right at the place where data is read from the sensors and to end where actuators are controlled. Further, the body of the robot has to be designed with a psychoanalytically inspired decision unit in mind.

5.7 Discussion

As already stated in the beginning of this chapter, the shown results are generated using a proof-of-concept approach. Thus, the implementation ARSi11 is evaluated on the basis of use-case 0 which addresses the investigated functionalities. Its outcome is compared to the model description. First, the three sub-systems that fit the focus of this thesis best are discussed. Step by step each module's function is explained by applying a set of input data, analyzing what happens to this data within the function, and forwarding the result to the next module. The second part of results is done by putting these three sub-systems in context of the whole model.

Both parts showed that the implementation works according to the developed model and that the innovations interact with already existing sub-systems. A big issue with the evaluation of the model is that the drives (self-preservation and sexual) built the base for decision making. Without a proper implementation of the defense mechanisms and the modules of the secondary process, they cannot be evaluated on a larger scale. To create a more detailed model description for these modules will be the task of following theses. As soon as the descriptions are available, the decision making can be implemented and the influence of the drives on it should be re-evaluated.

Results

The three described self-preservation drives added more and potentially conflicting goals in the form of the pairs of opposites *nourish–bite*, *relax–sleep*, and *repress–deposit*. The provision of conflicting goals is an important asset for the further development of the model. One of the core issues of meta-psychology is how to deal with inner conflicts.

The seeking sub-system proofed as useful. The interaction between the integrated libido and the incoming perceptions biased decision making without the need of changing anything in the modules of the secondary process. Thus, if something is remembered as being qualified to reduce drive tension it automatically attracts the focus of attention of the system.

The implementation of the model and the performed experiments can be seen as the third step in the modeling process as described in Section 1.2.4. The next step in this process is the reviewing of the gained insights of the implementation by engineers together with psychoanalysts. What has to be discussed in this step are the similarities of the implementations of the modules E42 and E5 respectively E44 and E38. E42 and E5 are implemented almost identically; they differ in the used parameters only. The same accounts for the second pair. It should be considered if these two pairs should not be merged to two single modules. Hence, after E43 and E4 the two sub-systems seeking system and self-preservation system should be merged.

An interesting experiment performed at the end of this chapter is the application of the psychoanalytically inspired decision unit to the real world robot NAO. It was possible to show that the developed model can be used with a standard robot platform up to some extent. The limitations arise from the simplicity of the robot's body and the utilization of an abstraction framework to access sensors and actuators.

To conclude, the introduced concepts to the model proved useful. The added self-preservation drives provide a richer base for decision making and the seeking system biases the perception towards preferred entities. Additionally, the minimal sub-set of the final functional model showed the expected bodily demand driven behavior. Thus, the proof-of-concept succeeded. Based on the shown realization of use-case 0, the other ten use-cases can be realized. Future work focusing on deliberation related modules in the secondary processes can such be evaluated.

> To you, a robot is a robot. Gears and metal;
> electricity and positrons. Mind and iron!
> Human-made! If necessary, human-destroyed!
> But you haven't worked with them, so you
> don't know them. They're a cleaner better
> breed than we are.
>
> Dr. Susan Calvin, robopsychologist,
> in Asimov's "I, Robot"

6 Conclusion and Outlook

The goal of extending and improving the psychoanalytically inspired decision making model was approached by using an interdisciplinary top-down modeling design process. With the focus on the psychoanalytical entity Id, concepts derived from psychoanalysis were transferred into technically feasible terms step by step. The resulting model was implemented into an artificial life simulation to evaluate them. The translation of psychoanalytic terms was done using an interdisciplinary approach. For a correct translation of the terms, scientists from both fields — engineers and psychoanalysts — were necessary. The model itself was designed as a functional model with a separated data layer.

After concluding and discussion of the work of this thesis, short and medium term future tasks are worked out as well as long term perspectives.

6.1 Discussions

Designing a general purpose control system based on psychoanalytic theories can be attributed to the young scientific field of Artificial General Intelligence (AGI). The aim of it is to create a system which models each step of the control loop in a coherent manner. It could be shown that in Artificial Intelligence (AI), usually isolated problems are solved which cannot converge to such a coherent model. Important AGI projects like Learning Intelligent Distribution Agent (LIDA) (see [FP06]) and Open Cognition (OpenCog) (see [Goe06]) are based on a more or less mash up of theories originating in sciences like neurology, psychology, or behaviorism. Artificial Recognition System (ARS) project and this thesis are following a different approach: using (neuro-) psychoanalysis in general and Freud's concept in particular as the foundation and deriving the model by interdisciplinary research. Others have used psychoanalysis too, but no other research project found has followed this approach more exhaustively and comprehensively.

Three different types of research projects were identified in this thesis that work in the interdisciplinary field of psychoanalysis and computer science. The first one consists of researchers coming from psychoanalysis, arguing that psychoanalysis can be useful for cognitive science and AI (e.g. [CS88, Tur89, RR96]). The second group consists of engineers comparing their AI solution to psychoanalysis (e.g. [Min05]). In the last group engineers try to build a control system based on (a subset of) psychoanalysis. These works do not go into depth of psychoanalytic theory and they are not using an interdisciplinary approach. Thus, works described in [NTMI99, PKP07] stay on a shallow level of psychoanalysis. Except Leuzinger-Bohleber and Pfeifer in [LBP02, LBP06] and publications by project ARS, no interdisciplinary publications could be found. The work of Buller [BJLS05, Bul05, Bul09] is the only one found which deals with the modeling of drives based on a subset of psychoanalysis — the psychodynamic. By doing so, important parts of psychoanalysis are left out. Further, the role of the body in combination with the psyche is not examined by Buller. The first research project found that works on a control architecture based on psychoanalysis using an interdisciplinary approach is project ARS.

Starting from results generated by previous dissertations (e.g. [Roe07, Pal08, Lan10, Zei10]) in project ARS, this work aimed at providing a solid concept of the psychoanalytic drive concept and the introduction of an explicit body with rich internal dynamics. Now, the drive system consists of self-preservation and sexual drives and each drive is represented by an aggressive and a libidinous component. The role of the body in psychoanalysis and in AI was analyzed. Based on the results a novel concept to embodiment was introduced in this thesis: the rich internal dynamics of the body itself. It extends the previous view on embodiment as seen by AI. With these internal dynamics present, the body operates as basic motivational source.

The presented model is derived step by step from the basic concepts provided by psychoanalysis. The first — oversimplificated — model is divided into an intermediate model. New or updated concepts with focus on the Id are presented which lead to the next iteration of the top-down modeling process. The result is the final functional model.

The presented artificial life simulation consists of a virtual environment in which virtual embodied autonomous agents roam. The purpose of this platform is to provide a test-tool. Use-cases are defined to which the agents are exposed to. By analysis of the observed behavior, insights on the created model can be extracted. These can be used to refine the model or to rethink the concepts provided by psychoanalysis. The agents can be equipped with different implementations of control systems. The body of the agent has an interface which enables to use these different implementations for comparison purposes. An operational implementation of the final functional model is presented and evaluated with the simulator.

An alternative implementation of the model is compared with the original one. It consists only of modules and functionalities which are necessary to produce at least a minimum response to the environment. In this way, the critical implementation path is identified. As long as this path is operational, the agent is able to produce at least some response. The created complex model — several feedback loops on different layers along with over 40 modules — might become instable or implementation errors might lead to blocked modules. The identified critical path should guide development of the next model/implementation by taking special care on the stability of the modules located on this path.

6.2 Research Considerations Revisited

After the above given synopsis, the six research considerations formulated in Section 1.4.2 are revisited. They are discussed in the light of the results produced by this work.

Statement 1.1 *The model of the human psyche as described by the theoretical framework of psychoanalysis — the metapsychology — can be transformed into a technically feasible model.*
This basic assumption of the ARS project holds true for this work too. By application of the design loop described in Section 1.2, the terms extracted from psychoanalysis are divided in submodules. This process has been continued until the description of each single module could be understood by an engineer. The — for engineers very abstract — narrative descriptions from psychoanalysis are now converted into "black box" modules. Input, output, and task of each module can now be implemented without further knowledge of psychoanalysis.

Although all module descriptions have reached the desired granularity, descriptions of modules belonging to secondary processes/decision making are not of the same quality as the Id related ones. This issue will be further discussed in the next section.

Statement 1.2 *The technical model as described in Statement 1.1 can be implemented in a computer.*
The implementation sketched in Section 4.5 shows that this statement is valid. Although not all modules have an implementation satisfying the full module description, a complete implementation is present. The fully implemented modules are showing a proof-of-concept of the whole implementation. Especially modules belonging to primary processes and the Id are part of this group. The other modules contain at least so called "dummy"-implementation. They provide a minimum implementation, usually passing data from the input to the output with a minimum of conversion done. The implementation of the rest is part of the tasks formulated in the future work section.

Statement 1.3 *A-Life simulations are best suited to perform evaluations of the implemented model based on Statement 1.1.*
In Chapter 5, the results of the simulation experiments are discussed. The defined use-cases together with the developed artificial life simulation provide a good platform for the experiments. The Artificial Life (A-Life) simulation proved useful for two different evaluation approaches. The first approach consists of a step by step analysis of the modules. Several types of sensory sensations can be applied which result in different results. These differences provide valuable input. The second type of evaluation executed is to define a world setup and to expose two different agents to it. This is done to compare the minimal implementation with the full set of modules. The overall performance of the agents over a time span of 100 simulation steps can be compared. Only the first of the eleven use-cases has been used for evaluation purposes. The current implementation is not suitable for the

CONCLUSION AND OUTLOOK

other ten yet. Nevertheless, with the progress of the model development and the continuation of the implementation, they can be added to the ARSIN world similarly to the shown use-case 0. Despite the proven usefulness, it can already be said that refinement of the defined use-cases is necessary. They are extracted from the psychoanalytic description of the functional modules. Thus, they are not derived from existing psychological tests. How this problem should be faced is shown in the next section.

Statement 1.4 *The Id implies a body and thereafter embodiment.*
According to the analysis of the psychoanalytic literature performed in Section 3.1.4, this statement has to be extended. The Ego is a reflection of the body. Thus, not only the Id implies a body but also the Ego. The reasons why the Id implies a body are that it communicates bodily needs/drives to the psyche. The view on embodiment by psychoanalysis is more advanced than the one usually used in AI. The psyche influences the body and the body influences the psyche. It is a constant loop of mutual influences. Further, robots and software agents have no or very limited inner dynamics in their body (if they are embedded). For robots, inner somatic sources for drives are usually battery level or motor temperature (cp. Section 5.6). If a robot should be equipped with a psychoanalytically inspired control system, its body dynamics have to get richer. This is further discussed in the final section of this work—outlook.

Statement 1.5 *The solution which satisfies Statement 1.4 satisfies Statement 1.1 too.*
If designing a system operated by a psychoanalytically inspired control system, a rich body fitting to psychoanalytical instance Id has to be considered. Otherwise, no inner somatic organic drive source would be present. This results in the problem that no drives are represented in the psyche. Without drive tension provided by inner somatic sources, the control system would not be able to make a decision—the basic motivation of such a system is to reduce drive tension. If the body is designed fitting to the Id, it fits to psychoanalytic theory and thus, it satisfies this statement by not violating Statement 1.1.

Statement 1.6 *A subset of the implemented model (see Statement 1.2) exists which provides a simpler, but still operational system.*
As shown in the results Section 5.5, it is possibly to define such a minimal model. The minimal model cannot be seen as a psychoanalytical model any more—Superego is an intrinsic part of the first structural model. Nevertheless, this technical view on the model is important for implementation purposes and has to be redone for each new version of the model. This will be discussed in the next section.

All six research considerations have been proven to be valid. The presented results evaluated that the behavior of the implementation of the model fits psychoanalytic descriptions. Although the overall results presented are satisfying the task at hand, new questions and problems have appeared. The modules belonging to the Id are well discussed in this thesis; the overall model is discussed and developed for the last 5 years. Modules of the defense mechanisms and decision making process are falling behind in their quality of description.

The reason for this is that without a solid definition of the drive system, these modules cannot be developed. With the work at hand, this border has been overcome and focus should be put on them. It is very likely that a third iteration of the top-down modeling process is necessary. To conclude: a lot has been done and a solid base is now present. Still, much has to be done as laid out in the following two sections.

6.3 Further Work

Short and medium term tasks are to be realized in the next stage of project ARS. Focus should be put on the following four points: use-cases defined according to psychology-based tests, a finer grained definition of the modules of the secondary processes, interplay of body with psyche, and which parts of the introduced concept of sexuality are needed.

The use-cases presented in Section 4.2 serve the tasks of model development and evaluation well. What they lack is their rooting in medical sciences. They are not based on tests taken from psychology, behaviorism, or psychoanalysis. The first tests utilized test-cases comparable to the ones known from software engineering. Each function is tested for the return of a correct result of a given input set. This approach is sufficient to test individual modules if they meet the requirements but fails in complex interactions with other systems. The next stage of tests is based on use-cases as described in this work. They define setups in the simulated world and expected behaviors of the agents. While they are suitable for evaluation of complex scenarios, they face a different problem. As discussed in Section 1.2, the task of creating a control architecture based on psychoanalysis can only be approached in an interdisciplinary way and should be based on a solid concept taken from psychoanalysis. As the evaluation is part of this task, the system has to be developed similarly to the model. Thus, the defined use-cases are sufficient for evaluation but do not meet the superior constraints. Psychoanalytic therapy focuses on the subjective experiences of individuals. Hence, for the evaluation task at hand, tests from other sciences like psychology have to be applied. The third type of tests would have to be based on adapted tests taken from psychology, and their results have to be analyzed together with experts from this field.

The secondary process function modules need a more detailed description. Although this subsystem of the model developed well since the version published by Palensky in [Pal08, p. 73] and the version described by Lang in [Lan10, p. 65], the quality of the description has to be increased. In comparison with the quality of the description the primary process related modules a lot of work has to be done still. The problem does not lie within the number of modules and interfaces, it lies within the description of how these modules interact and what data sets are passed. For example, the approach to thinking and dealing with complex decisions which take humans much time to think about are hardly explained by the current version of the model. Next, the influence of the sequential, non-parallel, implementation of the cognitive cycle has to be analyzed. Primary process related functionality react to incoming data from the various sensors at each cycle iteration. It is innate to these tasks that each module has to consider the last few steps only (independent of possibly much older information retrieved from memory). This is different for decision making. Short, medium, and long term plans have to be created and asset. The most promising ones are selected and executed. How this commitment to the selected strategy can be modeled in the ARS control architecture is an open question.

One important result of this thesis is the introduction of rich internal body systems. Without them, a psychoanalytically inspired decision unit would suffer from too few drive sources. The complexity of the control architecture has to meet the complexity of the internal and external body systems as well as the environment and the tasks it is designed to perform. Based on this foundation, the influence of the internal systems has to be researched by using other application areas. For example, what systems does a robot offer today has to be analyzed in respect of what kind of drive sources they offer and how these drives can be put in relation to the table given in Section 3.3.1. Next, changes in robot design which provide more internal systems should be researched. The possibility of introduction of such systems in software agents is another important research question. Other than A-Life agents and robots, they do not need a body. This makes it harder to determine possible internal systems. Finally, the embodiment of building automation systems has to be defined by answering questions like: "What is the body of a kitchen?"

The question of embodiment and how to integrate the ARS model into a pre-manufactured robot should be revisited in future with the availability of NAOs successor ROMEO [19]. This robot will be more than twice as large as NAO and be equipped with many more actuated joints and sensors.

The following two components of the drive system have to be refined: building of pair of opposites and the four modules responsible for accumulation of quota of affects and primal repression. Currently, there exist predefined lists of pairs of opposites for each bodily source in the modules E41 and E3. It would be interesting to find a more dynamic approach. If more than two drive representations are generated for a single source, the predefined, fixed link between two of them cannot be justified. It has to be researched how the drive representations can be built based solely on the drive source and the agent's experience on how the drive demand can be satisfied. The resulting interesting research question is "How can opposing drive representations be identified automatically?" The second improvement for the drive related part of the model is related to the modules that perform accumulation of quota of affects and primal repression. Now, the modules E42 and E5 perform the first task and the modules E44 and E38 the second task. The insights gained from the implementation and the experiments performed suggest that they should be merged. The differences between Module E42 and Module E5 are the incoming data and the parameters used. The algorithms and the data structures are identical. The same accounts for the other two modules. Thus, it has to be discussed with the psychoanalytical advisors if it is possible to merge E42 and E5 to Accumulation of affects for drives (E48) and E44 and E38 to Primal repression for drives (E49). If not, more differentiated descriptions for the four modules are needed.

Another future work related to embodiment is the development of a more human-like body. The body described in Section 4.3 is loosely inspired by mammals. It offers abstracted sensors and actuators along with internal systems like a stomach which can store different types of nutrition. While this is necessary for developing a first implementation of the control architecture, it may not be sufficient on the long term. Thus, a new body has to be designed. It should include sensors which provide only low level information. This would make the implementation of the neurosymbolization modules necessary. Currently, symbols instead of raw data are fed into the control cycle. Instead of abstract actuators, arms and legs with several joints should be added. This is necessary to discuss neurodesymbolization related matters and how motion sequences are stored and processed. Blood circulation along with a beating heart has a completely different impact on the agent's possibilities than the slow messenger system in combination with stamina in the current agent body. Also hormones and other messengers can be modeled more precisely if blood circulation is present. Additionally, the current digestion system can be replaced by a simplified version of the human gastrointestinal tract. This would diminish the direct impact of the consumed food. Depending on the state of this tract, a relatively long period of time can pass between feeding and resulting problems. The reason for introducing these complex internal systems is to evaluate their role in decision making. Using analogies from medical sciences makes it easier to compare the resulting system behavior with observations made in nature. Further, the drives listed in Table 3.1 can be directly applied to a human-like body. To apply them to a technical system like a kitchen needs a translation of the concepts. Which internal systems should be replaced and the ideal level of detail of the modeled tract has to be researched.

An element that already existed in the old ARS model is the explicit modeling of reactive actions and their inhibition. It has to be evaluated if this is still possible with the current version of the model. If not, the necessary changes have to be formulated and implemented. Reactive actions are a powerful tool that takes place in fast changing situations. As soon as the assessment of the situation has been performed it might turn out that the reactive action was the wrong choice. Thus, the possibility to inhibit it is necessary.

The fourth suggested future work is to research the role of the sexual drives in the context of a technical system. As described in Section 3.3.3, the sexual drives are part of the seeking system which is a motivational source. It drives the agent to do something. Next to the constant flow of libido which is produced by the body, libido can be produced by stimulation of erogenous zones. Exactly this type of stimulation has to be researched in more depth. For example, the question "What are the applications for sexual drives and erogenous zones in building automation?" is an open issue. Further, in case of a multi-agent system, the agents have to be prevented from misusing this concept. One solution might be to introduce fitting Superego rules. On the other hand, social interaction and team building among the agents could be aided by this concept.

A combination of the third and the fourth issues is the future work task to evaluate the listed drives (see Table 3.1) regarding their technical feasibility and necessity in technical control systems. Not all of them might be necessary or applicable.

A task not related to model development and thus not part of the four items listed at the beginning of this section is the continuation of the implementation of the A-Life simulator ARSIN world. As mentioned in Chapter 4, the simulator has been implemented only as so far as it is necessary to perform the evaluation tests in the next chapter. As the

CONCLUSION AND OUTLOOK

development of the secondary process related functional modules goes along, the other parts of the simulator have to be implemented as well (see Section 4.1).

The above given tasks aim at the next steps of the ARS project. In the next section more long term ideas and goals are formulated.

6.4 Outlook

The test application described in this thesis and as well as other applications like robots are different to the original goals of project ARS. The research questions which lead to the project as it is today originate in building automation and in the task of deriving meaning out of a data flood generated by hundreds of thousands of sensors. The long term goal has to be to return to these roots by applying the gained insights and the developed models to building automation tasks. A building control system that is able to understand the actions of its inhabitants — be it humans, pets, or independent robots — will be able to provide a more comfortable environment than systems which operate on a pure statistical approach. Next to comfort, the system will also be able to create a safe and secure world by using the same behavior prediction as used for comfort control. Additionally, it is expected that this system is able to reduce power consumption of the whole building by pro-actively influencing the temperature, heating, lighting, and others.

As an — again — intermediate step, a return to the project Smart Kitchen (SmaKi) should be reconsidered. Equipped with more and more powerful sensors it should be possible to research the question of embodiment. As shown in the results chapter with the robot NAO, these enhancements have to go far beyond of adding more sensors of the same type. A co-development of the SmaKi and the decision unit designed for it has to take place. The body related modules of the functional model have to be implemented right where the sensors are. A framework independent of the decision unit has to be avoided. Only if the sensors and actuators are tightly interwoven, the full power of a psychoanalytically inspired decision unit can be reached. Another usage for it is to evaluate the new type of psychological use-cases as described above.

Another field which requires understanding is natural language processing. The therapy provided by psychoanalysis is often referred to as the talking cure. How a human formulates thoughts, words, and speech are important concepts of metapsychology. Further, language influences significantly how thinking is organized. Memory contents are built of thing and word presentations. To conclude, language and how language is processed are important concepts to psychoanalysis. Thus, psychoanalysis is a good foundation for creating a system which is capable of processing natural language. Although, psychoanalysis seems to be overloaded with concepts not directly linked to language like drives, they are all necessary parts of understanding language and producing understandable language. Human communication is not bound to one channel — speech — alone. Various other channels like pitch and speed of the voice, facial expressions, and movement of body parts are utilized too. They are all influenced by internal states of the mind like unpleasure and tension. Hence, a model like the ARS model has to be used as foundation. Starting from the concepts described in this thesis together with the work on the secondary processes as proposed in the previous section it should be possible to build a system capable of natural language communication with humans.

In general, the proposed architecture aims at all automation tasks performed by humans today — be it flying, steering a car, safety and security surveillance, or safely guiding a space ship to a remote planet. These are tasks which are on one hand monotonous, but on the other demand human-like capabilities in case something goes wrong. Then, the control systems have to react to unforeseen situations. This can only be achieved if the systems can produce "creative" solutions. This includes the abilities to reflect the situation and made experiences and the ability to abstract the gained insights. Further, the system has to be able to decide what is more important at the moment: the task at hand or the protection of for example the steered vehicle. To include all this abilities, the designed control architecture has to be based on a holistic view on the human psyche. As argued in the first chapter, this is only provided by psychoanalysis.

Designing machines which are aimed to have human-like capabilities leads towards the question of the "singularity." This is a point in the future where machines have reached human-like "intelligence" and start to produce faster and better new machines, exceeding the capabilities of humans more and more with each new generation. While a thorough discussion of resulting ethical implications would exceed the scope of this thesis, it has been dealt with elsewhere: For example, Anderson and Anderson [AA07] discusses the topic from the point of view of a machine and by Bostrom [Bos03] who raises the question if the creation of these "superintelligent" machines should be enforced or slowed down. The idea behind this thesis and project ARS is that every aspect of the human psyche can be described in a functional model. As soon as this ambitious goal has been reached and the model has been implemented properly, the "singularity" has been reached as so far as the built machine has human-like capabilities. If the resulting machine can think as fast as a human and if better hardware will make it as fast or even faster than humans cannot be answered now. The same accounts for the question if these machines can exceed their human-like capabilities. Being faster than others may be necessary but it is not the only thing necessary to fulfill this goal. Thus, if these machines will be able to outsmart humans is an interesting question but it will not be answered before such a functional model has been created.

In the context of the future of control architectures and consciousness — a topic related to the "singularity" issue — Palensky et al. [PBTD09] discusses an interesting aspect: Will the computer hardware as we know it today be sufficient for machine consciousness? Alternatively, hardware which violates the von-Neumann concept could be necessary. Further, the question is raised if a conscious artifact can be turned off and on again like an ordinary computer. Or would turning it off "kill" the conscious artifact. This leads to the last topic discussed in this outlook. If a machine incorporating human-like capabilities is created, it will incorporate human-like problems too.

A machine controlled by an architecture inspired by psychoanalysis, which perceives the world through its own sensors and is using only grounded symbols, cannot be analyzed by looking in the state of the executed program code and the variables alone (if at all).

Conclusion and Outlook

Due to the complexity, richness, and subjectivity of the gained and stored knowledge, interpretation of the data stored in the various variables is difficult. A certain value could have meaning X for robot A and meaning Y for robot B. Thus, different methods have to be used to find the reasons for a certain behavior. Why did robot A perform better at task T? And why did it refuse to perform task I? Why does the robot cooperate with person P better than with person U? Looking at stored data structures and debugging the code will hardly lead to a human-interpretable answer. And if an answer is found, it might be impossible to change the data accordingly due to the fact that all memory entries are associated with many other entries. Thus, changing one entry may help removing one unwanted behavior but may result in many other — yet unknown — problems. A solution to this problem has been sketched by the science fiction author Asimov with the introduction of the fictional character Susan Calvin. She is a robopsychologist, talking with robots about their problems like psychoanalysts and psychologists talk with humans about their problems. Thus, the robot uses its own actuators and experiences to express its complex problems in natural language and a human operator influences the robot through the robots own sensors towards a solution for these problems. Although at this stage this concept seems very fictitious, it will be one of many tools to deal with human-like problems in psychoanalytically inspired control systems.

It is still a long way until the ambitious goal — creating a control architecture based on psychoanalysis — will be achieved. This is the very nature of each fundamental research project. Nevertheless, undergoing such an idealistic endeavor is worth the risks involved. If successful, the created insights give new impulses to the scientific fields AI and cognitive science. This thesis is hopefully a milestone on the path to this goal.

Literature

[AA07] Michael Anderson and Susan Leigh Anderson. Machine ethics: Creating an ethical intelligent agent. *AI Magazine*, 28 No. 4:4–15, 2007.

[Aub98] Michel Aubé. Designing adaptive cooperating animats will require designing emotions: Expanding upon toda's urge theory. *Papers from the SAB98 Workshop on Grounding emotions in Adaptive Systems, Fifth International Conference on Simulation of Adaptive Behavior (SAB): From Animals to Animats*, 5:7–12, 1998.

[BA08] Christian Becker-Asano. *WASABI: Affect Simulation for Agents with Believable Interactivity*. PhD thesis, Faculty of Technology, University of Bielefeld, 2008.

[Bad97] Alan Baddeley. *Human Memory: Theory and Practice*. Psychology Press, 1997.

[Bau06] Eric Baum. A working hypothesis for general intelligence. *Proceeding of the 2007 conference on Advances in Artificial General Intelligence: Concepts, Architectures and Algorithms: Proceedings of the AGI Workshop 2006*, pages 55–74, 2006.

[BAW09] Christian Becker-Asano and Ipke Wachsmuth. Affective computing with primary and secondary emotions in a virtual human. *Autonomous Agents and Multi-Agent Systems*, 20(1):32–49, 2009.

[BDK+04] Elisabeth Brainin, Dietmar Dietrich, Wolfgang Kastner, Peter Palensky, and Charlotte Rösener. Neuro-bionic architecture of automation systems : Obstacles and challenges. *Proceedings of 2004 IEEE AFRICON, 7th Africon conference in Africa, Technology Innovation*, 2:1219–1222, 2004.

[Ber08] M. J. Berryman. Review of software platforms for agent based models. Technical report, Defence Science and Technology Organisation, 2008. http://dspace.dsto.defence.gov.au/dspace/bitstream/1947/9306/1/DSTO-GD-0532PR.pdf.

[BF07] Bernard J. Baars and Stan Franklin. An architectural model of conscious and unconscious brain functions: global workspace theory and ida. *Neural Networks*, 20:955–961, 2007.

[BF09] Bernard J. Baars and Stan Franklin. Consciousness is computational: The lida model of global workspace theory. *International Journal of Machine Consciousness*, 1:23–32, 2009.

[BJLS05] Andrzej Buller, Michal Joachimczak, Juan Liu, and Katsunori Shimohara. Atr artificial brain project: 2004 progress report. *Artificial Life and Robotics*, 9(4):197–201, 2005.

[BKPLW08] Christian Becker, Stefan Kopp, Nadine Pfeiffer-Leßmann, and Ipke Wachsmuth. Virtual humans growing up: from primary towards secondary emotions. *KI - Künstliche Intelligenz*, 1/08:23–27, 2008.

[BKW04] Christian Becker, Stefan Kopp, and Ipke Wachsmuth. Simulating the emotion dynamics of a multimodal conversational agent. *In Proceedings Tutorial and Research Workshop on Affective Dialogue Systems (ADS-04), LNAI 3068*, pages 154–165, 2004.

[BKW07] Christian Becker, Stefan Kopp, and Ipke Wachsmuth. Why emotions should be integrated into conversational agents. In T. Nishida, editor, *Engineering Approaches to Conversational Informatics*. John Wiley & Sons, 2007.

[BL06] Bradley J. Best and Christian Lebiere. Cognitive agent interacting in real and virtual worlds. In Ron Sun, editor, *Cognition and Multi-Agent Interaction*, pages 186 – 218. Cambridge University Press, 2006.

[BLPV07] Wolfgang Burgstaller, Roland Lang, Patricia Pörscht, and Rosemarie Velik. Technical model for basic and complex emotions. *Proceedings of 2007 IEEE International Conference of Industrial Informatics*, pages 1033–1038, 2007.

[Bos03] Nick Bostrom. Ethical issues in advanced artificial intelligence. *Cognitive, Emotive and Ethical Aspects of Decision Making in Humans and in Artificial Intelligence*, 2:12–17, 2003.

[BP05] Simon Bovet and Rolf Pfeifer. Emergence of delayed reward learning from sensorimotor coordination. *IEEE/RSJ International Conference on Intelligent Robots and Systems*, pages 2272–2277, 2005.

[Bra87] Michael Bratman. *Intention, Plans, and Practical Reason*. Harvard University Press, 1987.

[Bre01] Cynthia Breazeal. Affective interaction between humans and robots. *Proceedings of the Sixth European Conference on Artificial Life (ECAL2001), Prague, CZ*, 1:582–591, 2001.

[Bre02] Cynthia Breazeal. *Designing Sociable Robots*. MIT Press, Cambridge, MA, USA, 2002.

[Bro86] Rodney A. Brooks. A robust layered control system for a mobile robot. *IEEE J. Robotics and Automation*, pages 14–23, 1986.

[Bro90] Rodney A. Brooks. Elephants don't play chess. *Robotics and Autonomous Systems 6*, 1:3–15, 1990.

[Bro92] Rodney A. Brooks. Artificial life and real robots. In *Toward a Practice of Autonomous Systems: Proceedings of the First European Conference on Artificial Life*, 1992.

[Bru07] Dietmar Bruckner. *Probabilistic Models in Building Automation: Recognizing Scenarios with Statistical Methods*. PhD thesis, Vienna University of Technology, Institute of Computer Technology, 2007.

[Bul02] Andrzej Buller. Volitron: On a psychodynamic robot and its four realities. *Pro-ceedings Second International Workshop on Epigenetic Robotics: Modeling Cognitive Development in Robotic Systems*, 94:17–20, 2002.

[Bul05] Andrzej Buller. Building brains for robots: A psychodynamic approach. *Invited talk on the First International Conference on Pattern Recognition and Machine Intelligence, PReMIT'05*, pages 17–20, 2005.

[Bul09] Andrzej Buller. Four laws of machine psychodynamics. In Dietmar Dietrich, Georg Fodor, Gerhard Zucker, and Dietmar Bruckner, editors, *Simulating the Mind – A Technical Neuropsychoanalytical Approach*, pages 320 – 332. Springer, Wien, 1 edition, 2009.

[Bur07] Wolfgang Burgstaller. *Interpretation of Situations in Buildings*. PhD thesis, Vienna University of Technology, Institute of Computer Technology, 2007.

[Can97] Dolores Canamero. Modeling motivations and emotions as a basis for intelligent behavior. In *AGENTS '97: Proceedings of the first international conference on Autonomous agents*, pages 148–155, Marina del Rey, California, United States, 1997. New York, NY, USA. ISBN: 0-89791-877-0.

[CB97] Hillel J. Chiel and Randall D. Beer. The brain has a body: adaptive behavior emerges from interactions of nervous system, body and environment. *Trends in Neurosciences*, 20(12):553–557, 1997.

[Chr03] Ron Chrisley. Embodied artificial intelligence. *Artificial Intelligence*, 149(1):131–150, 2003.

[CS88] Kenneth M. Colby and Robert J. Stoller. *Cognitive Science and Psychoanalysis*. The Analytic Press, 1988.

[CS04]   Andrew L. Coward and Ron Sun. Criteria for an effective theory of consciousness and some preliminary attempts. *Consciousness and cognition*, 13:268–301, 2004.

[Dam94]   Antonio Damasio. *Descartes' Error: Emotion, Reason, and the Human Brain*. Penguin, 1994. Published in Penguin Books 2005.

[DBM+10]   Dietmar Dietrich, Dietmar Bruckner, Brit Müller, Gerhard Zucker, and Friederich Kupzog. Abstraction levels for developing a model of an intelligent decision unit. *Proceedings of the 8th IEEE INDIN*, pages 77–83, 2010.

[DBZ+11]   Tobias Deutsch, Markus Bader, Heimo Zeilinger, Roland Lang, Markus Vincze, and Clemens Muchitsch. Cognitive decision unit applied to autonomous biped robot nao. *Proc. 9th IEEE International Conference on Industrial Informatics INDIN 2011*, 2011. to be published.

[DFKU09]   Dietmar Dietrich, Georg Fodor, Wolfgang Kastner, and Mihaela Ulieru. Considering a technical realization of a neuropsychoanalytical model of the mind – a theoretical framework. In Dietmar Dietrich, Georg Fodor, Gerhard Zucker, and Dietmar Bruckner, editors, *Simulating the Mind – A Technical Neuropsychoanalytical Approach*, pages 99 – 115. Springer, Wien, 1 edition, 2009. invited contribution for the 1st ENF - Emulating the Mind, 2007, Vienna.

[DFZB09]   Dietmar Dietrich, Georg Fodor, Gerhard Zucker, and Dietmar Bruckner. *Simulating the Mind - A Technical Neuropsychoanalytical Approach*. Springer, Wien, 2009.

[DGLV08]   Tobias Deutsch, Andreas Gruber, Roland Lang, and Rosemarie Velik. Episodic memory for autonomous agents. In *Proc. Conference on Human System Interactions*, pages 621–626, 25–27 May 2008.

[Die00]   Dietmar Dietrich. Evolution potentials for fieldbus systems. In *Factory Communication Systems, 2000. Proceedings. 2000 IEEE International Workshop on*, volume 1, pages 145–146, 2000. Invited Talk.

[DKM+04]   Dietmar Dietrich, Wolfgang Kastner, T. Maly, Charlotte Roesener, Gerhard Russ, and H. Schweinzer. Situation Modeling. *Factory Communication Systems, 2004. Proceedings. 2004 IEEE International Workshop on*, pages 93–102, 2004.

[DLB+10]   Dietmar Dietrich, Roland Lang, Dietmar Bruckner, Georg Fodor, and Brit Müller. Limitations, possibilities and implications of brain-computer interfaces. In *Proceedings of 3nd International Conference on Human System Interaction (HSI '10), Rzeszow*, pages 722–726, 2010.

[DLP+06]   Tobias Deutsch, Roland Lang, Gerhard Pratl, Elisabeth Brainin, and Samy Teicher. Applying psychoanalytic and neuro-scientific models to automation. In *Proc. 2nd IET International Conference on Intelligent Environments IE 06*, volume 1, pages 111–118, 5–6 July 2006.

[Doe09]   Benjamin Doenz. Actuators for an artificial life simulation. Master's thesis, Technische Universität Wien, Institut für Computertechnik, 2009.

[DS00]   Dietmar Dietrich and Thilo Sauter. Evolution potentials for fieldbus systems. In *Proceedings of 4th IEEE Int. Workshop on Factory Communication Systems*, pages 343–350, 2000.

[DTM+09]   Tobias Deutsch, Anna Tmej, Clemens Muchitsch, Gerhard Zucker, Christiane Riedinger, and Roland Lang. Failsafe aspects of a decision unit inspired by cognitive sciences - the id without ego and super-ego. *Proceedings of the 2nd International Conference on Human System Interaction*, Special Session 1 - 4th presentation:376–382, 2009.

[DZ08]   Dietmar Dietrich and Gerhard Zucker. New approach for controlling complex processes. an introduction to the 5th generation of AI. *Human System Interactions, 2008 Conference on*, pages 12–17, 2008. invited keynote speech.

[DZL07]   Tobias Deutsch, Heimo Zeilinger, and Roland Lang. Simulation results for the ars-pa model. In *Proc. 5th IEEE International Conference on Industrial Informatics*, volume 2, pages 995–1000, 23–27 June 2007.

[DZLZ08]   Tobias Deutsch, Tehseen Zia, Roland Lang, and Heimo Zeilinger. A simulation platform for cognitive agents. In *Proc. 6th IEEE International Conference on Industrial Informatics INDIN 2008*, pages 1086–1091, 13–16 July 2008.

[FG97]   Stan Franklin and Art Graesser. Is it an agent, or just a program?: A taxonomy for autonomous agents. In *ECAI '96: Proceedings of the Workshop on Intelligent Agents III, Agent Theories, Architectures, and Languages*, pages 21–35, London, UK, 1997. Springer-Verlag.

[FGSW06]   Stan Franklin, Ben Goertzel, Alexei Samsonovich, and Pei Wang. Four contemporary agi designs: a comparative treatment. *Proceeding of the 2007 conference on Advances in Artificial General Intelligence: Concepts, Architectures and Algorithms: Proceedings of the AGI Workshop 2006*, pages 25–35, 2006.

[FM04]   Stan Franklin and Lee McCauley. Feelings and emotions as motivators and learning facilitators. *In Architectures for Modelling Emotions. AAAI Spring Symposium, Stanford University, Ca., USA*, 2004. http://citeseerx.ist.psu.edu/viewdoc/download?doi=10.1.1.2.5301&rep=rop1&type=pdf.

[FP06]   Stan Franklin and F. G. Patterson. The lida architecture: Adding new modes of learning to an intelligent, autonomous, software agent. *Proceedings of Integrated Design and Process Technology, IDPT-2006*, 2006. http://www.theassc.org/files/assc/zo-1010-lida-060403.pdf.

[Fra97]   Stan Franklin. Autonomus agents as embodied ai. *Cybernetics and Systems: An International Journal*, 28:499–520, 1997.

[Fra03]   Stan Franklin. Ida: A conscious artifact? *Journal of Consciousness Studies*, 10:47–66, 2003.

[Fra06]   Stan Franklin. A foundational architecture for artificial general intelligence. *Proceeding of the 2007 conference on Advances in Artificial General Intelligence: Concepts, Architectures and Algorithms: Proceedings of the AGI Workshop 2006*, pages 36–54, 2006.

[FRD+07] Stan Franklin, Uma Ramamurthy, Sidney K. D'Mello, Lee McCauley, Aregahegn Negatu, Rodrigo Silva L., and Vivek Datla. Lida: A computational model of global workspace theory and developmental learning. In *AAAI Fall Symposium on AI and Consciousness: Theoretical Foundations and Current Approaches*. Arlington, VA: AAAI, 2007. http://ccrg.cs.memphis.edu/assets/papers/LIDApaperFallAISymposiumFinal.pdf.

[Fre94]   Sigmund Freud. The neuro-psychoses of defence. *The Standard Edition of the Complete Psychological Works of Sigmund Freud*, III:41–61, 1894.

[Fre95]   Sigmund Freud. Project for a scientific psychology. *The Standard Edition of the Complete Psychological Works of Sigmund Freud, Pre-Psycho-Analytic Publications and Unpublished Drafts*, I:281–391, 1950 [1895].

[Fre05a] Sigmund Freud. Drei abhandlungen zur sexualtheorie. In *Gesammelte Werke*, volume V. Fischer Taschenbuch, 1905.

[Fre05b] Sigmund Freud. *Three Contributions to the Theory of Sex*. 1905. 1920 translation by A.A. Brill.

[Fre08]   Sigmund Freud. Character and anal erotism. *The Standard Edition of the Complete Psychological Works of Sigmund Freud*, IX:167–176, 1908.

[Fre15a] Sigmund Freud. Instincts and their vicissitudes. *The Standard Edition of the Complete Psychological Works of Sigmund Freud*, XIV (1914-1916): On the History of the Psycho-Analytic Movement, Papers on Metapsychology and Other Works:109–140, 1915.

[Fre15b] Sigmund Freud. *The Unconscious*, volume XIV (1914-1916) of *On the History of the Psycho-Analytic Movement, Papers on Metapsychology and Other Works*. Vintage, 1915.

[Fre17]   Sigmund Freud. On transformations of instinct as exemplified in anal erotism. *The Standard Edition of the Complete Psychological Works of Sigmund Freud*, XVII:125–134, 1917.

[Fre23]   Sigmund Freud. The ego and the id. *The Standard Edition of the Complete Psychological Works of Sigmund Freud*, XIX (1923-1925):1–66, 1923.

[Fre26]   Sigmund Freud. Inhibitions, symptoms and anxiety. *The Standard Edition of the Complete Psychological Works of Sigmund Freud*, XX:75–176, 1926.

[Fre33]   Sigmund Freud. *New Introductory Lectures On Psycho-Analysis.*, volume Volume XXII (1932-1936): New Introductory Lectures on Psycho-Analysis and Other Works, 1-182 of *The Standard Edition of the Complete Psychological Works of Sigmund Freud*. Hogarth Press and Institute of Psych–Analysis, 1933.

[Fue03]   Clara Tamarit Fuertes. *Automation System Perception - First Step towards Perceptive Awareness*. PhD thesis, Faculty of Electrical Engineering and Information Technology, Vienna University of Technology, 2003.

[Gar70]   Martin Gardner. The fantastic combinations of john conway's new solitaire game "life". *Scientific American*, 223:120–123, 1970.

[Gar85]   Howard Gardner. *The mind's new science: a history of the cognitive revolution*. Basic Books, Inc., New York, NY, USA, 1985.

[GB07]   Ben Goertzel and Stephan Vladimir Bugaj. Stages of cognitive development in uncertain-logic-based ai systems. *Proceeding of the 2007 conference on Advances in Artificial General Intelligence: Concepts, Architectures and Algorithms: Proceedings of the AGI Workshop 2006*, pages 174–194, 2007.

[GHB+06]   Ben Goertzel, Arj Heljakka, Stephan Vladimir Bugaj, Cassio Pennachin, and Moshe Looks. Exploring android developmental psychology in a simulation world. *Proceedings of the ICCS 2006*, pages 27–30, 2006.

[GL09]   Robert M. Galatzer-Levy. A primer of psychoanalysis for alan turing. In Dietmar Dietrich, Georg Fodor, Gerhard Zucker, and Dietmar Bruckner, editors, *Simulating the Mind – A Technical Neuropsychoanalytical Approach*, pages 367 – 381. Springer, Wien, 1 edition, 2009.

[Goe06]   Ben Goertzel. Patterns, hypergraphs and embodied general intelligence. *Proceedings of the International Joint Conference on Neural Networks, IJCNN 2006*, pages 451–458, 2006.

[Goe07]   Ben Goertzel. Virtual easter egg hunting: A thought-experiment in embodied social learning, cognitive process integration, and the dynamic emergence of the self. *Proceeding of the 2007 conference on Advances in Artificial General Intelligence: Concepts, Architectures and Algorithms: Proceedings of the AGI Workshop 2006*, pages 217–252, 2007.

[Goe09]   Ben Goertzel. Opencogprime: A cognitive synergy based architecture for artificial general intelligence. *Proceedings of the 2009 8th IEEE International Conference on Cognitive Informatics*, pages 60–68, 2009.

[GP07]   Ben Goertzel and Cassio Pennachin. The novamente artificial intelligence engine. In Ben Goertzel and Cassio Pennachin, editors, *Artificial General Intelligence*, pages 63–129. Springer Berlin Heidelberg, 2007.

[GP08]   Ben Goertzel and Cassio Pennachin. An inferential dynamics approach to personality and emotion driven behavior determination for virtual animals. *Proceedings of the The Reign of Catz and Dogz. Symposium, AI and the Simulation of Behavior (AISB)*, pages 1–5, 2008.

[GP09]   Ben Goertzel and Cassio Pennachin. The collective pet unconscious: Balancing intelligence and individuality in populations of learning-enabled virtual pets. *ACM-CHI*, 2009. http://www.novamente.net/file/Goertzel.pdf.

[Grü00]   Adolf Grünbaum. Ein jahrhundert psychoanalyse. ein kritischer rückblick – ein kritischer ausblick. *Forum der Psychoanalyse*, 16:285–296, 2000.

[GW07]   Ben Goertzel and Pei Wang, editors. *Advances in Artificial General Intelligence: Concepts, Architectures and Algorithms*. IOS Press, 2007. ISBN-13: 978-1586037581.

[Har90]   Stevan Harnad. The symbol grounding problem. *Physica D: Nonlinear Phenomena*, 42:335–346, 1990.

[HDN03]   Wan Ching Ho, Kerstin Dautenhahn, and Chrystopher L. Nehaniv. Comparing different control architectures for autobiographic agents in static virtual environments. *Intelligent Agents, 4th International Workshop, IVA 2003, Kloster Irsee, Germany, September 15-17, 2003, Proceedings*, pages 182–191, 2003.

[HDN05]   Wan Ching Ho, Kerstin Dautenhahn, and Chrystopher L. Nehaniv. Autobiographic agents in dynamic virtual environments - performance comparison for different memory control architectures. *Proceedings of IEEE Congress on Evolutionary Computation IEEE*, pages 573–580, 2005.

[HDNB04] Wan Ching Ho, Kerstin Dautenhahn, Chrystopher L. Nehaniv, and Rene Te Boekhorst. Sharing memories: An experimental investigation with multiple autonomous autobiographic agents. *IAS-8, 8th Conference on Intelligent Autonomous Systems*, pages 361–370, 2004.

[HG08]   David Hart and Ben Goertzel. Opencog: A software framework for integrative artificial general intelligence. *Proceedings of the First AGI Conference, AGI 2008*, pages 468–472, 2008.

[HGS+07] Ari Heljakka, Ben Goertzel, Welter Silva, Cassio Pennachin, Andre' Senna, and Izabela Goertzel. Probabilistic logic based reinforcement learning of simple embodied behaviors in a 3d simulation world. *Proceeding of the 2007 conference on Advances in Artificial General Intelligence: Concepts, Architectures and Algorithms: Proceedings of the AGI Workshop 2006*, pages 253–275, 2007.

[HPC93]   Steve Hanks, Martha E. Pollack, and Paul R. Cohen. Benchmarks, test beds, controlled experimentation, and the design of agent architectures. *AI Magazine*, 14(4):17–42, 1993.

[HS02]   Ramin Halavati and Saeed Bagheri Shouraki. Zamin: An artificial ecosystem. *EurAsia-ICT*, pages 1008–1016, 2002.

[HS03]   Ramin Halavati and Saeed Bagheri Shouraki. A fuzzy artificial world: Zamin ii. *International Conference on Computational Science*, pages 601–609, 2003.

[HSZ+04]   Ramin Halavati, Saeed Bagheri Shouraki, Saman Harati Zadeh, Pujan Ziaie, and Caro Lucas. Zamin, an agent based artificial life model. *Proceedings of the Fourth International Conference on Hybrid Intelligent Systems (HIS, 04)*, pages 160–165, 2004.

[Kan99]   Eric R. Kandel. Biology and the future of psychoanalysis: A new intellectual framework for psychiatry revisited. In *The American Journal of Psychiatry*, pages 505–524. McGraw-Hill, 1999.

[Koh08]   Stefan Kohlhauser. Requirement analysis for a psychoanalytically inspired agent based social system. Master's thesis, Technische Universität Wien, Institut für Computertechnik, 2008.

[Kus97]   Nicholas Kushmerick. Software agents and their bodies. In *Minds and machines*, pages 227–247, 1997.

[Lan89]   Christopher G. Langton. Artificial life. *Artificial Life*, 6:1–47, 1989.

[Lan92]   Christopher G. Langton. Preface. In Christopher G. Langton, Charles Taylor, J. Doyne Farmer, and Steen Rasmussen, editors, *Artificial life II: proceedings of the workshop on artificial life*, pages xiii–xviii, 1992.

[Lan10]   Roland Lang. *A Decision Unit for Autonomous Agents Based on the Theory of Psychoanalysis*. PhD thesis, Vienna University of Technology, 2010.

[LBP02]   Marianne Leuzinger-Bohleber and Rolf Pfeifer. Remembering a depressive primary object: Memory in the dialogue between psychoanalysis and cognitive science. *International Journal of Psychoanalysis*, 83:3–33, 2002.

[LBP+03]   Sean Luke, Gabriel Catalin Balan, Liviu Panait, Claudio Cioffi-Revilla, and Sean Paus. Mason: A java multi-agent simulation library. *Proceedings of the Agent 2003 Conference*, 2003. www.cs.gmu.edu/~sean/papers/MASONSocialInsects.pdf.

[LBP06]   Marianne Leuzinger-Bohleber and Rolf Pfeifer. Recollecting the past in the present: Memory in the dialogue between psychoanalysis and cognitive science. In Mauro Mancia, editor, *Psychoanalysis and Neuroscience*, pages 63–95. Springer Milan, 2006.

[LBP+07]   Roland Lang, Dietmar Bruckner, Gerhard Pratl, Rosemarie Velik, and Tobias Deutsch. Scenario recognition in modern building automation. *Proceedings of the 7th IFAC International Conference on Fieldbuses & Networks in Industrial & Embedded Systems (FeT 2007)*, pages 305–312, 2007.

[LCRPS04] Sean Luke, Claudio Cioffi-Revilla, Liviu Panait, and Keith Sullivan. Mason: A new multi-agent simulation toolkit. In *Proceedings of the 2004 Swarmfest Workshop*, 2004. http://cs.gmu.edu/~eclab/projects/mason/publications/SwarmFest04.pdf.

[LGP04] Moshe Looks, Ben Goertzel, and Cassio Pennachin. Novamente: An integrative architecture for general intelligence. In *papers from AAAI Fall Symposium on Achieving Human-Level Intelligence through Integrated Systems and Research*, pages 54–61, 2004.

[LKZD10] Roland Lang, Stefan Kohlhauser, Gerhard Zucker, and Tobias Deutsch. Integrating internal performance measures into the decision making process of autonomous agents. In *Proceedings of 3nd International Conference on Human System Interaction (HSI'10)*, Rzeszow, 2010.

[Lor08] Emiliano Lorini. Agents with emotions: a logical perspective. *Association for Logic Programming Newsletter*, 21(2-3), 2008.

[MBLA96] Nelson Minar, Roger Burkhart, Chris Langton, and Manor Askenazi. The swarm simulation system: A toolkit for building multi-agent simulations - report no.: 96-06-042. Technical report, Santa Fe (NM): Santa Fe Institute, 1996. http://citeseerx.ist.psu.edu/viewdoc/download?doi=10.1.1.26.3075&rep=rep1&type=ps.

[MDD+10] Brit Müller, Klaus Doblhammer, Dietmar Dietrich, Dietmar Bruckner, Gerhard Zucker, Anna Tmej, and Georg Fodor. An engineering description of the freudian second topographical model. *Journal of the Neuropsychoanalytical Society*, 2010. in review.

[Min88] Marvin Minsky. *The Society of Mind*. Simon and Schuster, New York, 1988.

[Min05] Marvin Minsky. Interior grounding, reflection, and self-consciousness. *Proceedings of an International Conference on Brain, Mind and Society. Tohoku University, Japan.*, 2005. invited speech.

[Min06] Marvin Minsky. *The Emotion Machine: Commonsense Thinking, Artificial Intelligence, and the Future of the Human Mind*. Simon & Schuster Paperbacks, 2006.

[MP08] Heinz Müller-Pozzi. *Eine Triebtheorie für unsere Zeit*. Huber, 2008.

[NTMI99] Tohru Nitta, Toshio Tanaka, Kenji Mishida, and Hiroaki Inayoshi. Modeling human mind. In *Systems, Man, and Cybernetics, 1999. IEEE SMC '99 Conference Proceedings. 1999 IEEE International Conference on*, volume 2, pages 342 – 347, 1999.

[OT90] Andrew Ortony and Terence J. Turner. What's basic about basic emotions? *Psychological Review*, 97, No. 3(3):315–331, 1990.

[Pal08]	Brigitte Palensky. *From Neuro-Psychoanalysis to Cognitive and Affective Automation Systems*. PhD thesis, Faculty of Electrical Engineering and Information Technology, Vienna University of Technology, 2008.

[Pan98]	Jaak Panksepp. *Affective Neuroscience, the Foundations of Human and Animal Emotions*. Oxford University Press, Inc. 198 Madison Avenue, New York, 1998.

[PB07]	Rolf Pfeifer and Josh Bongard. *How the body shapes the way we think*. MIT Press, 2007.

[PBL03]	Alexander Pokahr, Lars Braubach, and Winfried Lamersdorf. Jadex: Implementing a bdi-infrastructure for jade agents. *EXP - in search of innovation (Special Issue on JADE)*, 3(3):76–85, 2003.

[PBTD09]	Peter Palensky, Dietmar Bruckner, Anna Tmej, and Tobias Deutsch. Paradox in ai – ai 2.0: the way to machine consciousness. In Mihaela Ulieru, Peter Palensky, and Rene Doursat, editors, *IT Revolutions*, pages 194–215. Springer Berlin/Heidelberg, 2009.

[PDHP07]	Gerhard Pratl, Dietmar Dietrich, Gerhard P. Hancke, and Walter T. Penzhorn. A new model for autonomous, networked control systems. *IEEE Transactions on Industrial Informatics*, 3:21–32, 2007.

[PDP05]	Peter Palensky, Dietmar Dietrich, and Gerhard Pratl. Die zukunft der gebäudeautomation. *LNO Brief*, 35:5–8, 2005.

[Per97]	Achim Perner. *Nach 100 Jahren: Ist die Psychoanalyse eine Wissenschaft?*, chapter 10, pages 226–256. Ernst Reinhardt Verlag München Basel, 1997.

[Pfe94]	Rolf Pfeifer. The fungus eater approach to emotion: A view from artificial intelligence. *Cognitive Studies*, pages 42–57, 1994.

[Pfe96]	Rolf Pfeifer. Building "fungus eaters": Design principles of autonomous agents. *In Proceedings of the Fourth International Conference on Simulation of Adaptive Behavior SAB96 (From Animals to Animats)*, pages 3–12, 1996.

[Pic95]	Rosalind Picard Affective computing. Technical Report 321, M.I.T Media Laboratory Perceptual Computing Section, 1995. http://citeseerx.ist.psu.edu/viewdoc/download?doi=10.1.1.63.432&rep=rep1&type=pdf.

[Pic99]	Rosalind Picard. Response to sloman's review of affective computing. *AI Magazine*, 20(1):134–137, 1999.

[PIG06]	Rolf Pfeifer, Fumiya Iida, and Gabriel Gómez. Designing intelligent robots – on the implications of embodiment. *Journal of Robotics Society of Japan*, 24(7):9–16, 2006.

[PKP07]   Kyung-Sock Park, Dong-Soo Kwon, and Mignon Park. A design of the mental model of a cognitive robot. In *Robot and Human interactive Communication, 2007. RO-MAN 2007. The 16th IEEE International Symposium on*, pages 905 – 911, 2007.

[Pop63]   Karl Popper. Science: Conjectures and refutations. In *Conjectures and Refutations: The Growth of Scientific Knowledge*, pages 43–77. Routledge, 1963.

[Poz06]   Dmitrij Pozdnyakov. An overview of the agent-based social system simulation tools. *Annual Proceedings of Vidzeme University College, ICTE in Regional Development*, pages 1–7, 2006.

[PP05]   Gerhard Pratl and Peter Palensky. Project ARS – the next step towards an intelligent environment. *Proceedings of the IEE International Workshop on Intelligent Environments*, pages 55–62, 2005.

[PPC09]   Peter Palensky, Brigitte Palensky, and Andrea Clarici. Cognitive and affective automation: Machines using the psychoanalytic model of the human mind. In Dietmar Dietrich, Georg Fodor, Gerhard Zucker, and Dietmar Bruckner, editors, *Simulating the Mind – A Technical Neuropsychoanalytical Approach*, pages 178 – 227. Springer, Wien, 1 edition, 2009. invited contribution for the 1st ENF - Emulating the Mind, 2007, Vienna.

[PPDB05] Gerhard Pratl, Walter T. Penzhorn, Dietmar Dietrich, and Wolfgang Burgstaller. Perceptive awareness in building automation. *IEEE 3rd International Conference on Computational Cybernetics*, pages 259–264, 2005.

[Pra06]   Gerhard Pratl. *Processing and Symbolization of Ambient Sensor Data*. PhD thesis, Faculty of Electrical Engineering and Information Technology, Vienna University of Technology, 2006.

[PS97]   Rolf Pfeifer and Christian Scheier. Implications of embodiment for robot learning. *Advanced Mobile Robots*, pages 38–43, 1997.

[PS99]   Rolf Pfeifer and Christian Scheier. *Understanding Intelligence*. MIT Press, 1999.

[QD99]   Tom Quick and Kerstin Dautenhahn. Making embodiment measurable. *Proceedings der 4. Fachtagung der Gesellschaft für Kognitionswissenschaft*, 1999. http://supergoodtech.com/tomquick/phd/kogwis.

[RBDF06] Uma Ramamurthy, Bernard J. Baars, Sidney K. D'Mello, and Stan Franklin. Lida: A working model of cognition. *Proceedings of the 7th International Conference on Cognitive Modeling*, pages 244–249, 2006.

[RDL+09] Charlotte Roesener, Tobias Deutsch, Roland Lang, Brit Müller, and Takahiro Yakoh. Artificial group mind, a psychoanalytically founded thought experiment. In Dietmar Dietrich, Georg Fodor, Gerhard Zucker, and Dietmar

	Bruckner, editors, *Simulating the Mind – A Technical Neuropsychoanalytical Approach*, pages 332 – 347. Springer, Wien, 1 edition, 2009.
[RHBP04]	Charlotte Roesener, Harald Hareter, Wolfgang Burgstaller, and Gerhard Pratl. Environment simulation for scenario perception models. *Factory Communication Systems, 2004. Proceedings. 2004 IEEE International Workshop on*, pages 349 – 352, 2004.
[Rie02]	Alexander Riegler. When is a cognitive system embodied? *Cognitive Systems Research*, 3(3):339–348, September 2002.
[RLFV06]	Charlotte Roesener, Brigitte Lorenz, Georg Fodor, and Katharina Vock. Emotional behavior arbitration for automation and robotic systems. *Proceedings of 2006 IEEE International Conference of Industrial Informatics*, pages 423–428, 2006.
[RLJ06]	Steven F. Railsback, Steven L. Lytinen, and Stephen K. Jackson. Agent-based simulation platforms: Review and development recommendations. *SIMULATION*, 82 No. 9:609–623, 2006.
[RN03]	Stuart J. Russell and Peter Norvig. *Artificial Intelligence: A Modern Approach*. Pearson Education, 2003.
[Roe07]	Charlotte Roesener. *Adaptive Behavior Arbitration for Mobile Service Robots in Building Automation*. PhD thesis, Vienna University of Technology, Institute of Computer Technology, 2007.
[RR96]	Juan Rodado and Marion Rendon. Can artificial intelligence be of help to psychoanalysis ... or ... vice versa? *The American Journal of Psychoanalysis*, 56(4):395–412, 1996.
[Rus03]	Gerhard Russ. *Situation-dependent Behavior in Building Automation*. PhD thesis, Vienna University of Technology, Institute of Computer Technology, 2003.
[SC05]	Aaron Sloman and Ron Chrisley. More things than are dreamt of in your biology: Information-processing in biologically inspired robots. *Cognitive Systems Reasearch*, 6(2):145–174, 2005.
[Sch71]	Thomas Schelling. Dynamic models of segregation. *Journal of Mathematical Sociology*, 1:143–186, 1971.
[SCS05]	Aaron Sloman, Ron Chrisley, and Matthias Scheutz. The architectural basis of affective states and processes. In M. Arbib and J-M. Fellous, editors, *Who Needs Emotions?: The Brain Meets the Robot*, pages 203–244. Oxford University Press, Oxford, New York, 2005.
[Sip95]	Moshe Sipper. An introduction to artificial life. *Explorations in Artificiul Life (special issue of AI Expert)*, pages pages 4–8, September 1995.

[Slo99] Aaron Sloman. What sort of architecture us required for a human-like agent? In Michael Wooldridge and Anand Rao, editors, *In Foundations of Rational Agency*, pages 35–52. Kluwer Academic Publishers, 1999.

[Slo00] Aaron Sloman. Models of models of mind. *Proceedings of symposium on how to design a functioning mind*, pages 1–9, 2000.

[Slo01a] Aaron Sloman. Beyond shallow models of emotion. *Cognitive Processing*, 2(1):177–198, 2001.

[Slo01b] Aaron Sloman. Varieties of affect and the cogaff architecture schema. *Proceedings Symposium on Emotion, Cognition, and Affective Computing AISB01 Convention*, pages 39–48, 2001.

[Slo04a] Aaron Sloman. Information-processing systems in nature. Technical report, University of Birmingham, UK, 2004.

[Slo04b] Aaron Sloman. What are emotion theories about? In *Symposium Technical Report*, pages 128–134. AAAI Spring, 2004.

[Sol96] Mark Solms. Was sind affekte (translated: What are affects). *Psyche*, 6:485–522, 1996.

[SSK97] Peter Schuster and Marianne Springer-Kremser. *Bausteine der Psychoanalyse*. WUV-Universitätsverlag, 1997.

[ST02] Mark Solms and Oliver Turnbull. *The Brain and the Inner World: An Introduction to the Neuroscience of Subjective Experience*. Karnac/Other Press, Cathy Miller Foreign Rights Agency, London, England, 2002.

[Tec05] Dan Tecuci. A generic episodic memory module. Technical report, University of Texas at Austin, 2005.

[TNH+06] E. Tatara, M.J. North, T.R. Howe, N.T. Collier, and J.R. Vos. An introduction to repast modeling by using a simple predator-prey example. *Proceedings of the Agent 2006 Conference on Social Agents: Results and Prospects*, 2006.

[Tod62] Masano Toda. Design of a fungus-eater. *Behavioral Science*, 7:164–183, 1962. Reprinted in Toda, 1982, 100-129.

[Tod82] Masanao Toda. *Man, Robot and Society*. Martinus Nijhoff Publishing, 1982.

[Tul72] Endel Tulving. *Organization of memory*, chapter Episodic and semantic memory, pages 381–403. New York: Academic Press, 1972.

[Tur50] Alan Turing. Computing machinery and intelligence. *Mind*, 59:433–460, 1950.

[Tur89] Sherry Turkle. Artificial intelligence and psychoanalysis: A new alliance. In S. R. Graubard, editor, *The Artificial Intelligence Debate: False Starts, Real Foundations*, pages 241–268. MIT Press, Cambridge, MA, 1989.

[Tur09]   Mika Turkia. A computational model of affects. In Dietmar Dietrich, Georg Fodor, Gerhard Zucker, and Dietmar Bruckner, editors, *Simulating the Mind – A Technical Neuropsychoanalytical Approach*, pages 277 – 290. Springer, Wien, 1 edition, 2009.

[Vel97]   Juan D. Velásquez. Modeling emotions and other motivations in synthetic agents. In *AAAI/IAAI*, pages 10–15, 1997.

[Vel98a] Juan D. Velásquez. A computational framework for emotion-based control. *5th International Conference of the Society for Adaptive Behavior*, 1998. http://www.ofai.at/~paolo.petta/conf/sab98/final/velasquez.ps.gz.

[Vel98b] Juan D. Velásquez. When robots weep: Emotional memories and decision-making. In *AAAI/IAAI*, pages 70–75, 1998.

[Vel08]   Rosemarie Velik. *A Bionic Model for Human-like Machine Perception*. PhD thesis, Vienna University of Technology, Institute of Computer Technology, 2008.

[VFK98]   Juan D. Velásquez, Masahiro Fujita, and Hiroaki Kitano. An open architecture for emotion and behavior control of autonomous agents. *Proceedings of the second international conference on Autonomous agents, Minneapolis*, 1:473–474, 1998.

[VLBD08] Rosemarie Velik, Roland Lang, Dietmar Bruckner, and Tobias Deutsch. Emulating the perceptual system of the brain for the purpose of sensor fusion. In *Proc. Conference on Human System Interactions*, pages 657–662, 25–27 May 2008.

[VM97]   Juan D. Velásquez and Pattie Maes. Cathexis: a computational model of emotions. In *AGENTS '97: Proceedings of the first international conference on Autonomous agents*, pages 518–519. ACM, 1997.

[Weh94]   Thomas Wehrle. New fungus eater experiments. In P. Gaussier and J.-D. Nicoud, editors, *From perception to action*, pages 400–403. Los Alamitos: IEEE Computer Society Press, 1994.

[WG06]   Pei Wang and Ben Goertzel. Introduction: Aspects of artificiel general intelligence. *Proceeding of the 2007 conference on Advances in Artificial General Intelligence: Concepts, Architectures and Algorithms: Proceedings of the AGI Workshop 2006*, pages 1–16, 2006.

[Wil96]   Patrick Wilson. Interdisciplinary research and information overload. *In Library Trends: Navigating Among the Disciplines: The Library and Interdisciplinary Inquiry*, 45(2):192–203, 1996.

[ZDML08] Heimo Zeilinger, Tobias Deutsch, Brit Müller, and Roland Lang. Bionic inspired decision making unit model for autonomous agents. In *Proc. IEEE International Conference on Computational Cybernetics ICCC 2008*, pages 259–264, 27–29 Nov. 2008.

[Zei10] Heimo Zeilinger. *Bionically Inspired Information Representation for Embodied Software Agents*. PhD thesis, Vienna University of Technology, 2010.

[Zie01] Tom Ziemke. Are robots embodied ? *Proceedings of the First International Workshop on Epigenetic Robotics: Modeling Cognitive Development in Robotic Systems Lund University Cognitive Studies*, 85:75–93, 2001.

[ZLL04] Saman Harati Zadeh, Abolfazl Keighobadi Lamjiri, and Caro Lucas. Zamin environment: Review and comparison. *WSEAS Transactions on Systems*, 3(1):316–327, 2004.

[ZLM09] Heimo Zeilinger, Roland Lang, and Brit Müller. Bionic inspired information representation for autonomous agents. In *Proceedings of 2nd International Conference on Human System Interaction (HSI '09), Catania*, pages 24–30, 2009.

[ZPK10] Heimo Zeilinger, Andreas Perner, and Stefan Kohlhauser. Bionically inspired information representation module. In *Proceedings of 3rd International Conference on Human System Interaction (HSI '10), Rzeszow*, pages 708–714, 2010.

[ZSH04] Saman Harati Zadeh, Saeed Bagheri Shouraki, and Ramin Halavati. A survey on zamin artificial ecosystem. *WSEAS TRANSACTIONS on SYSTEMS*, 3(4):1674–1681, 2004.

Internet References

[1] Artificial Recognition System. *Homepage*, 2009. `ars.ict.tuwien.ac.at`, accessed March 2009.

[2] Institute of Computer Technology. *Homepage*, 2009. `www.ict.tuwien.ac.at`, accessed March 2009.

[3] SmaKi Project. *Homepage*, 2009. `http://smartkitchen.ict.tuwien.ac.at`, accessed March 2009.

[4] Push Singh. *Why AI Failed — The Past 10 Years*, June 1996. `http://web.media.mit.edu/~push/why-ai-failed.html`, accessed April 2010.

[5] The Psychoanalytic Center of Philadelphia. *Frequently Asked Questions about Psychoanalysis*, 2010. `http://www.philanalysis.org/resources/psychoanalysis-faq.html`, accessed Dezember 2010.

[6] AGIRI Workshop. *Instead of an AGI Textbook*, 2010. `http://www.agiri.org/wiki/Instead_of_an_AGI_Textbook`, accessed Mai 2010.

[7] Cognitive Computing Research Group, University of Memphis. *LIDA Project Homepage*, 2008. `http://ccrg.cs.memphis.edu/tutorial/index.html`, accessed Mai 2010.

[8] OpenCog Foundation. *OpenCog Prime Wiki*, 2010. `http://opencog.org/wiki/OpenCog_Prime`, accessed June 2010.

[9] OpenCog Foundation. *OpenCog Prime - Roadmap*, 2010. `http://www.opencog.org/wiki/OpenCogPrime:Roadmap`, accessed June 2010.

[10] AnyLogic - Xjtek. *Homepage*, 2009. `http://www.xjtek.com/anylogic/`, accessed March 2009.

[11] Swarm Development Group. *Homepage*, 2010. `http://www.swarm.org/index.php/Main_Page`, accessed March 2010.

[12] RePast. *Homepage*, 2010. `http://repast.sourceforge.net/`, accessed March 2010.

[13] Mason. *Homepage*, 2010. http://cs.gmu.edu/~eclab/projects/mason/, accessed March 2010.

[14] ODE—Open Dynamics Engine. *Homepage*, 2011. http://www.ode.org, accessed March 2011.

[15] 2D Physics in MASON. *Homepage*, 2011. http://cs.gmu.edu/~eclab/projects/mason/extensions/physics2d/, accessed March 2011.

[16] JGraph. *Homepage*, 2011. http://www.jgraph.com/jgraph.html, accessed March 2011.

[17] protegé. *Homepage*, 2011. http://protege.stanford.edu/, accessed May 2011.

[18] Aldebaran Robotics. *Homepage*, 2011. http://www.aldebaran-robotics.com/, accessed May 2011.

[19] Project ROMEO. *Homepage*, 2011. http://www.projetromeo.com/, accessed May 2011.

A UML Notation

In Chapter 4 the important parts of the implementation ARS implementation number 11 (ARSi11) and the ARSIN world simulator are described using a Unified Modeling Language (UML) like notation. At some points, the rich UML notation is reduced not to occlude the diagrams. From the 14 types of diagrams defined in UML 2.2 the following three are used: Class diagram, sequence diagram, and package diagram.

A.1 Class Diagram

This type of diagram is used to describe the structure of the system and the relation among the classes. The attributes of each class and the relations are left out.

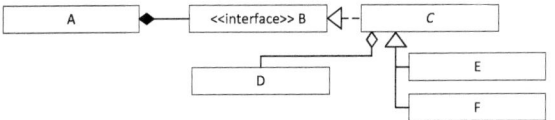

Figure A.1: UML class diagram example

The rectangles with letters A, D, E, and F represent classes in Figure A.1. C is an abstract class and <<interface>> B an interface class. Interface classes are used in Java instead of multiple inheritance. The arrow with the dashed line between C and <<interface>> B defines that class C is implementing <<interface>> B. The arrow with the solid line connecting E and F with C defines that the classes E and F are of type C.

The line with the black diamond between A and <<interface>> B denotes that class A is composed of a set of instances of the class <<interface>> B. Composition refers to a strong dependency of the container and its components. Hence, the life time of objects of type <<interface>> B is usually controlled by the containing object of type A.

An aggregation — represented by a line with a white diamond — refers to a weak dependency. For example, an instance of class E contains a set of references to instances of class D. The life times of the container instance and the contained instance are independent.

UML NOTATION

Each occurrence of an aggregation or a composition defines a one to one relationship in the UML figures in Chapter 4.

A.2 Sequence Diagram

A sequence diagram is used to describe the interaction between two or more objects. It gives a time line of the events and function calls that occur.

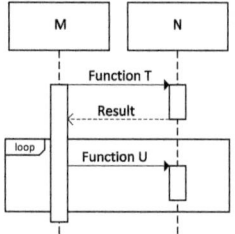

Figure A.2: UML sequence diagram example

The given sequence diagram example (see Figure A.2) contains of two objects. The first one is M and it calls functions provided by N. The vertical dashed lines beneath M and N are the time lines. The rectangles along a time line depict the activity. In this example, object M is always active, whereas object N is only active if one of its functions is called by M. Two different types of function calls are depicted. Function T provides a return result and function U that has not return result. Both function calls are blocking. Thus, object M waits until T or U has finished before it continues. The rectangle with the label "loop" attached to its upper left side denotes that function U is called repeatedly until the loop is finished.

A.3 Package Diagram

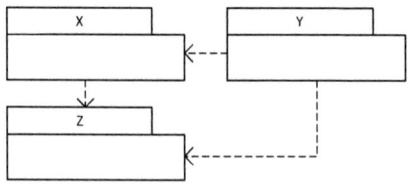

Figure A.3: UML package diagram example

The package diagram is used to show package dependencies. Figure A.3 shows three packages (X, Y, and Z). The dashed arrow defines that the package at its origin includes the package it points at. Hence, package Y includes the packages X and Z; package X includes only package Z. The package Z includes no other package. Classes in package Y can access classes in package Z but not the other way round.

Die VDM Verlagsservicegesellschaft sucht für wissenschaftliche Verlage abgeschlossene und herausragende

Dissertationen, Habilitationen, Diplomarbeiten, Master Theses, Magisterarbeiten usw.

für die kostenlose Publikation als Fachbuch.

Sie verfügen über eine Arbeit, die hohen inhaltlichen und formalen Ansprüchen genügt, und haben Interesse an einer honorarvergüteten Publikation?

Dann senden Sie bitte erste Informationen über sich und Ihre Arbeit per Email an *info@vdm-vsg.de*.

Sie erhalten kurzfristig unser Feedback!

VDM Verlagsservicegesellschaft mbH
Dudweiler Landstr. 99
D - 66123 Saarbrücken
www.vdm-vsg.de

Telefon +49 681 3720 174
Fax +49 681 3720 1749

Die VDM Verlagsservicegesellschaft mbH vertritt

Printed by Books on Demand GmbH, Norderstedt / Germany